DEVELOPING EXECUTIVE LEADERS

This is the fourth and final volume of articles selected from the *Harvard Business Review* for the series entitled The Business Administrator.

DEVELOPING EXECUTIVE LEADERS

Edited by Edward C. Bursk, Editor, Harvard Business Review, *and*
Timothy B. Blodgett, Associate Editor, Harvard Business Review

Harvard University Press
Cambridge, Massachusetts
1971

CONTENTS

INTRODUCTION

Few would accept without reservation the notion that what is good for business is also good for the country. But few would deny that what is good for the country depends to a large extent on how business performs as a major element in the economic and social environments.

Improvement of administrative competence and broadening of the administrator's viewpoint have been the goals of the Harvard Business School since its founding more than six decades ago. For nearly five of those decades the *Harvard Business Review* has extended that educational function in printed form to practitioners of administration throughout the world.

In this book we present sixteen important articles (which have been printed from reproduction proofs of *HBR*) dealing with the vital subject of executive development.

In an age when business in the United States has reached pinnacles of technical achievement, the capacity of its leaders to play a key role in surmounting the awesome problems we face is still open to question. In 1953 Donald K. David, then Dean of the Harvard Business School, considered this point in an introduction to a little book on building executive leadership. His words are just as true today:

The scales are coming into balance as managements awake to the importance of continuous growth and its need for day-by-day attention. This is good, for executive ability is needed in many places. Already short in American business, it is needed in local and national government and in business overseas. Here is a quality the world much requires, for the economy of nations and of the free world cannot long proceed without the participation of professional administrators. Perpetuation of a free society depends upon prompt and equitable industrialization of undeveloped countries, upon freer trade, and upon the extension of American productivity to the world in which

American has risen to leadership. Leadership is nothing without the men who lead. Those men must know *how* to be continually more effective.[1]

The italicized word is the critical one here. "How" to become more effective in selling more goods, improving the precision of a tool, or automating a routine function is not at issue here; we are supereffective in such endeavors. But when there is a human element in the equation, when accomplishment of the task demands securing the cooperation of others and sometimes changing their minds, our much-celebrated American know-how is not always adequate.

The historical rationale for more effective leadership has been to make the system work better, to market more aggressively, or to adapt to new technology. But in these times, when organizations are increasingly being called to account for their actions and the system itself is being questioned, effective leaders are those who are capable of change and growth. They view change as a natural process, rather than as something to be feared and resisted.

Because they know their powers and the limits on those powers, and, more important, because they know themselves, these leaders are less authoritarian, more "human." These qualities, incidentally, synchronize with the self-interest of the organization in increasing efficiency and productivity. Managers view satisfaction of workers with their jobs as a major factor in achieving those goals, and it is generally agreed that individual performance on the job and the "openness" of the organization are linked.

The purpose of this book is to encourage organizations to look beyond the mechanical task

1. Edward C. Bursk (ed.), *How to Increase Executive Effectiveness* (Cambridge, Mass., Harvard University Press, 1953), p. 5.

of supervising production of X widgets a day and to help executives transcend the viewpoint of them and their associates as merely units making the machines run smoothly.

A clue to the rationale for this book can be found in a sampling of the chapter titles: "The Management of Ideas," "Conditions for Manager Motivation," "Power and Politics in Organizational Life." The authors of these chapters can of course give no definitive answers to the question of how to be an effective leader; management will never be reduced to a science. But they do provide some useful signposts, as well as much food for thought.

We have divided the book into three sections, "Personal Growth," "Coping with the Job," and "Motivation for Growth." Part I is the broadest in scope, and we have chosen an article by Kenneth R. Andrews, who has long been concerned with executive development, as a kind of keynote address for the book as well as the section. This chapter, "Toward Professionalism in Business Management," is useful in showing businessmen where they stand now in the opinion of society—measured by criteria beyond mere financial success—and what they can become. Does the businessman wish to be measured in terms of knowledge and application of it, in terms of self-control and social responsibility? Does he want the esteem of society? Our premise is that he does. To quote Andrews: "The commitment of the individual depends on the clarity and quality of the personal, corporate, and professional goals of his life, his company, and his business. So long as purposes are defined in narrow, conventional terms, obscuring or limiting their importance, the ability, initiative, and dedication of the individuals assigned to achieve them are not likely to remain impressive or to grow."

How managers view themselves is a good starting point for transcending the "narrow" and "conventional"; from there growth begins. That is the subject of the second chapter, "The Power to See Ourselves." Other chapters in this section concern how to turn to advantage the inevitable disappointments that a manager experiences; the prospect of extending the thoughts we have on Sunday to other days of the week; and the intellectual demands of today's world that force the executive to do more than merely manage productive resources.

The theme of Part II is well summed up in the title of its first chapter, "Skills of an Effective Administrator." This section of the book deals with the tools the executive needs to handle the problems that come across his desk every day. Robert L. Katz, the author of the first chapter in this section, contends that effective administration is founded on three basic skills: technical, human, and conceptual. He stresses development of these skills on the job.

Other chapters discuss the task of management from the point of view of the chief executive, in the perspective of the power relationships inherent in any organizational structure, and in terms of the constructive and aggressive drives in the manager's psychological makeup. Finally, we have included a chapter devoted to the demands placed on executives by the advent of electronic data processing and sophisticated mathematical techniques of analysis.

In Part III, "Motivation for Growth," the focus shifts from that of the manager and his domain to that of training and motivating those who have taken on, or who are scheduled to be given, greater responsibility in the organization.

Leading off is "Pygmalion in Management," by J. Sterling Livingston, whose purport is the influence that the top manager has on the careers of those immediately below him: he tends to make them in his own image. The succeeding chapter continues the theme of the critical effects of top management attitudes and policies on rising subordinates.

In other articles rounding out this section, their authors report the results of a survey of more than 1,000 managers in a large corporation, which sought to uncover the most important elements in motivation of managers; analyze corporate career-planning programs; and suggest ways in which the administrator can lay out his own "learning agenda." The final chapter considers the training programs of multinational U.S. companies in underdeveloped nations of the world.

A vital part of administrative effectiveness, Dean David wrote in the introduction quoted earlier, is "the ability to strike continual balances among responsibilities to oneself, one's company, associates, industry, and community." We hope this book will give the executive insight into finding ways to achieve those balances, for the better fulfillment of his responsibilities.

E. C. B.
T. B. B.

PERSONAL GROWTH

1

TOWARD PROFESSIONALISM
IN BUSINESS MANAGEMENT

Kenneth R. Andrews

Foreword

In this article the author examines business management in terms of the attributes of professionalism, finding that management falls short in some technical respects but qualifies surprisingly well, all criteria considered. Then he moves on to what is for him a more important question: *In what ways* is business becoming more professional? In particular, *how* can it serve society better?

Whether business in our society can be characterized as a *profession* is a question which has been debated for the last 50 years. The proponents sometimes have been distinguished individuals like Louis Brandeis, A.A. Berle, Jr., and David Lilienthal, all with no axe to grind. More often the affirmative has been argued by the idealistic founders and committed leaders of graduate schools of business, by partisan business journals and associations, and by business leaders of stature. The usual academic response has been, "No, not yet, but some day perhaps."

3

Although neither business education nor business leadership appears cast down by this verdict, good reason exists to reopen the subject. In this article I shall attempt to:

1. Review the definitions and criteria essential for consideration of the status question.

2. Identify the nature and direction of such professionalization as may be found in business practice.

3. Propose contributions from educators and practitioners that might most constructively continue or institute whatever is desirable in the process of professionalization.

Whether in the course of my argument anyone concludes that business is or is not a profession is not of the first importance, for reasons that will become clear.

Defining professionalism

In 1912, Louis D. Brandeis described business as a profession shortly after the establishment of graduate business education at Dartmouth in 1900 and at Harvard in 1908. The attributes of a profession, in his judgment, were that the training for its practice be intellectual in character, that it be pursued not for one's own sake but for others, and that the amount of financial reward not be considered the measure of success.[1] Abraham Flexner, popularly credited with professionalizing medical education almost single-handedly, wrote in 1915 that a profession should be intellectual, learned, practical, expert in relevant technique, formally organized, and altruistic.[2] He concluded, incidentally, that medicine, law, engineering, literature, painting, and music qualified, but that social work (about which he was writing) did not. Ernest Greenwood, still writing about social work in 1953, described the consensus of distinguishing attributes to be "(1) systematic theory, (2) authority [accorded by clients], (3) community sanction, (4) ethical codes, and (5) a formally sustained culture."[3]

Bernard Barber, writing ten years later, identified four essential characteristics:
1. High degree of generalized and systematic knowledge.
2. Orientation primarily to community rather than individual interest.
3. High degree of self-control through internalized codes and voluntary organizations.
4. System of rewards viewed as symbols of work achievement, not as ends in themselves.[4]

Morris L. Cogan directly addressed the problem of definition in 1953. After reviewing the whole range, he offered a distillation which is comprehensive and unbiased:

"A profession is a vocation whose practice is founded upon an understanding of the theoretical structure of some department of learning or science, and upon the abilities accompanying such understanding. This understanding and these abilities are applied to the vital practical affairs of man. The practices of the profession are modified by knowledge of a generalized nature and by the accumulated wisdom and experience of mankind, which serve to correct the errors of specialism. The profession, serving the vital needs of man, considers its first ethical imperative to be altruistic service to the client."[5]

Leading criteria

The criteria accumulating from these representative definitions take us far from sole reliance on formalities of education, admission, ordination, and licensing. These processes in an earlier time confined recognition to the three "learned professions"—theology, law, and medicine. To evaluate the professional quality of any occupation it is clear that we must give attention to five criteria:

1. *Knowledge*—The knowledge pertinent to a professional field involves more than information or historical fact. Whether derived from empirical experience, experiment, or recorded history, it has been subjected to disciplined analysis. It has produced and been tested by concepts extending its usefulness and determining its possible meanings. Already sufficiently extensive to bear on most of the problems of the profession, it is capable of being extended further by systematic research.

2. *Competent application*—The knowledge just described is competently applied to a class of practical problems of considerable complexity

1. *Business—A Profession* (Boston, Hale, Cushman & Flint, 1933; originally published by Small, Maynard in 1914), p. 2.

2. "Is Social Work a Profession?" *School and Society*, June 20, 1915, p. 901.

3. Quoted in Howard W. Vollmer and Donald L. Mills, *Professionalization* (Englewood Cliffs, New Jersey, Prentice-Hall, Inc., 1966), p. 10.

4. "Is American Business Becoming Professionalized?" in *Sociological Theory, Values, and Sociocultural Change: Essays in Honor of Pitirim A. Sorokin*, edited by Edward A. Tiryakien (New York, Harper & Row, 1967), pp. 121-145.

5. Quoted in Vollmer and Mills, op. cit., p. vii (note).

and of major concern to organized society by individuals taking responsibility for the applicability of what they know to the problems at hand. The application of knowledge is a complex exercise of practical judgment and skill facilitated by attitudes like pride in competence, pleasure in performing the work of the field, and sympathy for the individuals or groups being served.

3. *Social responsibility*—The practicing professional is not only knowledgeable and competent, but is motivated less by his own aggrandizement than by the desire to satisfy needs, solve problems, or accomplish goals appropriate to his field. Whether we call this altruism, community interest, enlightened self-interest, or selflessness, *it is not primarily self-serving*. The material or monetary rewards attending successful performance, though varying widely in and among professions, are not valued primarily for their own sake.

4. *Self-control*—The membership of a profession should have an effective means for setting standards of conduct, influencing behavior, and disciplining poor performance. Except where behavior is illegal and thus comes under the jurisdiction of the courts, this review will be performed and discipline will be administered by members of the profession, not to protect poor practice from adverse judgment by laymen, but to ensure the technical validity of the criticism.

5. *Community sanction*—As a consequence of knowledge, skill, responsibility, and self-control having been made manifest, the individuals and segments of society served by a profession grant its practitioners respect, authority, and considerable freedom within which to pursue their practice. In turn, the status won by professional activity gives it a high position in the hierarchy of occupations.

Problems of evaluation

When we begin to measure business against either the accepted professions or their attributes, we are immediately put off by the heterogeneity of business activity. Business is hardly a single occupation. It comprises the congeries of occupations and organization form which perform all the functions of industry, commerce, and finance. Its purpose in Western societies is to produce and distribute the interrelated products and services comprising material existence, making life agreeable, and permitting the pur-

suit of nonmaterial goals. In industrially developed countries these activities multiply, change, die out, and spring up in an unstable complexity affected by entrepreneurial energy, developing technology, increasing expectations of material well-being, and ideals of social justice.

The institutions of business are more prominent than the individual businessman. They are similarly diverse in size and kind, in competence and integrity, in purpose and morality, in technology and complexity. Their leadership is not all trained to the same traditions, exposed to the same disciplines, or persuaded by compulsory

education to the same ideals. Variety in the work of the world and in the institutions organized to perform it makes it impracticable to argue that all of business is professional. To a greater degree than in law and medicine, there is much hewing of wood and drawing of water.

For our present purposes the two most important strands in the pattern of business are the proliferation of the technical functions of business and the development of the process called management. Functions like research and development (including basic science, engineering, and technological forecasting), production functions (including engineering, linear programming, and the more esoteric operations research), a cluster of logistical functions resulting in the storage and distribution of goods, and electronic data processing have joined older specialties like marketing, manufacturing, accounting, control, finance, and personnel and labor relations to comprise the sophisticated division of labor made possible by organization. These specialties have found or established bases of knowledge in the physical sciences, mathematics, economics, and the behavioral sciences. The successful operation of a moderately complex organization requires the services of many specialists who have formed societies devoted to the extension of knowledge, the development of standards, and the achievement of professional status.

It would be an interesting but endless task to examine and rank all of these technical specialties against the attributes of professionalism. The ultimate conclusion would doubtless be that although the rate and nature of their development differ widely, the direction of their striving is unmistakably toward the status enjoyed by the professions and toward the qualities of professional activity that earn the recognition sought.

Is management professional?

Rather than take up the technical functions, it is more practicable for us to examine the *management* of business organizations against the essential criteria of a profession. The more intricate the division of labor in a corporation, the more essential becomes the coordination of specialized activity to keep the specialism of the functions in balance, to serve the principal purposes of the organization, and to sustain the motivation and development of its membership. The managers of business have responsibility for all that goes on from the entrepreneurial evaluation of opportunity to the development and achievement of organization purposes. Without detailed knowledge of more than one or two functional specialties, and probably already behind the times in these, executives must somehow achieve the convergence of all the technical ramifications of business activity.

If the general management function cannot be viewed as professional, then it is of little importance whether the functional specialties can be. Management is the most important and most nearly central process in the operation of effective business organizations. It is being recognized as the central process in the successful conduct of other kinds of organizations.

To evaluate the professionalism of management, let us examine the five criteria.

Knowledge requirement

That the practice of management in business rests on a body of knowledge meeting the first criterion is today beyond argument. Business administration constitutes a curriculum in three different kinds of business schools:

1. A vocational group which undertakes to combine a basic undergraduate general education and a useful introduction to the functions of business and to the administrative process.

2. A small number of graduate schools in which the curriculum stresses the core disciplines of business, with some attention to the functions but little to general management.

3. The schools which as "professional" rather than "graduate" schools present a nondepartmental curriculum conceived primarily with the requirements of practice in mind; i.e., the curriculum comprises the study of (a) functions like marketing, production, and finance which cut across all industries; (b) the organization processes like quantitative analysis, control, and organizational behavior which cut across all functions; (c) the social, economic, political, and technical environmental forces affecting the individual firm; and (d) the policy processes leading to the formulation and achievement of purpose.

The disciplines that underlie these studies include principally economics, mathematics, statistics, individual and social psychology, applied anthropology, sociology, history, and political science. In addition, all areas of the business curriculum now draw on original and applied research of their own, and on the already developed literature of the functions, of organization theory, of the human problems of organization, and of leadership.

The aim of the professionally oriented business school is to apply to the purposes and problems of business the presumed outcomes of liberal undergraduate education. These I take to be the ability to use language and mathematics, to think logically, to understand in depth some discipline, to appreciate the methods of science, and to recognize the range of human capability, accomplishments, and values. The professional school attempts to inculcate such qualities as willingness to accept responsibility, energy in action, and reasoned judgment in crises of decision. It aims further to empower its students to act effectively and responsibly and to equip them to lead. No responsible critic of the remaining imperfections of business education will deny that management practice now rests on a developing body of knowledge being systematically extended by valid research methods.

Questions of certification: But is management unprofessional to the degree that its practitioners are not *required* to study this curriculum? Perhaps so, but we should be careful not to let too literal a definition distract us from the spirit of professionalism. Note, for instance, that most lawyers graduate from law schools which Professor David F. Cavers of Harvard University describes as "Stratum III," hardly distinguished for their quality.[6] Their graduates pass bar exams after cram courses directed to that hurdle. They learn more law in law offices and in practice, through apprenticeship and emulation, than in the classroom. Lawyers, doctors, preachers, and teachers are like businessmen in that they *all* learn more from their practice than from their academic preparation.

Moreover, certification for practice would appear to be more crucial for the accepted professions than for business. The doctor or lawyer usually deals with a client who needs the reassurance that his adviser has had at least a minimum of preparation and has been licensed to practice. But management occurs only in organizations which have checks, measures, and competition to discourage malpractice. In these organizations, decisions are the outcome of group processes, tradition, and analysis of special circumstances. The judgment required in reaching decisions is subject to review by a hierarchy organized (in healthy companies) to equate competence and breadth of experience with status and power. The surveillance of junior managers by executives of higher rank, and the subjection of senior executives to the test of results under competition in the marketplace, may be thought of as a kind of certification process. Like admission to the bar, such a trial by experience does not guarantee but establishes the presumption of competence.

At the same time it is clear that formal education in business administration meets the test of enabling the graduates to learn faster and more accurately from their practice than they otherwise would, and to acquire sooner the values that professionalize their work. As business education becomes more relevant to practice, it is in fact more highly valued and more widely sought. But the diversity of business practice, the market mechanism rewarding successful and penalizing unsuccessful entrepreneurship, and the organization means for supervising competence in management all make it impracticable and unnecessary to erect educational requirements in imitation of the formality of law, medicine, and the ministry.

Earlier I mentioned the requirement that the concern of a profession is for practical problems of vital importance. The practice of management indeed requires adaptation of knowledge (however acquired) to practical problems of major concern to mankind. It goes without saying that a material standard of living which frees people from drudgery is vital to human happiness and attainment. Until such a standard is achieved, it takes priority over everything else.

Doubts about responsibility

The criterion of social responsibility presents more difficulty than all the others in appraising the degree of professionalism attained by the members of the "executive elite" of our business system. Judgment is obscured by the persistence of classic economic theory, which postulates self-interest and profit-maximization as the primary motive and duty of businessmen and thus also of the managers of business.

The issue is complicated also by the poverty of understanding, objectivity, and information in the transactions of the academic and business communities. The lack of firsthand knowledge of the motives, purposes, and ideals of businessmen, the suspicion of personal and corporate power originating in earlier eras of our industrialization, and inability of businessmen as men of action to conceive and to express the precise import of what they intend and what they are doing—all these insulate belief from evidence and make us blind to changes taking place.

Adam Smith's "invisible hand" of competition in atomized markets serving consumers who were presumed to have complete knowledge and were motivated to make only the most economical purchases was once supposed to ensure that the general good could best be served by the self-centered striving of the individual firm and entrepreneur. Yet in real life large corporations have power over their markets. Consumers do not have perfect knowledge of their economic alternatives and are not always motivated to search for the lowest price. The inadequacy of the laissez-faire doctrine has been so often commented on, however, that we need not go into it again. The principal point is that the increasing sophistication of economic theory has not eliminated the tendency to describe the principal motive of the corporate manager as the relentless pursuit of profit at the expense of society. This notion distorts reality.

6. "Legal Education in Time of Change," scheduled for publication in *Theological Education*, May 1969.

Illusions about profit: The managers of present-day corporations, which indeed cannot survive without profit or attract capital without producing return, see profit variously as (a) the avoidance of loss, (b) the result rather than the principal purpose of successful operation, (c) the measure of success, (d) the reward for entrepreneurship or patentable innovation, (e) the source of money to be invested in growth and, to the extent which is necessary or "fair," distributed to stockholders. Profit over the long term requires forgoing profits in the near term. Profit maximization has thus become nearly meaningless as a concept in legitimate business.[7] The profit motive in business does not necessarily mean personal greed and acquisitiveness, or exploitation of the public.

The corporate executive, with his firm, his stockholders, his suppliers, and his customers, all with some claim to be his clients, is in any case not producing profit for his personal account—not when separation of ownership from management has taken place. His share in profit is not his main motivation. He does not retire to a life of ease as soon as his economic future is assured. He does not fight against the high rate of taxation of personal income. His satisfaction in increased compensation (incrementally of small value in the higher tax brackets) appears to be of considerable *symbolic* value in providing recognition of attainment and performance.[8]

In the meantime the income of physicians, professors, and lawyers is rising rapidly to reduce or close the gap between the practicing manager and the members of the established professions. No one argues now that professionalization is inversely proportional to monetary reward.

Inept philosophers: The reality of corporate power cannot be denied. The issue is whether under sound and moderately restrictive governmental regulation the public can be assured that this power will be responsibly exercised. Businessmen themselves contribute to doubt on this matter. They sometimes embrace the purely economic rationale prepared for them by economists and used against them by their critics. In contesting the extension of government regulation, in maintaining their "prerogatives" to raise prices when the Council of Economic Advisers would prefer otherwise, or just in describing their firms' objectives in simplistic terms, they assert the philosophy of nine-teenth-century capitalism. Indeed, they are advised to do so by some members of professional school faculties,[9] by some economists, and by such students of the corporation as Eugene V. Rostow of the Yale Law School.[10]

Traditionally, American businessmen, for reasons which I believe are understandable, have not been articulate or persuasive either in rejecting outworn philosophies of corporate leadership or in advancing new ones. Their principal preoccupation is their work, which is relatively much more demanding than the daily schedules of their critics. Their métier is organization, conflict, competition, and the problem-strewn arena of action. They are not theorists or philosophers. They usually leave their speech-writing to underlings. Their actions speak louder than their words; their critics, who read words but do not study action, are deaf to the message.

Delusive criticism: A study by Bernard Barber [11] illustrates the academics' attitude toward management responsibility. Taking note of assertions that businessmen attempt to balance the public and corporate interest and to act as if these were convergent in the long run, Barber notes in a remarkable understatement that "at least in some business quarters the older 'public be damned' attitude has been condemned and the interests of the community at large sometimes become an element in business decisions." The increase in corporate philanthropy, community service, and support to education that he acknowledges seems to him to be at the margin of the businessman's role, not at the center "in his decisions with regard to procurement, production, and pricing." This community concern seems to him only a small part of the direct community orientation required of the practitioner in the accepted professions.

Barber's conclusion that business is insufficiently concerned with community interest to be considered professional is a matter of opinion. The evidence and illustrations used to support the conclusion, however, are far out of date.

7. See Robert N. Anthony, "The Trouble With Profit Maximization," HBR November-December 1960, p. 126.

8. See Crawford H. Greenewalt, *The Uncommon Man* (New York, McGraw-Hill Book Company, Inc., 1959), pp. 87-103.

9. For example, see Theodore Levitt, "The Dangers of Social Responsibility," HBR September-October 1958, p. 41.

10. See "To Whom and for What Ends are Corporate Managements Responsible?" in *The Corporation in Modern Society*, edited by Edward S. Mason (Cambridge, Massachusetts, Harvard University Press, 1959), pp. 46-71; other papers in this volume elaborate the economists' distrust of the doctrine of responsibility.

11. Op. cit., p. 121.

A clue to the communication lag between practice and criticism so characteristic of the evaluation of business by outsiders may be found in Barber's reliance for corroboration on *The American Business Creed*.[12] This book, appearing in 1956, describes an ideology which is clearly inconsistent with professional aspiration.

The evidence of the existence, nature, and alleged dominance of the ideology are drawn largely from advertisements, brochures, and published statements of the National Association of Manufacturers. This organization was at an earlier time not only one of the most reactionary established institutions in American life but one of the least influential, even among its own membership. To determine the degree of professionalization of American management from such source material would be like evaluating the concern of the medical profession for the aged and the indigent on the basis of the American Medical Association's passionate subscription to the ideology of reaction (e.g., its once stubborn refusal to consider subsidy of medical care, new methods like group practice, and ways to reduce the cost of drugs).

The NAM itself has changed rapidly in the last two decades, as will the AMA in time, in response to the more progressive views of its membership. The published remnants of its philosophers were even at the time of their use in *The American Business Creed* not representative of the practices of most of the members and almost wholly without influence in those segments of the business community to which the future belonged. The authors take no note of the publications of the professional business school of their own university, including HBR, the books of its Division of Research, or the writings of its deans and faculty.

Contemporary concept: The strong current in today's leading business practice, as indicated, for example, in A.A. Berle's *Twentieth Century Capitalist Revolution*[13] and David Lilienthal's *Big Business: A New Era*,[14] is to undertake the reconciliation of conflicting responsibilities. These responsibilities arise out of the relationship of the firm to its own members, to its owners (now typically subdivided and unable themselves to control the balance), and to the communities that it serves or is served by. From the time of Chester Barnard's *The Functions of the Executive*,[15] the firm has been properly conceived as a system operating within larger systems in intricate interdependence. Its equilibrium is not principally the product of chance or of impersonal forces; it is capable of being designed, directed, influenced, and changed. The interests of the corporation and the systems of which it is a part are capable of being combined in ways quite satisfactory to both, depending in large part on the capability, good will, initiative, and morality of the men in charge.

Emergence of self-control

The hectic variety of business makes difficult the establishment of intraprofessional standards of conduct. Because of public concern, the courts, Congress, and administrative agencies of the government (like the Federal Drug Administration, the Antitrust Division of the Department of Justice, and the Federal Trade Commission) maintains a surveillance of industry which it is not moved to duplicate.

One by one, however, industry trade associations are adopting codes of conduct expressing the rules of fairness and specifying standards of quality and safety. (Surely in the older professions the emergence of standards of competence and ethics were at first spontaneous developments which were later formalized.) Whatever may be said of the limited punitive provisions of these codes, they serve as visible signs of a much more massive force. This may be described as the development of corporate due process, which serves as a "corporate conscience," establishing norms of what is acceptable and insuring through preventive disapproval that these norms are not ignored.

Studies of organization have produced convincing evidence that group norms are often more effective than is external force in influencing behavior. As standards have been formalized in business, it has not seemed imperative, in the interests of pluralism and innovation, that professional managers should be examined by a public agency and their behavior supervised by business groups with punitive power. Competitive pressure, obsolescence, financial loss, and failure have seemed adequate punishments for incompetence. The law deals with crimes and misdemeanors; organization conscience and corporate due process deal with ethical and moral

12. Francis X. Sutton, Seymour E. Harris, Carl Kaysen, and James Tobin, *The American Business Creed* (Cambridge, Massachusetts, Harvard University Press, 1956).

13. New York, Harcourt, Brace & Company, 1954.

14. New York, Harper & Brothers, 1958.

15. Cambridge, Massachusetts, Harvard University Press, 1938.

questions not covered by law. The force of public opinion plays over the whole scene.

Community sanction

This final attribute of a profession follows from the demonstration of more fundamental characteristics. It is for that reason not central to our inquiry.

Used car lot operators, repairmen, and hucksters are commonly viewed by the public with a certain reserve. The hinterland of shady practice is much more extensive in business than in the accepted professions. But at no time has general acceptance and tacit approval of the management of corporate enterprise risen higher than the level of today. This acceptance does not mean that corporate executives are viewed as heroes, but neither is there any public complaint—as curiously enough there is among academics—that corporate leaders are "faceless." The depression which appears to afflict our society in the presence of such problems as Vietnam, rebellious youth, the problems of the cities, and the balance of international payments has not extended to disillusion about the management of our enterprise system.

There is good reason for this acceptance of business. Significantly, it will authorize the entry of business into new areas of service to which it is drawn because of social needs and from which it would have been barred in earlier days of distrust.

Becoming professional

It is clear by this time that I believe an already impressive degree of professionalism marks the management of business. The criteria we have used have been derived from the historical development of law and medicine. They were not designed to accommodate the special complexities, forms of organization, and variety of function in business. It is remarkable, therefore, that except on quite technical grounds business management is not clearly disqualified by any of the criteria. It falls short formally in the relation of practice to educational and admission requirements and in institutional arrangements for disciplining conduct.

The differences between business, on the one hand, and law and medicine, on the other, are such that the natural organic development of business's role in society may not be well served by artificially making it more similar to the older professions. Rather than measuring the technical discrepancy between the attributes of business and the older professions, it is more important for us to note—and, if we approve, to support—the *direction* in which business leadership is taking its functions and institutions (and with them our whole society). "Is business a profession?" is not really the question which we should address further. *How* business and the established professions can better serve society is a much more important question.

We would do better to join Everett C. Hughes, who records his own experience with this issue as follows:

"In my own studies I passed from the false question, 'Is this occupation a profession?' to the more fundamental one, 'What are the circumstances in which the people in an occupation attempt to turn it into a profession, and themselves into professional people?' " [16]

If this progression is appropriate, then we must turn away from arguments about attainment to the *process* of professionalization. The process itself is well described by Harold Blumer:

"Professionalization seeks to clothe a given area with standards of excellence, to establish rules of conduct, develop a sense of responsibility, to set criteria for recruitment and training, to insure a measure of protection for members, to establish collective control over the area, and to elevate it to a position of dignity and social standing in the society." [17]

A number of trends attest to the progressive professionalization of business. Let us look at five especially important ones.

1. More sophisticated practice

The growth of business education, the tradition of openness in communicating management discoveries made in practice, and the constant pressure for effectiveness from intra- and inter-industry competition have advanced the art. Intuitive practice derived from routine and tradition has given way to more analytical and studied approaches to problems. Planning has been accepted as essential in business. As the management of the economy by government has stabilized cyclical variation, growth and im-

16. *Men and Their Work* (Glencoe, Illinois, Free Press, 1958), p. 45.

17. Quoted in Vollmer and Mills, op. cit., p. xi.

provement in performance measured in annual increments have been institutionalized as goals. As free trade has admitted low-cost goods to U.S. markets, many industries have been stimulated to maintain or improve their positions.

2. Leadership in change

Far from defending established investments, practices, and privileges, business is responding to and initiating change at a rate which is visibly faster than that prevailing in any other segment of society. The pace may be glacial, as in the case of U.S. Steel, steady, as in the case of General Motors, or frenetic, as in the case of IT&T, but in almost all instances it seems to be accelerating.

Innovation is seen as the best route to growth. Product diversification (through acquisition and merger, new product development, market research, and increasing competence) introduces changes into the ways of a business organization and ultimately into the lives of its customers. The search for new opportunity releases imagination, authorizes creativeness, and permits experiments. The destructive implications of change for its own sake are kept in check by the need to estimate the risks attending investment in innovation and to compare opportunities with each other before allocating limited resources.

The wastefulness of planned obsolescence, the disorderly duplication resulting from free initiative, and the inefficient regulation of growth and change by antitrust action do not obscure the transformation of business from a conservative to an innovative orientation. The by-product of material well-being is proving to be heightened aspirations and ideals of social justice, liberation from drudgery, and more education—all leading ultimately to a transformed society, whatever the interim upheaval.

3. Relations with government

In a day when business was business and competence was intuitive, the wider the distance and the less the traffic between business and government, the better everything was thought to be. This attitude is on the way out. The old hostility which limited business interest in public problems has diminished in the face of these developments:

☐ In the long-established defense business, extensive and constructive relationships have developed between private firms and contracting agencies of the Defense Department.

☐ In the space business, NASA-sponsored contracts have markedly increased the experience of private firms in cooperating with the government. The creation of COMSAT, as original a combination of private and public interests in satellite communications as was the old concept of the regulated utility illustrated by AT&T, is a new chapter in this history.

☐ The participation by individual businessmen in the Treasury, Defense, and Commerce departments has gradually brought more adaptable and effective executives into important public posts.

☐ The service of innumerable businessmen on presidential task forces and commissions has lately led to surprisingly liberal positions, like the endorsement of East-West trade by the commission headed by Irwin Miller, the proposal for a negative income tax (later recommended for serious study by Arjay Miller, then president of the Ford Motor Company), and the participation by business in the problems of the city. Old stereotypes of the business leader have faded because of the roles played by Thomas Watson of IBM, Joseph Wilson and Peter McColough of Xerox, David Rockefeller of The Chase Manhattan Bank, Charles B. Thornton of Litton Industries, and the late Gerald Phillippe of General Electric in government-sponsored inquiries or undertakings dealing with socioeconomic problems.

4. Action on public problems

Business is increasingly active in educational activities contributing to community development and in turning the corporation's organized resources to social problems. Its many efforts along these lines can be regarded as an entrepreneurial enlargement of the economic function of business. Activities like the following are becoming increasingly numerous:

☐ The Job Corps centers of many companies are not undertaken only to make money, but also to bring corporate competence to bear on a specific need, to acquire experience, and to enlarge the skilled labor force.

☐ The related entry of companies like IBM, General Electric, Time, RCA, Raytheon, Litton Industries, and the New York Times into education reflects an extension of corporate activity into growth areas expected to produce profits in return for new kinds of service rendered.

☐ The progress of civil rights in the South owes much to the willingness of business leaders in Birmingham, Atlanta, Houston, and elsewhere to persuade segregated firms to change their policies for economic and social reasons.

☐ U.S. Gypsum, Aerojet, Lockheed, Ford, and now innumerable other companies have been working out feasible ways to rehabilitate housing, establish factories and training facilities in the ghettos, and provide skills and jobs to hardcore, Negro unemployed. Such activities manifest a genuine and widespread recognition of obligation to the community; they also reflect businessmen's satisfaction in helping to solve the urgent problems of society.

Especially complex social problems—urban renewal, for instance—are at this stage so baffling that efforts to cope with them are somewhat inhibited for lack of knowledge of how to be effective. But as inquiry, experience, and the innovative skills of corporate enterprise make the problems more clear, corporate involvement with them will increase. Examples like the following indicate the *kind* of thing we can expect to see more often in the future:

☐ The Kaiser Foundation Hospitals and Health Plan, originating in a company medical service and now serving over a million persons in four Western regions, is providing high-quality medical care in 42 outpatient centers and 13 hospitals; it employs 1,000 well-qualified and well-paid physicians. This organization may itself expand to new regions and attract imitation. As a nonprofit organization, the incentive for expansion and emulation is altruistic; we may ask one day whether society will be better served if such corporations could be allowed returns which would attract investment.

☐ On a smaller scale, the Mississippi Delta Test Facility of the General Electric Company hopes to convert its mission, when its missile testing is over, in part to the economic and social development of a depressed rural region. It has already undertaken pilot projects in community development.

A generation ago such ventures would have been inconceivable. Tomorrow private corporations may be running public school systems and the Federal Post Office. Such developments cannot take place, of course, without sufficient professionalization of business to justify public trust and without adequate regulation to ensure propriety.

At any rate, industry and society are redefining the legitimate areas of business. If goodwill, management skill, and corporate power result in important accomplishments in education, social justice, economic rehabilitation of cities and regions, and the organization problems left unattended by medicine, law, the church, and education, the relationship between business and nonbusiness elements of our society will change. One outcome will be the consensus that such accomplishments deserve recognition and are motivated primarily by concern for society.

5. Internationalization

The expansion of business activity into other countries has been importantly aided by the desire for growth, increased sophistication, a willingness to consider new modes of cooperation with overseas companies and governments, and the desire to contribute to the economic development of the world. The simple motive of disposing of surplus inventories or of maintaining 100%-U.S. subsidiaries abroad has long since given way to more systematic adaptation to the needs of foreign markets, the organization of joint ventures with other private firms or with foreign governments, and the training of foreign nationals to operate and manage these ventures.

The involvement of oil companies with the national states which their revenues maintain, the role of American banks in contributing to local economic progress, and the accumulating experience of formerly provincial Americans in culturally and economically different environments should ultimately educate U.S. businessmen to a world view far more extensive than that of the accepted professions. Entry into the world arena tends to reduce doctrinaire decision making. It liberalizes the prejudices of insular companies and industries. Internationalization requires greater imagination in discovering and greater organizational skill in developing opportunity. It makes vivid the extent to which industrialization can serve humanity, and it is indispensable to meeting the material needs of the world's populations.

Opportunities for progress

This hasty review of some of the major current developments in business is intended to indicate the *scope* for professionalization in business and to suggest its *direction*. Utopia has not been achieved. Much more can be done both by business and by business education to clarify the kind of professionalization most appropriate to the new role of business in our society. Some business schools are rendered impotent in this undertaking by a crisis of purpose. Are they to retain or enlarge their attachment to the "graduate" school, accumulating and interpreting knowledge within the limited framework of one academic discipline or another? Or are they to orient their research and teaching toward practice, study the interdisciplinary problems of the application of knowledge, and identify themselves as much with the values of the profession as with the values of the university?

Aims of education

Greater professionalism will be best served by acceptance in business education of greater professionalization as an institutional goal. This will not be an easy task. The economists' recognition of the inadequacy of classical doctrine in the face of "managerialism" has not yet been followed by a rationale taut enough to be persuasive or binding enough to be reliable.[18] The doctrine of social responsibility needs much more hard work. The idealism implicit in new definitions of the role of business needs to be identified and embraced, not extolled in one place and ridiculed in another.

The principal curricular developments now under way in the professional school of business include:

○ Growth of new methods of quantitative analysis associated with the computer.

○ Study of organizational behavior.

○ Better concepts for analyzing, understanding, and reacting responsibly to the social, economic, technological, and political environment of business.

○ Study of policy formulation.

These subjects all bear importantly on both the abilities and responsibilities of professional managers, as long as they are taught with concern for the complexities and problems of practice. The programs of continuing education, more extensive in business than elsewhere, will clearly continue. Their relevance to increased professional skill and the promulgation of professional ideas is quite clear.

The principal present responsibility of the

business school for the progress of professionalization appears to be through research and teaching to assist the applications of organized corporate resources to the solutions of the newly recognized problems of society. The business executive does not work alone on the problems of clients. He is a leader of organized effort that should be applied to purposes before which the single individual is helpless. He is willing to turn to logistical problems like air and water pollution, transportation, and the decay of the city. But he needs help in defining and solving the new kinds of problems. It is the new task of the professional school to study them and to create the combination of concepts necessary for approaching them effectively.

Better self-regulation

It is properly the function of the professional school, in addition, to develop and maintain the standards appropriate to performance. Whether it is feasible to develop some form of certification of qualification for the executive taking office at a prescribed level in a particular kind of corporation, or to establish special or quasi-public authorities for the examination of practice, deserves more than the cursory attention it is getting today. If the cumbersome and uninformed regulation of business from outside is not to be increased or is to be made less formal, then business must be able to satisfy the public that self-regulation can meet the need.

Opportunity for greater self-regulation on the part of business can be found in the organization both of the firm itself and of its industry. Within the firm, the largely dormant or only occasionally active board of directors, typically now an institution using only a small part of the talent of its membership, could begin inquiring continuously into the legal and social implications of the corporation's activities. These activities should be considered not only in the light of today's laws but of tomorrow's higher standards and broader definitions of economic opportunity. The perspective of conventional boards can be expanded by:

○ Reducing the average age and increasing the diversity and caliber of directors.

○ Reducing the number of "inside directors."

○ Adding representatives from education, government, or other industries who have demonstrated concern and competence in dealing with modern definitions of the functions of private business.

18. See Edward S. Mason, "The Apologetics of 'Managerialism,'" *The Journal of Business*, January 1958, p. 1.

○ Redefining the board's responsibility and agenda.

Since selecting the membership and planning the activity and role of boards in the publicly held corporations are in the hands of its management, it is the chief executive who has the opportunity to provide for more searching and critical self-examination. *If he wants it, he can have it.*

The constrained efforts of several industries to regulate the practices of their own members suggests the feasibility of industry councils, manned by individuals from representative companies. Such councils could review without publicity whatever practices of the industry seem most vulnerable to criticism, develop codes of conduct, and exercise through moral suasion or more punitive measures (e.g., publicity) effective influence on firms that are open to criticism. Much diffidence and confusion of conscience remain to be overcome before industry councils can be useful.

Coping with the risks: To be sure, formalization of industry institutions for self-regulation brings with it dangers of real or imputed collusion and of confusion between self-discipline and the pursuit of special privilege. All professionalization, however, implies increasing obligations and competence in the complex disentanglement of right from wrong; the problem of telling one from the other carries with it no release from responsibility.

To deal with the possibility of having council proceedings deteriorate gradually toward self-serving rationalization or improper collaboration of competitors, management can resort to practical measures like recording the proceedings of discussions or inviting the scrutiny of minutes or meetings by representatives of regulatory agencies or neutral organizations. Increased self-regulation would not eliminate, in any case, the role of governmental supervisory agencies in seeing to it that private self-regulation does not run off with the public interest.

Conclusion

Further progress toward professionalization in the practice of management turns mainly on the forthright acceptance of the desirability of professionalism and the clarification of the purposes of business. The corporation is now at least partially understood as a social system. More attention needs to be given to the satisfactions and incentives available to its members. The commitment of the individual depends on the clarity and quality of the personal, corporate, and professional goals of his life, his company, and his business. So long as purposes are defined in narrow, conventional terms, obscuring or limiting their importance, the ability, initiative, and dedication of the individuals assigned to achieve them are not likely to remain impressive or to grow.

What business is for and what a given company is trying to accomplish are of vital importance to making professionalization a process influential in the progress of a particular person or organization. Attention to the quality of organization purpose, to the terms in which it should be stated, and to the criteria by which its worth should be judged may be the most important next stage in the formal progress of business.

Deliberate attention by both business and business education to the encouragement of professionalization is thus vitally important. If the corporation is to attract the kind of specialized and executive talent that is required by the complexity and magnitude of the problems to be solved, the rewards of a career in business must be more than money, status, and power. The satisfactions it offers in terms of work worth doing over a lifetime career must be not only real but evident. Business is not innately less challenging, less rewarding, or less vital to society than the accepted professions.

Much hard work will be needed to make clear what the new role of business is in the world, and to show how business offers to men and women of intelligence, ability, and morality the the opportunity to solve problems *beyond the reach of other professions.* But the task should not be as difficult tomorrow as it was yesterday. As purpose and performance become clear and as institutions are developed to articulate, apply, and perhaps enforce standards, the progress of professionalization in business will be no less rapid than it is today. And it will be attended by more honor.

2

THE POWER
TO SEE OURSELVES

Paul J. Brouwer

A psychological fact is that manager development means change in the manager's self-concept. Each of us, whether we realize it or not, has a self-image. We see ourselves in some way — smart, slow, kindly, well-intentioned, lazy, misunderstood, meticulous, or shrewd; we all can pick adjectives that describe ourselves. This is the "I" behind the face in the mirror, the "I" that thinks, dreams, talks, feels, and believes, the "I" that no one knows fully. In this article we will explore the meaning of the self-image, particularly in relation to changing behavior in the growing manager, and how changes in self-concept come about.

One reason this self-concept is crucial is that it has a great deal to do with manager development — with being a growing person and eventually realizing one's self-potential. Note the term *manager* development rather than *management* development; the purpose of such development is to help individual managers to grow. After all, they have to do most of the job themselves. As a member of a firm of consulting psychologists to management, I can report that fact from experience — and add the further observation that no one can tell a manager exactly how to grow. Rather, the most one can do is to help the manager understand himself

AUTHOR'S NOTE: This article is drawn from material that will appear as a chapter in *Managers for Tomorrow*, to be published in 1965 by The New American Library of World Literature, Inc., New York.

in his own situation, and then trust him to find the best direction himself.

Filters for Reality

In the first place, the self-concept is important because everything we do or say, everything we hear, feel, or otherwise perceive, is influenced by how we see ourselves. For example:

A businessman, who had traveled in many parts of the world, was incorrigibly curious about the customs, speech, local places of interest, history, and traditions of any place he visited. However, on a one-week visit to London — his first — on a delicate mission for his company, he might just as well have been in Indianapolis for all he learned of English ways of life. Being on a business trip, he saw himself as a businessman, and actually perceived little of what was around him. But as a vacationer in London he would have seen England in depth, because he would have seen himself coming to London for that purpose.

Photographers often slip a reddish filter over the lens when snapping pictures of clouds on black and white film. The filter prevents some of the light rays from reaching the film, so that the final picture shows much darker skies and more sharply whitened clouds. The self-concept is like a filter that screens out what we do not want to hear and see, passes through what we do want to see and hear. In the reverse

15

direction, it gives an idiosyncratic flavor to our behavior. Who among us doesn't usually pick his name out of a jumble of words on a page? Or hear his name announced at an airport amidst all of the other announcements that he fails to hear? This is called selective listening, and it is a function of our self-concept. Thus, how we see ourselves determines generally what we react to, what we perceive, and, in broad terms, how we behave in general.

And this shows up in business situations too. Imagine two executives, A and B, in identical situations. Each calls in a subordinate and delegates an assignment. The italicized words below give partial indications of their self-concepts. Executive A says:

"Tom, I'm *concerned* about our relations with the XYZ Company. Its *purchases* from us have fallen off lately and *rather abruptly*. You know our history with it. *Will* you *investigate* and find out the cause of the reduced volume? *Let me know* if you run into anything you don't understand."

Executive A is confident of his ability to handle the situation. He sees himself as unthreatened, able to cope with whatever Tom's investigation discloses, and willing to delay action until the facts are gathered and studied.

Executive B, on the other hand, says:

"George, the XYZ Company has cut back its purchases from us for the third month in a row. *We've got to get on this and quick.* Now, you go visit it. *I wish I could but I'm tied down here.* Talk to the purchasing agent — uh, what's his name again? Uh . . . (shuffling papers) . . . here it is . . . Bailey. *See* Bailey. Oh . . . and you'd better see the chief engineer, a nice guy . . . named . . . uh . . . his name slips me *for the moment* . . . you can get it from Bailey. But don't go near Sam Awful — he'll cover up whatever's happening anyway, and might use your visit as a sign we're scared of old XYZ. *I've got to have some answers on this one, George.* The boss is on my neck but good. So. . . ."

Executive B is obviously less confident. He feels threatened by the situation. He doesn't trust George to use his own common sense — as indicated by his explicit "do"s and "don't"s — probably because he himself lacks confidence.

Continuing Changes

Although the self-concept is important in understanding human behavior *generally*, it becomes critically so in understanding *manager development*, where changes in behavior are the objective. As a matter of cold, hard, psychological fact, a change in behavior on the job, for better or worse, means a change in self-concept. Thus, we are dealing with an immensely and immediately practical consideration.

Human beings constantly change their behavior, as we see if we examine ourselves (and others) critically enough. It is a superficial observation to say that so-and-so is the same person he was five years ago. Technically, he isn't exactly the same today as he was even yesterday. For one thing, he is one day older. He has learned something new, however negligible, that becomes incorporated in his apperceptive mass. As a result, his perception of today's events is different, however slightly and undetectably, from what it was yesterday. He may have had nothing "significant" happen to him — no promotion, no accident, no soul-searching upset — but he will be different, even though only a person with Solomon's wisdom would know it. Change in behavior is constant.

The difficulties managers have in thinking about changes in behavior come from their inability to detect change, and from fuzzy thinking behind such comforting, though fallacious, notions as, "You can't teach an old dog new tricks," "He was born that way," or "He's been like that ever since I've known him."

On the other hand, sometimes superficial behavior changes are erroneously thought to be basic. For example, consider the simplest level of change in behavior, which is brought about by increased knowledge or skill:

The newly appointed foreman learns his new duties, dons a white shirt, delegates jobs he used to do himself, and learns to participate in his superintendent's meetings. His company provides him with instruction through manuals, books, conferences, sessions with his boss, and management training courses. He joins the National Foremen's Association, attends lectures, and may even be sent to a two-week seminar at the local university. He learns much and becomes suitably skillful in discharging his new functions. This new way of life changes the foreman's behavior, of course; but only peripherally, just as living in a new house does not basically alter the marriage relation. He knows more, sees more, has more and better skills.

If companies do want such "simple-level" changes, and only these, then management training is called for. The girl learns to type; the boy learns how to sell; the new zone manager learns the policy manual; and the new vice president of manufacturing learns how the company's controller figures costs. These specific learnings are the objectives of training, and can become changes in behavior produced by training.

Keystone for Growth

If, however, a company wants growth in the *deeper* sense, then something more subtle and basic in its impact is called for in the manager development effort. Such deeper growth is, of course, a change in self-concept. The manager who once was unreliable in his judgment or who lacked drive *grows* toward reliability in judgment or toward stronger drive. Growth in this sense brings observable changes in outward behavior, because each person is now inwardly different — different, for example, in his perception of himself, in his attitude toward his job and his company as both relate to his own life, or in his feeling of responsibility for others.

But experience shows that such growth is as difficult to achieve as it is desirable. It demands the full-fledged participation of the manager. Actually the trite expression, "Management development is self-development," is psychologically sound. The growing manager changes because he wants to and because he has to in response to new insights and understandings that he gains on the job. He does not change because he is told to, exhorted to, or because it is the thing to do.

Such growth implies changes in the man himself — in how he uses his knowledge, in the ends to which he applies his skills, and, in short, in his view of himself. The point is clear that the growing person examines himself; and as he does so, he emerges with new depths of motivation, a sharper sense of direction, and a more vital awareness of how he wants to live on the job. Growth in this sense is personalized and vital. And such growth in self-concept is at the heart of a real manager development effort.

But growth in self-concept is not always simple and clear.

Conflicts in Self-Concept

Each human being is several selves. He lives comfortably in the role of father, husband, businessman, president, golfer, bridge player, the life of the party, and so on. But if there are conflicts among any of these roles, then discomfort arises. And such conflict brings with it such dynamics as tension, guilt feelings, and compensation. Let us illustrate with a familiar example:

A man sees himself both as a good father and as a good businessman. As a father, he spends time with his children; but as a businessman, he finds the demands on his time overwhelming. Now what does he do? He obviously cannot be home most evenings with his family and also be out of town on necessary business trips. He cannot realize both self-concepts simultaneously. So what happens? He compromises by giving his business his time Monday through Friday, and his family the weekend.

This seems like an easy resolution. What, then, is the problem? The man in our example has had to modify both self-concepts and may feel deeply dissatisfied with such a necessity. So his dissatisfaction, his psychological discomfort, his basic conflict in self-concepts, may show in his behavior. He may be unduly critical of business associates (or subordinates) who will not follow his example and give up their family life during the week. Or he may resent his children, who blithely go about their own activities on the weekend, ignoring him. And if by chance his teen-age son develops any emotional problems which are ascribed to "parental neglect," our man really hits the ceiling! "Neglect? How can that be? Haven't I given my boy every weekend?" he asks.

In the deeper sense, conflicts lie behind many self-concepts, but it is beyond our scope to explore them. In an individual case, this is a matter for professional study and expert handling. By definition, effective, consistent behavior is integrated behavior, while unintegrated behavior is the behavior of conflict.

Unrealism in Self-Concept

In addition to conflicts between self-concepts as a cause of ineffective behavior, there is the crucial matter of disparity between "how I see myself" and "how others see me." Unrealistic self-appraisal has cost many a manager his job. Think of men you know who have been fired, eased out, or moved laterally because they no longer "seemed up to the job." Has there not been in many such cases the subtle flavor of unadaptability, of a rigid inability in a manager to adjust his sights to a new role as times have changed?

Most familiar are the unnecessarily tragic cases of men who cannot grow old gracefully. Next are those uncounted misfits who fail through lack of realistic insight into their true worth. For example, take the good vice president who flunks as president because he never realized his inability to endure the rigors of being top man. There are endless instances of failures owing to a disparity between "who I am" and "who I think I am."

Unfortunately, not only outright failure may come from disparities in self-concept; more insidious is the effect of partial or fuzzy self-appraisal. In fact, if the proposition is right that realism in the individual's view of himself has a one-to-one relationship with effectiveness on the job, then it surely follows that all of us can improve our effectiveness by the simple expedient of developing a more realistic, more accurate self-concept!

In short, the more realistic one's view of himself, the more guaranteed is personal effectiveness. Here is an example that underscores this point:

George H., the vice president of sales for a $50-million company with a staff of 250 sales and service men, was in serious organizational trouble. The group had increased in size so rapidly that it had long since outgrown its organizational pattern. There were constant complaints such as: "Whom do I work for?" "Nobody knows whether I'm doing well or poorly." "We haven't any system to follow in service to customers." The executives under George tried manfully to do twice and three times as much as they had always done. The situation was, frankly, a mess.

George as a person was well liked and respected. He was democratic, attentive to others, soft-spoken, unlikely to "order," always likely to "suggest," and unsure of himself as an administrator. In general he was a man who saw himself as a stimulator and coordinator of his men, an excellent personal salesman, but not a supervisor. Somehow he had completely missed sensing that his men waited for directions from him. He felt that a sensible district sales manager should know what to do. His own perception of himself and his men's perception of him as vice president of sales were poles apart.

The impasse was breached when an outsider on whom George relied heavily (and who also had the confidence of the top men in the department) finally told him bluntly, "George, your people are waiting for you to clear the air. They'll follow any organizational plan you want them to. This step only you can take. They respect you and want your leadership. They value you. Don't ask them; tell them, for goodness' sake, how you're going to organize their activities."

George tried to integrate this new dimension into his self-concept. At first, he swung to one extreme and "got tough." He made explicit, directive demands; he swore; he told everybody, in effect, "I want what I want when I want it — and that's right now!" But soon he abandoned his pretense and absorbed into his self-concept the new "take-charge" aspect of his functioning. He defined an organizational plan, set up policies and procedures which sorted out sales and service duties, discussed them fully with all involved, and said, in effect, "This is it. Let's go."

This example is, of course, an oversimplification; it highlights the fact that disparity in perception can reduce managerial effectiveness. What George saw himself to be in the office of vice president of sales precluded his seeing the needs of his men. And this blind spot nearly cost him prolonged chaos, if not the loss of his job.

Finally, it is manifestly clear that change in self-concept as a function of executive growth has a payoff. Recall situations where a critical appointment has to be made. Who gets the nod? Usually it is the man who *as a person* is thought to have potential and who is able through his style of life on the job to make a contribution to the "mix" of key executives. Consequently, many companies, in selecting their handpicked future executives, feed in "trainees" with liberal arts degrees. They are looking for the *man,* not his knowledge or special skills. By the same token, as the young man grows, it is his self-concept that will change and come more into line with what he is becoming in relation to his potential. It is on the basis of his self-concept that he emerges as a top executive. To twist an old adage, it isn't what you know that finally counts; it's who you *are.*

Natural Resistance

But there is still one big question to answer. If changes in the self-concept of the executive are desirable, just what brings them about? In fact, are changes in self-concept possible? Of course changes are possible, but there is one obvious block to growth.

Even when executives want to change, the lurking suspicion that such effort is futile tends to vitiate the process of change. Faint mutterings of self-discontent tend to get quashed by the notion that "an old dog can't learn new tricks." And the basic comfort of the status quo seems to outweigh the value of the new mode of behavior.

One reason for such feelings of resistance is

that, psychologically, the mature person resists change. By definition, the self-concept is an organization or patterning of attitudes, habits, knowledge, drives, and the like. And also, by definition, the fact of organization means a cementing together of all these complex components.

For example, the man who for many years has been highly and aggressively competitive cannot, except with difficulty, either suddenly or gradually become insightfully cooperative; he will still tend to see himself as needing to surpass the other fellow. The individual retains his pattern, his consistency, his basic characteristics; and in this sense resists change. Indeed, this is a good thing, or we still would all be going through the throes of "finding ourselves" as we did as adolescents.

When the mature person changes, therefore, he does so against a natural resistance; but whether this resistance is a deeply stabilizing influence that helps him to retain his basic direction and character, or whether it is a cocoon that makes him unreachable, is a moot question. Resistance, though built in, may thus be either a roadblock or a gyroscope.

We have noted that changes in the self-concept of the executive are "gut-level," not peripheral. They are changes in perception and attitude and understanding, not changes in knowledge or experience or skills. So our exploration of how change occurs must include those factors which seem to operate more deeply within the individual and which polarize new directions and behaviors. We are looking for those basic, vital factors which, as they operate, really change the person beyond his power of dissimulation or pretense. This is change in the fundamental makeup of the person, not change in his apparel. When such changes occur, the man is different.

Steps to Maturity

Let us be clear about one point. Growth does not proceed in clear-cut, discrete, logical steps. Sometimes it occurs in inexplicable spurts; at other times, with agonizing slowness. There are cases where real learning is so deeply unconscious that no overt behavioral change shows up for a long time. Even regressions will occur, as when an adolescent girl, perhaps troubled by her day's activities, will sleep with a doll as she did at age six. The process of growth is a nebulous, multifactored, fluid, dynamic process, often astounding, and usually only partially controllable.

But for the sake of discussion, and understanding, we can postulate a sequence of steps.

Self-Examination

If we were to attempt a systematic analysis of what happens when growth in a manager occurs, we would need to begin with self-examination. For here the individual first knows he *doesn't know* or first gets an inkling that he wishes his behavior were different in some respect. He is forced, either by circumstance or his own conscious introspection, to look at himself critically. This is what happens when a golfer sees movies of his swing, or when a mother scolds her child by saying, "Just look at yourself — all dirty." Or when the supervisor's thinly veiled anger over a subordinate's sloppy work finally becomes known. Every man sees himself each time he shaves, but does he really examine what he sees? Does he appraise and evaluate and study what manner of man he is?

The function of self-examination is to lay the groundwork for insight, without which no growth can occur. Insight is the "oh, I see now" feeling which must, consciously or unconsciously, precede change in behavior. Insights — real, genuine glimpses of ourselves as we really are — are reached only with difficulty and sometimes with real psychic pain. But they are the building blocks of growth. Thus self-examination is a preparation for insight, a groundbreaking for the seeds of self-understanding which gradually bloom into changed behavior.

Self-Expectation

As an individual raises his sights for himself, as he gets an insight into the direction in which he wants to grow, as he "sees" himself in a particular respect that he does not like, then he is changing his self-expectation. (This is the next step.) New demands on himself are set up, not by anyone else, just by himself. This is another way of saying what the theologians insist on, namely, that a conviction of sin precedes salvation. Or, as the psychologists put it, first accept the fact that *you* have the problem — not anyone else — and then you are ready to find a solution. Here are two cases that illustrate the importance of self-expectation through insight.

❧ John P. was a chronic complainer. Nothing was ever his fault. He frequently and self-pityingly inveighed against his boss, his subordinates, his peers, and the competition. He was capable, knowledgeable, a hard worker, critical. And never once, when he sang the old refrain, "Why does this always happen to me?" did an inner voice whisper back, "It's no different for you, old boy, than for anyone else. It's just the way you take it."

Efforts by his boss and his friends to develop some insight in John seemed wasted. Logical explanations, patiently made, were of course futile. Anger toward him only proved to him he was picked on. Gentle tolerance only gave him a bigger pool to wallow in.

One day in a meeting of executives to find answers to a particular crisis that had hit everyone (an unexpected price slash by a major competitor), he held forth at length on the uselessness of market research, on the futility of keeping a "pipeline" on the competitor's situation, on how his department (sales) couldn't be blamed for not anticipating the vagaries of the competition's pricing policy, and so on. He finally stopped. And, as though by prearrangement, the whole group, perhaps in complete disgust at his immaturity and irrelevance, sat in stony silence.

At length the silence became so oppressive that it suddenly dawned on the complainer that he was just that — an immature complainer. He recalled the words of his colleagues and his own dim awareness that he did complain a lot. Insight finally occurred.

At long last he was ready to begin to grow out of his immaturity. He saw (and disliked) himself at this point. Now his growth could become self-directed; he could easily find many opportunities to quash feelings of self-pity and to face reality in a more statesmanlike fashion, because now he expected more statesmanlike attitudes of himself.

❧ Pete B., age 58, was vice president of engineering of a company that made fine-quality capital goods equipment. He had been with his company 35 years. He was a good engineer, who knew the product inside out; and through the years he had learned to know the customers, too. He felt proud of and personally involved in each installation of the product. It was not unusual to see him on an evening, coatless and with his tie loose, perched on a stool before a drafting board, surrounded by young engineers, digging at a tough installation problem. While some thought Pete did too much himself, others felt that with him on the job the customer would be satisfied.

About four years ago, however, the president, whose family owned the company, sold it to a large corporation, and the company became a wholly owned subsidiary. One allied product line was acquired, then another. Finally Pete's department was asked to do the engineering work for several subsidiaries that were not set up to do their own.

Now Pete's job had changed, subtly but surely, and trouble began to brew for Pete because he couldn't seem to change with the situation.

Psychologically, Pete saw himself as a one-man department (with assistants as trainees) who personally engineered the product for the customer, his friend. He resisted the impersonality of working on engineering problems of "sister companies" whose customers and products he barely knew and cared less about. The new-fangled system of a "home office" engineering vice president who was "staff" seemed to him just another unnecessary complication. Nothing worked the way it used to. He saw himself bypassed by progress and change.

So, unconsciously, he began to resist and to fight. His yearning for the "good old days" subconsciously forced him to run faster and faster in order to know more customers and more product lines; to work more evenings; to press new systems into the form of old procedures. And, of course, he began to slip, and badly. Gradually, Pete was viewed by his superiors as "good old Pete, but let's not get him in on this matter or he'll have to take it over himself and we'll get bogged down," and by his subordinates as a fine fellow, but stodgy and old-fashioned.

Fortunately, before the situation compelled a major organizational shift, Pete took stock of his situation, and really saw himself as he was. He got the insight that his self-image of a kind of personal engineer was no longer applicable to the corporation's greatly expanded needs. And right then, with this new glimpse of himself (and the courage and self-honesty to face it), he began to change. He started by focusing on how his years of experience could be applied to the coaching of his subordinates. He put himself in the shoes of the staff vice president and could then see how to mesh gears better. Then he stopped resisting the new-fangled data processing and automation procedures. His growth began with a new self-expectation.

Change in Self-Expectation

How does one get a new self-demand, a new self-expectation? How does one find out that his present self-concept is inadequate? How does one know not only that he can be different but should be as well? Unfortunately for those who like recipes or formulas, such questions are perennially bothersome because there is no one best way.

What can be done to stimulate change in self-expectation besides honest, realistic, self-appraising introspection? In the business context, the constructive pointing up of an executive's needs for growth by his superior is a tremendous source of insight. The emphasis, of course, is on the word *constructive*, which means helpful, insightful ideas from the superior and not, as so often happens, a ceremonial, judgmental, "I'll tell you what I think about you" appraisal.

A further source of insight is wives — the perceptive ones, that is. Perceptive wives have unique ways of jerking husbands up short when their self-images become distorted.

In fact, anything which enables the man to get a new perception — reading, observing, studying, going to conferences, attending meetings, and participating in clubs — can provide insight into himself. *Out of insight comes change in self-expectation.*

And, of course, life situations which are kaleidoscopic always enable the perceptive person to see himself in a new light. Here is another example:

Paul W. was acutely self-critical, often to the point where his fear of failure immobilized him. He delayed decisions, fussed endlessly with details, and generally strained to be perfect. In time his relation with the psychologist, who genuinely accepted him without criticism, praise, blame, or hostility, enabled him to "see" how his self-critical attitudes really stemmed from his self-pride. He felt he had to be perfect because it was "safer" to be free from criticism and failure. But he finally "rejoined the human race" and demanded of himself only that he do his best. The insight that he was human after all freed him to change his self-expectations.

Self-Direction

A man is master of his own destiny in the sense that he takes charge of his own development if he wants to grow. Nothing can be done to him to make him grow; he grows only as he wants to and as his own insights enable him to.

The change in self-concept that an executive undergoes must continue primarily through his own self-direction. It is clear that many development programs miss their mark badly at this point. They make the naive assumption that exposure to experiences or people or books or courses is enough to produce growth. Not so. They effect change in the participant only

as he reaches out and appropriates something — a bit of wisdom, a new idea, or a new concept — that stretches him, and gives him an answer to his own self-generated problem.

Put another way, we might say that, just as learning is impossible without motivation, so real executive development is impossible unless the executive seeks it. Furthermore, the strength of his desire is infinitely stronger if he seeks development because he wants to develop than if he is merely trying to please his boss or do what is expected of him. As any teacher knows, the pupils who listen and learn merely in order to pass the course are far poorer learners than those who want to learn.

Fundamentally, this is the age-old problem of motivation, of keeping steam up in the boiler. The maintenance of a growing edge, as an executive emerges from insight to insight to realize his potential, is a consequence of intrinsic motivation. He is driven toward unrealized objectives, perhaps toward unrealizable goals; this is what keeps the executive honing his growing edge.

After he develops insight into himself *in relation to what he wants to be*, the power that keeps him growing is the veritable necessity of doing something that to him is intrinsically, basically, and lastingly worthwhile. Growing executives are so because they derive their strength and desire and drive from inner, unachieved goals; and their satisfactions from self-realization. This is intrinsic motivation as it relates to self-concept.

Broadened Perceptions

The dynamics of this factor of growth are very clear: anyone must see himself in relation to his environment, both personal and impersonal, and must develop his image of himself partly in response to what he sees around him. So if he sees a very small world (as a child does), his concept of himself must necessarily be narrow; if he sees himself as a citizen of the world (as a world traveler might), his self-concept embraces the world. This is the difference between the real provincial, such as a hillbilly, and the true sophisticate.

A most common complaint of superiors is that a subordinate is too narrow in his outlook. For example, the sales manager promoted to vice president of sales irritates his peers in manufacturing or research by having "only a salesman's point of view." The former production supervisor, now a vice president, is derided by the people in sales for his attitude of "We'll make it at low cost; it's up to you to sell it, and don't bother me with special runs for special customers or model changes — sell 'em." Both men suffer from constraint of the self-concept: they perceive their jobs (and themselves) too narrowly. For instance:

A vice president of sales was brought in from outside the company to gear up the effort of merchandising a new line of products. He did a magnificent job, old pro that he was, of shaping up and vitalizing a sales force. Volume of sales picked up excellently, and he was the hero of the hour.

But after a year, when he felt on top of his job, some of his attitudes and habits reasserted themselves, annoying others and stalling progress. For instance, he persisted in making frequent references to his former (and larger) company. He climbed on manufacturing for delivery delays, and on research and engineering for perfectionism before releasing the specifications for what he felt were needed product changes. The time it took to explain to him, pacify him, and argue with him was ill-spent and futile. He was rapidly becoming a block in the path of progress.

One day the president approached him directly. "George," said the president, "what's your title?"

"Why," said George, puzzled, "vice president of sales."

"Right. And what does vice president mean to you?"

George paused. What was the president getting at? "Well," he said, "it means lots of things, I guess. Responsibility for sales, building a. . . ."

"Stop right there," interrupted the president. "Responsibility for sales, you say. True in a way. But the sales manager also has this responsibility, doesn't he?"

"Well, yes."

"Then what does the word *vice president* mean in your title?"

"Oh, I see. . . . Well, I guess it means seeing or having responsibility for the sales function of the company from the point of view of the company . . . that part of your office."

"You got my point before I mentioned it, George," said the president. "A vice president speaks from the company point of view, not just that of his department. He tries to keep the overall good of the company in mind."

George thought this conversation over. He got the point. He realized the narrowness of his own view. He had been thinking of himself as "on loan" from his former employer to straighten things out here. As he pondered the president's comments, he broadened his perception of his job

— and of himself. And sometime later he began to act as an officer of the total company.

Self-Realization Power

It is not enough, however, just to see ourselves as we are now. Such understanding is a necessary starting point, or basis on which to build. But we must also see what our real selves *could* be, and grow into that.

The strong men of history have had one psychological characteristic in common: they seem always to have been themselves as persons —

. . . Michelangelo, fighting against odds for a chance to sculpt;

. . . Beethoven, continuing to compose after he became deaf;

. . . Milton, who didn't allow blindness to interfere with his writing.

Such men have given meaning to the phrase, "fulfilling one's destiny."

In less dramatic form, any strong executive fulfills himself as he lives a life that is an unfolding of his potential. He must be himself. In this sense, the self-concept of the strong executive is a constantly evolving, changing thing as he continuously realizes himself. This is, indeed, genuine growth and the kind that continues until senescence sets in.

Can all men aspire to be this strong — to accomplish such self-realization? Of course not. But a growing person (by definition) has unrealized power if his self-concept, his self-expectation, his self-direction, and his constantly broadening perceptions (wisdom) allow him to find it. The difference between a strong man and a weak man may not be a difference in ability, for many clerks have keen intelligence; or in drive, for many ambitious men get nowhere; or in opportunity, for somehow, strong men *make* opportunity. No, the difference lies in self-concept. How much do I value my life? What do I want to do with it? What must I do to be myself? Strong men have emerged with clear-cut answers to such questions; weak men equivocate and temporize and never dare.

Thus growth, finally, is the evolvement of personal goals and the sense of venture in pursuing them. This is the meaning of the dedicated man. His personal goals, his company goals, and his job goals have coincidence to a great extent; and his personal power is directed single-mindedly toward seeing himself in relation to the fulfillment of his executive potential.

3

MANAGEMENT OF DISAPPOINTMENT

Abraham Zaleznik

Foreword

While no one is immune to encounters with disappointment, men who want power and responsibility are especially vulnerable to episodes in which reality does not conform to their wishes or intentions. But, far from disappointment being a prelude to continued failure in their careers, these episodes may be occasions for accelerated personal growth and even the beginning of truly outstanding performance. The author discusses these immanent possibilities, illustrating his points with the reactions of well-known business and public leaders to the demands and stresses of responsibility.

A recent issue of *Life* magazine presented some unusually astute reflections on the leadership of President Johnson. Seen in the broadest possible perspective, these observations provoke a new set of questions about the motivation of leaders and, indirectly, fresh thinking about organizations, business as well as political.

The Editors of *Life* begin with the comment that President Johnson is not equally at home in each of the wide range of problems facing him. He would rather act on domestic problems than international issues; and if events force him to look beyond our borders, he would much prefer to deal with the new nations, the "have nots" in Asia, Africa, and Latin America as compared with the "haves" of the established industrial societies in Europe. In brief, President Johnson is propelled by an identification with the underdog and, if left to his own devices, would attack the problems of poverty, disease, education, and related concerns which seem at their core to cause human suffering. The thrust of his intentions to lead invariably aims at nurturing those for whom he feels strongly empathetic.

While these observations involve inevitably some oversimplification, they appear justified by the record of his Presidency thus far. The Editors of *Life* conclude with these comments:

"It can be argued—and is by many presidential scholars—that the man in the White House does not have a great deal of choice about the problems he gets or even how to deal with them. Perhaps that is so, but the Presidency still is a highly personal office. What pleases and placates, what intrigues and gratifies, what stimulates and flatters the man in the Oval Office subtly regulates the push and the priorities in the affairs of state that in the long run shape the era."[1]

Two points strike the reader of these editorial comments. The first is the rather tragic sense of leadership implied in the notion that events outside of one's control may not allow a man to do those things which he dearly wishes to do and for which his dispositions make him eminently suited. The second is the suggestion, even if only by inference, that we have here something more than a special situation or the idiosyncrasies of one man at one time and in one place.

We are not dealing with just the problems of political leaders, such as Johnson, although in many of the examples to follow I have used public figures, since their careers are well documented; if anything, we are more concerned with the problems of the head man of a business. For him, particularly, there may be some important generalizations about leadership in the idea that a man's inclinations, unknown to himself, channel him in a certain direction. A chief executive may therefore count himself lucky if he is able to utilize those tendencies with which he feels most comfortable, and over which in the end *he may have the least conscious control*. If we follow these leads, we soon delve into the borderland between personality and action in organizations.

It is my intention to take an excursion into this borderland, to leave the relatively safe, if somewhat arid, territory of organization theory which chooses to see management in terms divorced from the issues of personality. While, from a purely rational standpoint, a chief executive should be able to adjust the style and substance of his actions to the problems which press for solution, he is above all else a human being. The strategies and policies offered in his name, and the rationalistic terms with which they are advanced, often obscure the personal commitment in back of those formal programs. And, in fact, without the convictions drawn from personal commitment, the chief executive's attempts at persuasion and influence often leave others cold. On the other hand, while the conviction may be apparent, the direction of policy may appear so inconsistent and even unreal as to perplex subordinates and arouse wonder at the apparent displacement of personal concerns onto the business of the organization.

In effect, then, a corporate executive may face a paradoxical situation where he must live with himself and be himself while attempting to formulate realistic goals and means for implementing these goals.

Personal equation

Almost two decades ago, a young businessman exemplified some of the hazards involved in this paradox. Charles Luckman came to the presidency of Lever Brothers evidently intent on making a personal impact on the company and on the business community. His career ended abruptly when it became clear that his efforts at personal role building had far outstripped the sound development of business strategy and structure.[2]

In more recent times, the career of John Connor, former president of Merck & Co., Inc. and Secretary of Commerce, illustrated another aspect of this paradox: the gap between personal initiatives and the practical opportunities offered by the power structure for expressing these initiatives. As *Fortune* commented in "The Paradoxical Predicament of John Connor":

"Jack Connor took office with an ebullience he has been hard put to maintain. Within the Commerce Department, Connor is something

1. May 12, 1967, p. 46b.
2. See "The Case of Charles Luckman," *Fortune*, April 1950, p. 81.

less than the complete boss: his chief lieutenants are answerable less to him than to the President, who appointed them, has the power to promote, and holds their political loyalties. And despite his resounding Cabinet title, Connor finds he has a lot less influence on policy than he was once accustomed to." [3]

This gap between what a leader wants to do and the practical possibilities of action within the realities of power relationships poses a severe test for the individual. In Connor's case, according to *Fortune*, he endured the frustrations by a sense of optimism: "Putting the best possible face on what could have only been a severe disappointment, Connor made no complaint." [4] But there is a limit to any man's endurance, as indicated in Connor's later decision to resign his post and return to private enterprise.

For some executives, leadership is the conscious effort to suppress or subordinate their personal expression while meeting the standards and expectations others set. These executives usually do not provide remarkable case histories of business failure, but neither do they stand out as achievers. More significantly, they, along with a few intimates, measure the costs of unrealized hopes.

Where an individual expects, because of his ability, position, or wealth, to exert influence over events, there is no escape from the personal commitment to action. And, where such commitment is great, the potential for loss and disappointment is equally great. Consider:

□ In the spring of 1966, Howard Hughes sold his holdings in Trans World Airlines. While he realized enormous monetary gains in this transaction, he endured high personal costs because he gave up his intention to influence, if not control outright, one of the major international airlines. The decision to end a battle for corporate control implied a personal reappraisal of the potential gains and losses in continuing a set of tactics. That it was no simple outcome of investment logics was reflected in the comments of Charles Tillinghast, President of TWA, who explained Hughes' actions this way: "Perhaps he is a proud personality and wanted to divest voluntarily." [5]

As these illustrations suggest, the executive career turns on the subtle capacity to take personal risks in making decisions and putting them into action. This personal view of the executive career can, by extension, provide

the ideas for understanding better what actually goes on in organizations and in the exercise of leadership. Someday this personal view may also provide a theory which can be articulated and used in building organization structures. In the meantime, we need to know considerably more about the many sides of an individual's leadership style.

In studying effective executives, one usually asks: What were the man's experiences with success, and how did he build on them in his career? Psychological studies of creative people, including leaders, suggest that preoccupation with success may be less important than the role of disappointment in the evolution of a career. [6] Both the great strengths and weaknesses of gifted leaders often hinge on how they manage the disappointments which are inevitable in life.

The experience with disappointment is a catalytic psychological event that may foster growth or retardation in development. When the individual faces disappointment, he usually has to pull back his emotional investments in people and activities and reexamine them before reinvesting them in a new outward direction. The key idea, however, is in the *facing* of disappointment. If disappointment and the pains attendant on it are denied or otherwise hidden from view, the chances are great that the individual will founder on the unresolved conflicts at the center of his experience with disappointment.

Leadership style

In weighing ideas on the management of disappointment in the development of the executive career, we need to start with a clearer picture of the relationship between personality and leadership. This relationship involves the evolution of the individual's style of leadership. The concept of style refers to a widely noted observation that individuals who occupy the position of chief executive in similar organizations vary widely in the way they utilize the authority of their office.

The clearest illustration of this finding is offered in Richard E. Neustadt's study, *Presidential Power: The Politics of Leadership*. [7] In this

3. February 1966, p. 188.

4. Ibid., p. 152.

5. "Howard Hughes' Biggest Surprise," *Fortune*, July 1966, p. 119.

6. See Gregory Rochlin, *Griefs and Discontents* (Boston, Little, Brown and Company, 1965).

7. New York, John Wiley & Sons, Inc., 1960.

book Neustadt compares Roosevelt, Truman, and Eisenhower in their responses to the problem of power in executive relations. For Eisenhower, the use of power was a highly charged and ambivalent experience. His style, therefore, featured formalization of relationships within a staff system. The job of the staff, headed by Sherman Adams, was to screen and decide issues before they reached the personal level of the President. When top subordinates could not reach consensus, Eisenhower inadvertently allowed his power to be diffused and eroded through alternating responses which seemed to favor one side and then the other, as illustrated in the controversy over the 1957 budget.

In contrast to Eisenhower, who sought harmony, consensus, and tranquillity in the exercise of his responsibilities, Franklin D. Roosevelt was a man bent on taking the initiative. He was intent on making new departures, and he exploited every power base available to him to rally support for his decisions. Thus:

"The first task of an executive, as he [Roosevelt] evidently saw it, was to guarantee himself an effective flow of information and ideas. . . . Roosevelt's persistent effort therefore was to check and balance information acquired through official channels with information acquired through a myriad of private, informal, and unorthodox channels and espionage networks. At times he seemed almost to pit his personal sources against his public sources." [8]

In doing this, however, he not only checked and balanced the flow and validity of his information, but ensured for himself a position of the utmost centrality at every stage of the decision-making process. He could assess who wanted what and why he wanted it. He could establish his priorities and make his choices guided by clear indications as to where and at whom his power should be directed in order to secure support. At the same time, Roosevelt's style of leadership not only was that of an initiator, but involved the use of ambiguity in interpersonal relations. The use of ambiguity provided the means for maintaining his central position in the communications network and his flexibility in negotiation and decision making.

Similar observations about differences in style can be made about business leadership. Alfred P. Sloan, Jr. as head of General Motors functioned quite differently from his predecessor, William C. Durant.[9] Sloan was an organizer, while Durant was an entrepreneur. The entrepreneurial style of Durant was also quite different from the innovative pattern epitomized in the leadership of Henry Ford in the automotive industry. Ford's innovations depended on his ability to focus his goals, even to the point where they appeared to be fixations or obsessions. However much Ford operated with a one-track mind, he selected a profitable track that resulted in a major revolution in consumer behavior and industrial structure.

Differences in leadership style seem to revolve around differences in basic orientations to ideas, things, and people. Turning for help once again to Neustadt, we see how Roosevelt invested in ideas and political processes in a way that was free of conflicted attitudes toward people. For whatever reasons, Roosevelt was psychologically free to achieve his objectives through the use of all the bases of power available to him. He could *use* people. Consider:

"His [Roosevelt's] favorite technique was to keep grants of authority incomplete, jurisdictions uncertain, charters overlapping. The result of this competitive theory of administration was often confusion and exasperation on the operating level; but no other method could so reliably insure that in a large bureaucracy filled with ambitious men eager for power, the decisions and the power to make them would remain with the President." [10]

"Eisenhower's use of men tended to smother, not enhance, the competition roused by overlapping jurisdictions. Apparently this was intentional. . . . Eisenhower seemingly preferred to let subordinates proceed upon the lowest common denominators of agreement than to have their quarrels—and issues and details—pushed up to him." [11]

Patterns of investment in ideas, in things, and in people are relatively independent. An idea man may frequently experience personal conflict with people, but, as indicated in the case of Roosevelt, he may also be conflict-free in his relationships with others. A psychological study of Woodrow Wilson by Alexander and Juliette George [12] showed that Wilson's style of leader-

8. Neustadt, op. cit., p. 156.

9. See A. Chandler, *Strategy and Structure: Chapters in the History of Industrial Enterprises* (Cambridge, The M.I.T. Press, 1962).

10. A.M. Schlesinger, Jr., *The Age of Roosevelt, Vol. II: The Coming of the New Deal* (Boston, Houghton Mifflin Company, 1959). Quoted in Neustadt, op. cit., p. 157.

11. Neustadt, op.cit., p. 161.

12. *Woodrow Wilson and Colonel House: A Personality Study* (New York, Dover Publications, Inc., 1964).

ship reflected an emotional attachment to abstract ideals such as justice and democracy. But at an interpersonal level, Wilson had difficulty managing his competitive-aggressive strivings. He could work well with those few men, such as Colonel House, who flattered and openly adored him—or, interestingly enough, with those men who were his enemies. This polarization of relationships involving love and hate is more common than one would suppose and is found with considerable frequency among charismatic leaders.

Role of conflict

To achieve psychological understanding of the motives underlying a leadership style, one must be prepared to deal with the unexpected. In human affairs, relationships seldom persist for the simple reasons that appear on the surface. The central problem in the case of leadership styles is to grasp the meanings of the behavior and the multiple causes of action.

The concepts of *meaning* and *cause* when applied to human activities have at least two points of reference. The first is the relation of the leader's acts to some problem or tension in his environment. For example, Sloan's actions in establishing a rational formal organization can be analyzed in relation to the problems of constructing a balance between centralized and decentralized functions within a company made up of complex marketing, engineering, and production strategies. The second point of reference for behavior is the inner world of the actor. Here, we are concerned not only with the goals the individual seeks to achieve, but also with the nature of the stimuli that constantly threaten the individual's capacity to tolerate painful sensations and experiences.

Studying the external meanings of behavior requires a historical examination of institutions and their environments. The internal meanings also require a historical study, but of the individual and the legacies of his development. Leadership style is essentially the outcome of the developmental process and can be defined, following the psychoanalytic concept of "character," as *the patterned modes of behavior with which an individual relates himself to external reality and to his internal dispositions.*

One of the major contributions of psychoanalytic psychology has been to demonstrate the place of conflict in the development of the individual. Each stage in the life cycle involves personal conflict because the individual has the task of giving up one set of gratifications and searching for alternatives that take account simultaneously of biological, psychological, and social challenges. Failure to relinquish gratifications impedes development, while overly rapid learning establishes a gap between instinctual-emotional processes, on the one hand, and cognitive-rational capacities, on the other. This gap leads often to low tolerance for drives and emotions and to a highly rigid set of conditions for the exercise of competence.

Forrestal tragedy

The life and tragic death of James Forrestal is a case in point. Forrestal built a successful career on Wall Street and in government service. Toward the latter part of his service as the first Secretary of Defense, he developed a series of symptoms which later, when he left his post, took the form of manic-depressive psychosis with paranoid delusions. He took his life while under treatment, an end not uncommon in this type of illness.

Throughout his life, Forrestal, according to one biographer,[13] developed his capacity for work, but at the expense of achieving intimacy in his family. Forrestal broke with his parental family after completing college, in effect renouncing his past. Such breaks with the past do not usually occur apart from basic disappointments in the individual's experience with his development and his position in the family.

In Forrestal's case, while the data permit only reasoned speculations, they suggest the kinds of disappointments one finds in a harsh mother-child relationship. As the result of a complex psychological process, the individual renounces nurturance and other tender emotional exchanges, and substitutes instead a burning ambition and drive to achieve. If the individual has ability, as Forrestal clearly had in abundance, he may achieve leadership and success by any of the standards we use to evaluate performance. But the individual is vulnerable to continuing disappointment that may lead to breakdown. For Forrestal, the major disappointment in his career in government was probably his failure to achieve a power base independent of the President of the United States. He may even have harbored strong ambitions for the Presi-

13. A.A. Rogow, *James Forrestal: A Study of Personality, Politics, and Policy* (New York, The Macmillan Company, 1963).

dency—a position beyond his reach, given the political realities in our society.

Consequently, Forrestal's relationship with Truman became competitive and led to his replacement following the 1948 election. Forrestal fell ill immediately on the acceptance of his resignation and Louis Johnson's appointment as Secretary of Defense. As an active, ambitious man stripped of his power, he suffered a major deprivation with the severance of the channels formerly used in guiding his energies. Unfortunately, he had no alternative channels and no human relationship with which he could heal his wounds and rebuild his life.

Mastery process

The end need not have been tragic. Many great men work through their disappointments and emerge with greater strength and a heightened capacity for leadership. Winston Churchill must have suffered a similar disappointment during World War I. The disastrous campaign at Gallipoli became Churchill's responsibility and interrupted abruptly the career of this ambitious and powerful man. But he mastered this disappointment to become a leader during the supreme crisis of World War II.

The process of mastery must have demanded the kind of psychological work which usually occurs in psychoanalysis. Here, the individual withdraws and refocuses energy and attention from the outer world to himself. The outcome, if successful, is reorganization of personality based on insight, and then the renewal of active concern with the use of one's energy in work.

We know all too little about the self-curative processes which occur for "great men" in their struggle with disappointment.[14] But Churchill must have been aided immeasurably by his range of talents, not the least of which was writing. In other words, he did not have all his eggs in one basket. He also found strength in his relationship with his wife.

Similar processes must have occurred in the emergence of Franklin D. Roosevelt as a great leader. The injury he suffered, and I refer now to psychological injury as a result of the polio attack, was the critical episode in his career. But, again unlike Forrestal, he had the psychological resources and the relationships for performing the curative work necessary in a personal crisis.

Two final examples will clarify the complex way disappointment acts in the adult years as the developmental crisis of a career. Disappointment is not simply a condition where the outer evidences of success are absent or where the failure to realize ambitions is the critical event:

☐ In his autobiographical writing John Stuart Mill described the onset of his late adolescent depression. He was reflecting on life and his ambitions, and asked himself this question: "Suppose that all your objects in life were realized; that all the changes in institutions and opinions which you were looking forward to could be completely effected at this very instant: would this be a great joy and happiness to you?"[15] His answer was negative, and the outcome of his personal honesty was an intense depression which lifted only after he was able to mourn and express the grief underlying the psychological loss connected with his disappointments in fantasy.

☐ Henry Ford seems to have experienced a similar disappointment in fantasy on the success of the Model T. That great achievement marked a turning point in his career. Where formerly he could channel energies and direct others, he became increasingly rigid and unrealistic in his thinking. He entertained omnipotent and somewhat paranoid ideas, as evidenced by the ill-fated venture on the Peace Ship and his acceptance and support of the anti-Semitic campaigns of the newspaper, *The Dearborn Independent.*[16]

There are men who are spoiled by success and, as Sigmund Freud pointed out, develop symptoms only after major accomplishment.[17] To the naive observer, this consequence of achievement seems perverse or inexplicable. But it becomes comprehensible when analyzed in relation to the individual's investment in his fantasies. To produce a car, become president of a company, or make a great scientific discovery is not a simple dream.[18] Such dreams may also contain the

14. See, for example, Erik H. Erikson, *Young Man Luther* (New York, W.W. Norton & Company, Inc., 1958).

15. See John Stuart Mill, *Autobiography* (New York, The New American Library of World Literature, Inc., 1964), p. 107.

16. See Anne Jardim, *The First Henry Ford: A Study in Personality and Business Leadership* (unpublished doctoral dissertation, Harvard Business School, 1967); see also Allan Nevins and F.F. Hill, *Ford: The Times, the Man, and the Company; Ford: Expansion and Challenge;* and *Ford: Decline and Rebirth* (New York, Charles Scribner's Sons, 1954 [Vol. I], 1957 [Vol. II], 1963 [Vol. III]).

17. See Sigmund Freud, "Those Wrecked by Success," in *The Standard Edition of the Complete Psychological Works of Sigmund Freud,* edited by J. Strachey (London, The Hogarth Press, 1957), Vol. 14, pp. 316-331.

18. See Helen H. Tartakoff, "The Normal Personality in Our Culture and the Nobel Prize Complex," in *Psychoanalysis—A General Psychology, Essays in Honor of Heinz Hartman,* edited by R.M. Lowenstein, L.M. Newman, M. Schur, and A.J. Solnit (New York, International Universities Press, Inc., 1966).

hopes for restoring the individual to some state of happiness which he may have felt he once had and then lost. Or he may be enveloped by a sense of entitlement from which he views other persons as barriers to getting what he feels he justly deserves. These infantile wishes contained in the current actions of leaders are the most dangerous. Hell hath no fury like a woman scorned, or a man whose ambitions are frustrated because his dreams are incapable of realization no matter how hard he works or how tangible his achievements. Ambitions which contain hopes for changing the past and reversing the psychological disappointments encountered in development are self-defeating. The best that any of us can do is to understand the past. It cannot be changed.

Attachment to self

All human beings experience disappointment. If this hard fact of development were not so, it would be very difficult to explain the attractions of myth and legend. In myth we temporarily heal the wounds of disappointment and find ourselves restored to wishes once held and reluctantly abandoned in the interests of preserving attachment to reality and the objects we love. The psychology of the leader is therefore not different from that of other human beings in sharing an initial fate of injury and disappointment. But the psychology becomes different in the consequences of injury.

Most human beings accept disappointment and more or less content themselves with a collective engagement in which ritual and myth, along with work and human relationships, permit them to bear pain and loss. For creative people and those leaders endowed with special abilities, a sense of estrangement follows the early experiences with developmental conflicts. Like Narcissus, who caught his image in a reflecting pool and fell in love with this ideal self—in their childhood, leaders often direct their emotional investments inward. Their dreams and fantasies, translated as adults into ambitions, maintain their sense of being special. Very often these fantasies are part of an experience of destiny; their fate is to perform a great deed like Oedipus, who solved the riddle of the Sphinx, or the biblical Joseph, who interpreted the Pharaoh's dreams and predicted the famine.

The attachment to self leads to achievement, but only in conjunction with sharply developed talents. Without other qualities, such as the power to reason, to perceive the interplay of events in the environment, or to invent new solutions to old problems, the heightened sense of self would amount only to heightened frustration and, in the extreme, even madness. But the sense of self enters strongly into the personality of the leader and the ties others establish with him. What the leader does both with his abilities and with his investment in self is effectively the manifestation of what we call his style, with its special consequences for institutional management.

Resource or hazard?

The nature of policy and strategy in business organizations is a direct outcome of the actions of leaders. I do not believe it squares with reality to imagine that decisions are made in an impersonal way. They are made by men who think and act in relation to the influence of authority figures who themselves are, as I have tried to indicate, bound to a general process of human development.

In reaching decisions and charting a course for a corporation, considerable clarity of vision and accuracy in perception are necessary. The heightened sense of self that I have identified as a major factor in the psychology of leaders is both a resource and a hazard in corporate management and the fate of the individual. It is a resource in that the investment in self preserves the independence necessary to weigh opinions and advice of others. While it is good common sense to encourage subordinates to offer recommendations, in the final analysis a major policy cannot be advanced apart from the convictions of the chief executive. How does he achieve the conviction necessary to seal a decision? If he is dependent on others as a result of an impoverishment of self-confidence, it will be very difficult indeed for him to foster a position that will guide the destiny of the organization.

The problem of investment in self as a psychological quality of leadership is one of degree. Too little amounts to overdependence and often diffusion of purpose. The other extreme, overinvestment in self, poses problems as well, but in a more complex way than overdependence.

Freud, in his study "Group Psychology and the Analysis of the Ego," [19] described the primal leader as an individual who loves no one but himself. This imagery suggests the autocrat who

19. See Sigmund Freud in Strachey, op. cit., Vol. 18, pp. 67-143.

keeps subordinates equidistant from himself and relatively deprived of independent action. This primal leader is not an archaic figure in business management. He is not idealized now as he was in the late nineteenth and early twentieth centuries; nevertheless, he still persists with all his strengths and weaknesses in small enterprises as well as in large corporations. The autocrat provides a direction, and if he selects a correct path, he usually manages a successful enterprise. As a leader, he tends to select subordinates in his own image, and they reflect all his virtues and vices.

The hazard facing the autocrat stems from the tendency for new ideas, information, and vision to find limited acceptance. Subordinates tell the primal leader only what he wants to hear, and the opportunities for communication are limited by his distance. If an incorrect or outdated strategy continues to direct the organization, then the future is in doubt. Precisely this set of conditions occurred in the Ford Motor Company, leading to its decline in the industry and to serious financial losses from the 1920's until World War II.

Balance & perspective: At a more personal level the problem the primal leader faces is maintaining balance and perspective through the inevitable disappointments when they occur—and especially those which he may experience at the height of his career. These disappointments may range from business setbacks to family problems—including the discovery that his sons and heirs are not made in his image and have distinct personalities and problems. The experience with these latter-day disappointments may produce a kind of psychic injury that reopens old wounds. The response may be rage and restitutive thought patterns that we recognize as a false sense of omnipotence and even delusions.

Evidently Harry Truman had some insight into the hazards of disappointment, particularly when a leader becomes aware of the limitations of his power to control events and actions of others. Neustadt describes Truman's sympathetic anticipation of Eisenhower's problems with the Presidency. Truman said, "He'll sit here and he'll say, 'Do this! Do that!' And nothing will happen. Poor Ike—it won't be a bit like the Army. He'll find it very frustrating." [20] What Truman evidently recognized is that no matter how powerful the leader's position, the issue of influence is still problematic. Whether

20. Neustadt, op. cit., p. 22.

things get done is beyond the magical thinking that equates authority with influence.

The Narcissus-like leader who invests only in himself does not necessarily behave overtly like an autocrat, nor does he necessarily detach himself from others. Frequently one observes leaders who have close relationships with subordinates. We cannot conclude from superficial observation that the presence of these relationships indicates a balance between investment in self and others. Closer observation often shows that the ties are not in reality between two separate individuals who cooperate in a rational and purposive endeavor. Instead, the individuals position themselves around the leader as reflected images of himself taken from his infantile past. These executive structures then become dramatic reenactments of fantasies that existed to restore the self-esteem of the individual during his early experiences with disappointment.

The structure and dynamics of these relationships have a variety of unconscious meanings that are carried forward into major episodes of corporate life. While the relationships may have adaptive value, they may also become central to the outbreak of pathological processes within the leader and other key executives in the organization. And again I suggest that the pathologies involve the reexperience of disappointment and loss when the relationships shift or, under the influence of reality, fail as restitutive episodes.

While subordinates may be related to a leader in ways which become significant in the reenactment of fantasies, there is still room for modification. I am reminded of the tragedy of King Lear, who had to drive away those individuals who loved him most because he could not tolerate the intensity of his love for his youngest daughter, Cordelia. The only figure who remained close to Lear and who would tell him the truth was his fool. But the only way the fool could exist and speak the truth was to take the position of the castrated object who himself posed no threat to the power of the leader.

With this observation our problem shifts. Why would anyone give up his self-esteem to serve another, even though in a paradoxical way he performs noble work in helping the narcissistic leader maintain his fragile hold on reality? To be the king's fool strikes me as an excessive price to pay for another man's contributions to society. There is still another way, and that is to maintain one's integrity, to speak the truth, and to let the chips fall where they may. Subordinates to narcissistic leaders sometimes succumb to their own restitutive fantasies as a way of rationalizing their position. We can be sure that where a close relationship persists, there are more reasons than we know to account for the willingness of people to maintain object ties.

Self-examination need

Business managers, whether they know it or not, commit themselves to a career in which they have to work on themselves as a condition for effective working on and working with other people. This fact of the business career is so often neglected that we would do well to re-examine the implications of the need to work on oneself as a condition for the exercise of power.

The analysis presented in this article suggests that a significant area for the personal and inner work on oneself is the experience with disappointment. The question we now have to explore is: How does an executive make the management of disappointment a catalytic experience for personal growth? Here are some leads and suggestions.

Preventive aspects

First, as a preventive measure, examine carefully the personal goals in back of the decision to assume responsibility in a position. If the goals are themselves unrealistic, then major disappointment is inevitable.

A number of years ago, one man decided to change his career and take over a small enterprise. He told me that his reason for entering business was to put into practice the conceptions of good human relations in leadership to which he was personally dedicated. My question to him was this: How about going into business to manage a successful company and to make money? The intent of my question was not to insult his noble purposes but, rather, to suggest that the way one formulates his personal goals has something to do with the way he will practice his profession. In other words, a noble intention may enlighten work, but it is no substitute for competence. The investment in noble purposes may even prevent success and finally

21. *Leadership and Motivation* (Cambridge, The M.I.T. Press, 1966).

set the stage for the traumatic experience with disappointment.

McGregor's theories: A collection of essays by Douglas McGregor, published in 1966 following his death, offers by indirection some clues on how the clash between personal ideology and reality may obscure insight.[21]

McGregor, as you know, was the man who pointed out the difference between what he called *Theory X* and *Theory Y*. According to persuasive arguments, many managers of complex organizations are acting on the basis of an outmoded conception of human nature and institutions. This conception, Theory X, sees man as a stubborn, recalcitrant being who has to be motivated to work in directions consonant with organizational goals. Believing in this conception of man produces a self-fulfilling prophecy. That is, the type of leadership fostered by this "mechanical" man is apt to produce stubborn, recalcitrant individuals who sabotage the organization rather than contribute to its well-being.

In advocating the opposite view, Theory Y, throughout his essays, McGregor proposed that leaders should change their ideas about human nature. The content of this altered view is supported, according to McGregor, by the findings of behavioral science, particularly psychology. McGregor appealed to managers to adopt a philosophy of leadership based on the assumption that individuals want to be self-actualizing and want to participate in harmony with their environment. In this view the leader is an agronomist who cultivates the organizational environment in which this more optimistic picture of man will be fulfilled.

The message is powerful and at the root of McGregor's considerable stature as a management theorist. Its appeal lies in its humaneness and in the subtle way it addresses itself to the underlying guilt which plagues men who exercise power in modern organizations. All too often, leaders are uneasy about the power they have over men and decisions. The uneasiness is accompanied by a sense of guilt and a desire for reassurance, love, and approval from associates. It is as though leaders listen for the voices outside themselves which will testify to their humanity in opposition to the disquieting inner voices that disapprove, depreciate, and accuse. In short, McGregor's message was designed to deal as much with a bad conscience as with the realities of work, authority, and decisions in organizations.

But how lasting and relevant are these external cures for a bad conscience? Whether in the name of religion or science, the cure is temporary as compared with the more arduous route of self-knowledge and mastery. Socrates' advice to "know thyself" is exceedingly relevant today for men of responsibility. Unfortunately, McGregor's theories avoid the inner conflicts and resolutions of leadership problems in their almost singular dedication to creating an ideal organization climate.

McGregor missed the point in the study of leadership because, while he was keen on talking to managers, he failed in a basic sense to identify with them. His identification was largely with subordinates; and in talking to managers, McGregor communicated the wish in all of us for benign and benevolent power figures. But to love and to be loved is not enough in the painful process of choice while exercising leadership.

McGregor did capture this idea in what must have been for him a period of intense stress. In his essay "On Leadership," written as he was about to leave the presidency of Antioch College, a position he held for six years, he said:

"Before coming to Antioch, I had observed and worked with top executives as an advisor in a number of organizations. I thought I knew how they felt about their responsibilities and what led them to behave as they did. I even thought I could create a role for myself that would enable me to avoid some of the difficulties they encountered. I was wrong!...I believed, for example, that a leader could operate successfully as a kind of advisor to his organization. I thought I could avoid being a 'boss.' Unconsciously, I suspect, I hoped to duck the unpleasant necessity of making difficult decisions, of taking responsibility for one course of action among many uncertain alternatives, of making mistakes and taking the consequences. I thought that maybe I could operate so that everyone would like me—that 'good human relations' would eliminate all discord and disappointment. I could not have been more wrong...." [22]

The essay from which this quotation was taken appeared in May 1954. The subsequent essays, written while McGregor continued a distinguished career as Professor at M.I.T., suggest he had not assimilated the insight underlying his sense of disappointment. I suspect the insight

22. Ibid., p. 67.

got lost because McGregor was too hard on himself, as the brief quotation above suggests. In the later essays in this book, McGregor returns to the message through which he appealed to authority figures on behalf of subordinates.

Had he pursued the insight imbedded in the Antioch essay, he might have recognized that the essence of leadership is choice, a singularly individualistic act in which a man assumes responsibility for a commitment to direct an organization along a particular path. He might also have recognized that as much as a leader wishes to trust others, he has to judge the soundness and validity of the positions subordinates come to communicate. Otherwise, the leader is in danger of becoming a prisoner of the emotional commitments his subordinates demand, frequently at the expense of judging the correctness of policies and strategies.

McGregor's problem, I would suspect, developed out of his noble purposes. But nobility of purpose is not the first order of business in establishing one's position as chief executive of an organization. In the personal assessment of one's intention to lead, it is far better to assign the highest priority to discovering those things that need to be done, and then to devote oneself to engaging the commitments of others toward these goals. Of course, this does not rule out the possibility that historians can later look at this executive's work and discover the nobility which surrounded his leadership.

But no matter how hard one works on the preventive aspects, sooner or later disappointments occur, and the personal working through of these events then becomes the first order of business.

Facing issues

The second suggestion I shall make is to face the disappointment squarely. The temptation and the psychology of individual response to disappointment is to avoid the pain of self-examination. If an avoidance pattern sets in, the individual will pay dearly for it later. Usually, avoidance occurs because this mode of response is the individual's habitual way of dealing with disappointment from childhood days on. It also seems clear that those people who are lucky enough to have learned from childhood days how to face loss are best equipped to deal with the personal issues that arise during experiences with disappointment in the executive career. Consider:

□ One line manager in a large corporation worked closely with a vice president, who in the course of events in business life came out second best in a rivalry. The vice president resigned, and his department was left in a vulnerable position, without a leader, and with a loss of status. The line manager, who was in his early forties, had spent his entire working career with this large corporation. He had an excellent reputation, and the senior executives were genuinely hopeful that he would remain with the company.

He thought the issue through and decided to resign, recognizing that his commitments to the deposed vice president were so strong that they would not permit him to reestablish ties with others and to work effectively without paying too high a personal price. He discovered that his experience and talents were indeed in high demand, and he made a successful transition to another corporation where, after demonstrating his competence, he became a vice president and senior executive in his own right.

The decision to remain or to leave was not the significant test of whether the line manager was actually facing the disappointment he had endured. Rather, the significant test came in his silent work of self-examination which he shared only with his wife, who matched his personal courage and willingness to take risks. In effect, this line manager learned to face events and to follow the principle of finance of writing off a loss and then setting forth on a new program.

Emotional awareness

The key factor in mastering disappointment is the capacity to experience the emotions connected with the personal career losses.[23] The flight from the work leading to mastery is usually connected with the individual's limited capacity to tolerate painful emotions. The third suggestion, therefore, is to become intimately acquainted with one's own emotional reactions.

An example of the issues implicit in attempting to face the emotional reactions following disappointment is poignantly described in Volume II of *The Diaries of Harold Nicolson*.[24] Nicolson, a member of Parliament, held the post of Parliamentary Secretary in the Ministry of Information during the early years of World War II. Churchill asked for his resignation in connection with a series of top-level changes in the ministry resulting from public criticism and charges of mismanagement. Nicolson resigned, and the following day (July 19, 1941) he noted this entry in his diary:

"I wake up feeling that something horrible has happened, and then remember that I have been sacked from the Government. Go to the Ministry and start clearing out some of my private possessions. Then attend the Duty Room, probably for the last time. I meet Gerald Campbell in the passage. 'I hear,' he says, 'that you have been thurtled?'[a] Everybody expresses dismay at my going.[b] I have a final drink in the Press Bar with Osbert Lancaster, and then lunch at the Travellers with Robin Maugham. He is as charming as he could be.

"But I mind more than I thought I should mind. It is mainly, I suppose, a sense of failure. I quite see that if the Labour leaders have been pressing to have my post, there is good cause why they should have it. But if I had more power and drive, I should have been offered Rab Butler's job at the Foreign Office,[c] which I should dearly have loved. As it is, I come back to the bench below the gangway having had my chance and failed to profit by it. Ever since I have been in the House I have been looked on as a might-be. Now I shall be a might-have-been. Always up till now I have been buoyed up by the hope of writing some good book or achieving a position of influence in politics. I now know that I shall never write a book better than I have written already, and that my political career is at an end. I shall merely get balder and fatter and more deaf as the years go by. This is an irritating thing. Success should come late in life in order to compensate for the loss of youth; I had youth and success together, and now I have old age and failure.[d] Apart from all this,

---

a. Nicolson was replaced as Parliamentary Secretary by Ernest Thurtle, Labour M.P. for Shoreditch, who retained the office till the end of the war. Duff Cooper was succeeded as Minister by Brendan Bracken.

b. Duff Cooper wrote to him, "I think you have received very shabby treatment, and I find that everybody shares that view."

c. R.A. Butler, Under-Secretary of State for Foreign Affairs since 1938, was now appointed Minister of Education, and was succeeded at the Foreign Office by Richard Law.

d. Nicolson was then 54.

23. See Elizabeth R. Zetzel, "Depression and the Incapacity to Bear It," in *Drives, Affects, Behavior*, edited by Rudolph M. Loewenstein (New York, International Universities Press, Inc., Vol. II, 1965).

24. *The War Years, 1939-1945*, edited by Nigel Nicolson (New York, Atheneum Publishers, 1967).

I mind leaving the Ministry where I did good work and had friends.

"This space indicates the end of my ambitions in life. 'Omnium consensu capax imperii nisi imperasset.' [e] "

According to the editor of the diaries, it took Nicolson some time before he could assimilate the disappointment and plunge anew into lesser responsibilities. But Nicolson's apparent honesty, and his gifts as an observer and recorder of events, evidently helped him during a difficult personal crisis.

Studies of individuals who get into trouble and present themselves for treatment to a psychoanalyst frequently show that the roots of their difficulties lie in a limited capacity to tolerate emotions, especially those connected with loss and disappointment. The business executive is especially vulnerable because he may have developed an unconscious strategy of forced activity or, more accurately, hyperactivity, as a defense against emotional awareness. The hyperactive executive is of course rewarded for his hyperactivity, since, in the conventional understanding of how an executive should behave, busyness is generally considered a good thing.

However good it is in some respects, it is also bad if busyness serves to build and maintain the wall between the inner worlds of thought and feeling. In the treatment of such individuals who are in trouble, the most positive indicator of progress is the appearance of sadness and depression. As the individual consciously assimilates the depression and relates it to his experiences with disappointment throughout his development, he becomes capable of undoing the ineffective patterns and of substituting more effective ways of dealing with the demands and stresses of responsibility.

Conclusion

No one is immune to encounters with disappointment. More significantly, individuals who want power and responsibility or seek creative expression are especially vulnerable to episodes in which reality does not conform to one's wishes or intentions. As I have indicated in this article, far from disappointment being a prelude to continued failure in career, these critical episodes may actually be occasions for accelerated growth and even the beginning of truly outstanding performance.

But much depends on the quality of the psychological work the individual accomplishes under the stress of the sense of loss and bewilderment which frequently accompanies disappointment. As in all matters of personal development, the outcome turns on the quality of the man, the measure of courage he can mobilize, the richness of his talents, and his ability for constructive introspection.

It is no easy task to examine one's own motivations. In fact, the necessity seldom arises for many people until they meet an impasse in life. At this juncture, they are confronted with two sets of personal concerns: those connected directly with the present disappointments and those related to the experiences with disappointment in the past. Usually a crisis in the present reopens problems from the past, and, in this sense, the individual experiences a telescoping of time in which the psychological past and present tend to merge.

But the degree of telescoping is critical in judging the intensity of stress involved in the management of disappointment. It is usually difficult enough to solve a current problem, with all its demands for accurate observation and realistic thought. The difficulty increases, however, when the route to solving current problems involves examination of one's history with loss or deprivation. Here the most effective step the individual can take is to seek competent help.

In the course of examining reactions to disappointment, a subtle change may take place in the individual's perspectives and attitudes. While he may come to recognize the impossible quality of certain goals and wishes, and be willing to relinquish their demands on his behavior, he may at the same time discover uncharted possibilities for productive work and pleasure. These immanent possibilities usually remain obscure so long as the individual is intent in his quest for restitutive rewards to make up for his felt losses of the past.

There is irony in all of human experience and no less in the solutions to the problem of disappointment. The deepest irony of all is to discover that one has been mourning losses that were never sustained, and yearning for a past that never existed, while ignoring one's own real capabilities for shaping the present.

---

e. Tacitus on the Emperor Galba. "Had he never been placed in authority, nobody would ever have doubted his capacity for it."

4

"SKYHOOKS"

O. A. Ohmann

Foreword

This "HBR Classic" was first published in the May-June 1955 issue of HBR. It won immediate acclaim in the business community and started off a new line of thinking about the nature of effective leadership.

During the last several years, while my principal job assignment has been management development, I have become increasingly impressed with the importance of intangibles in the art of administration. With the managerial revolution of the last generation and the transition from owner-manager to professional executive, there has appeared a growing literature on the science and art of administration. A shift in emphasis is noticeable in these writings over the past 30 years.

Following the early engineering approach typified by the work of Frederick Taylor and others, there next developed a search for the basic principles of organization, delegation, supervision, and control. More recently, as labor relations became more critical, the emphasis has shifted to ways of improving human relations. The approach to the problems of supervisory relationships was essentially a manipulative one. Textbooks on the techniques of personnel management mushroomed. Still later it became more and more apparent that the crux of the problem was the supervisor himself, and this resulted in a flood of "how to improve yourself" books.

Meanwhile the complexities of the industrial community increased, and the discontents and tensions mounted.

It seems increasingly clear, at least to me, that while some administrative practices and personnel techniques may be better than others, their futility arises from the philosophical assumptions or value judgments on which this superstructure of manipulative procedure rests. We observe again and again that a manager with sound values and a stewardship conception of his role as boss can be a pretty effective leader even though his techniques are quite unorthodox. I am convinced that workers have a fine sensitivity to spiritual qualities and want to work for a boss who believes in something and in whom they can believe.

This observation leads me to suspect that we may have defined the basic purposes and objectives of our industrial enterprise too narrowly, too selfishly, too materialistically. Bread alone will not satisfy workers. There are some indications that our people have lost faith in the basic values of our economic society, and that we need a spiritual rebirth in industrial leadership.

Certainly no people have ever had so much, and enjoyed so little real satisfaction. Our economy has been abundantly productive, our standard of living is at an all-time peak, and yet we are a tense, frustrated, and insecure people full of hostilities and anxieties. Can it be that our *god of production* has feet of clay? Does industry need a new religion—or at least a better one than it has had?

I am convinced that the central problem is not the division of the spoils as organized labor would have us believe. Raising the price of prostitution does not make it the equivalent of love. Is our industrial discontent not in fact the expression of a hunger for a work life that has meaning in terms of higher and more enduring spiritual values? How can we preserve the wholeness of the personality if we are expected to worship God on Sundays and holidays and mammon on Mondays through Fridays?

I do not imply that this search for real meaning in life is or should be limited to the hours on the job, but I do hold that the central values of our industrial society permeate our entire culture. I am sure we do not require a bill of particulars of the spiritual sickness of our time. The evidences of modern man's search for his soul are all about us. Save for the communist countries there has been a world-wide revival of interest in religion. The National Council of Churches reports that 59% of our total population (or 92 million) now claim church affiliation. The November 22, 1954 issue of *Barron's* devoted the entire front page to a review of a book by Barbara Ward, *Faith and Freedom*.[1]

Perhaps even more significant is the renaissance in the quality of religious thought and experience. Quite evidently our religion of materialism, science, and humanism is not considered adequate. Man is searching for anchors outside himself. He runs wearily to the periphery of the spider web of his own reason and logic, and looks for new "skyhooks"—for an abiding faith around which life's experiences can be integrated and given meaning.

Why 'skyhooks'?

Perhaps we should assume that this need for "skyhooks" is part of man's natural equipment—possibly a function of his intelligence—or, if you prefer, God manifesting Himself in His creatures. It seems to me, however, that the recent intensification of this need (or perhaps the clearer recognition of it) stems in part from certain broad social, economic, political, and philosophical trends. I shall not attempt a comprehensive treatment of these, but shall allude to only a few.

Abundance without satisfaction: I have already indicated that on the economic front we have won the battle of production. We have moved from an economy of scarcity to one of abundance. We have become masters of the physical world and have learned how to convert its natural resources to the satisfaction of our material wants. We are no longer so dependent and so intimately bound to the world of nature. In a way we have lost our feeling of being part of nature and with it our humble reverence for God's creation.

While the industrialization of our economy resulted in ever-increasing production, it also made of individual man a production number—an impersonal, de-skilled, interchangeable production unit, measured in so many cents per hour. For most employees, work no longer promotes the growth of personal character by affording opportunities for personal decision, exercise of judgment, and individual responsibility. A recent issue of *Nation's Business* quotes the modern British philosopher, Alexander Lindsay, on this point as follows:

"Industrialism has introduced a new division into society. It is the division between those who manage and take responsibility and those who are managed and have responsibility taken from them. This is a division more important than the division between the rich and poor."[2]

Certainly the modern industrial worker has improved his material standard of living at the cost of becoming more and more dependent on larger and larger groups. Not only his dignity but also his security has suffered. And so he reaches out for new "skyhooks"—for something to believe in, for something that will give meaning to his job.

1. New York, W.W. Norton & Company, Inc., 1954.

2. John Kord Lagemann, "Job Enlargement Boosts Production," December 1954, p. 36.

Retrospective commentary

It's time I level with HBR readers about how "Sky-hooks" came about. In a very real sense, I did not write it. It came as a stream of consciousness—but only after I had worked very hard for several weeks at putting my ideas together. I wrote the paper mainly to clear my own thinking, and to try it out for criticism on the Cleveland Philosophical Club. After much reading and thinking, I got absolutely nowhere. In desperation I was about to abandon the idea and write on a different subject. Deep inside my consciousness I said in effect to my silent partner within, "Look, if you want me to do this, you better help." About 2 a.m. that morning the ideas flowed in a continuous stream, and I put them down in shorthand notes as fast as I could.

The word "Skyhooks" for the title came in the heat of a discussion with a group of business executives attending the Institute of Humanistic Studies at Aspen, Colorado. As we debated the limits of the rational and scientific approach to life, it occurred to me that science appears rational on the surface, but at its very foundation typically lies a purely intuitive, non-rational assumption made by some scientist. He just hooked himself on a "piece of sky out there" and hung on. It was a complete leap of faith that led him.

In my studies of exceptional executives I had found a mystery not easily explainable by rational elements. These men, too, were hanging on skyhooks of their own—hidden and secret missions which went way beyond their corporate business objectives. Sometimes the mission was a "nutsy" one. Often it had long roots back in the executive's childhood and was emotional, intuitive, beyond rationality, selfless—but it stuck. For example, it might be like John F. Kennedy's determination to become President; reportedly he was doing it for his older brother, who had the ambition to be President but never made it because he was a war casualty.

Or perhaps the mission was like that of the president of one of our largest corporations. When he was 12 years old, his father died. He promised his mother he would help her work the farm in the hills so that his eight younger brothers could go through school. This is what he continued to do all of his life—helping other young men to make something of themselves. He was a great developer of managers.

I could fill a book with such examples. Many great executives I have known have something deep inside that supports them; something they trust when the going gets tough; something ultimate; something personal; something beyond reason—in short, a deep-rooted skyhook which brings them calm and confidence when they stand alone.

There is another interesting aspect to this question. In our rational, analytical, and highly successful Western culture, we have come to place great value on the material gains which represent the end results of our achievements. This is what our kids are complaining about: that we have gone overboard on material values and made a culture of *things*. But the *results* of our strivings are dead works; the life is in the *process* of achieving, in the leap of faith. David was great not when he slew Goliath, but when he decided to try.

So it seems to me that the skyhooks mystique is also characterized by a commitment to value the *process*, the working relationships with others, the spiritual bonds growing out of the faith in the God-potential deep within another person, and the basis of genuine community. The rest is the means, not the end.

In 1955, when my article was published, the generation gap had not been invented, and Marshall McLuhan had not alerted us to the fact that "the medium is the message." Yet a quick look backward reveals the considerable impact of youth and "McLuhanism" on our history and our future. The "McCarthy Kids" have ousted a President and his party, halted the military domination of our foreign policy, radically changed our educational and religious institutions, revised industry's approach to management recruiting, and made the Peace Corps type of job competitive with the "goodies" offered by business. Generalizing about the medium having greater impact than the message, they have pointed out that our values are dictated by our social systems—especially the technological, political, and managerial systems. More important than the things we create in industry, they say, is the *way* we create them—the kind of community we establish in our working together.

Without debating the merits of "pot" versus liquor, or anarchy versus order, I believe their emphasis on social process is introducing a new dimension into our corporate life and values.

"Skyhooks" was written for myself and not for publication. For a while I refused to give anybody a copy, but under pressure I duplicated a small number of copies for my friends, and they wanted copies for their friends. When the Editor of HBR got his copy and asked, "How about publishing it?" I answered, "Only if you take it as it is; I don't want to revise it." I see little need for revising it now—except perhaps the reference to the increase in membership in the institutional church. The search for ultimate values and meanings is keener than in 1955, but it is apparently no longer satisfied merely by church affiliation.

Disillusionment with science: A second trend which seems to bear some relation to our urgent need for a faith grows out of our disillusionment with science. As a result of the rapid advance of science, the curtains of ignorance and superstition have been pulled wide on all fronts of human curiosity and knowledge. Many of the bonds of our intellectual enslavement have been broken. Reason and scientific method were called on to witness to the truth, the whole truth, and nothing but the truth. We were freed from the past—its traditions, beliefs, philosophies, its mores, morals, and religion. Science became our religion, and reason replaced emotion.

However, even before the atom bomb there was a growing realization that science did not represent the whole truth, that with all its pretensions it could be dead wrong, and, finally and particularly, that without proper moral safeguards the truth did not necessarily make men free. Atomic fission intensified the fear and insecurity of every one of us who contemplated the possibility of the concentration of power in the hands of men without morals. We want science to be in the hands of men who not only recognize their responsibility to man-made ethical standards (which are easily perverted) but have dedicated themselves to the eternal and absolute standards of God. Thus, while the evidence of material science has been welcomed, our own personal experiences will not permit us to believe that life is merely a whirl of atoms without meaning, purpose, beauty, or destiny.

Trend toward bigness: A third factor contributing to our insecurity is the trend toward bigness and the resulting loss of individuality. This is the day of bigger and bigger business—in every aspect of life. The small is being swallowed by the big, and the big by the bigger. This applies to business, to unions, to churches, to education, to research and invention, to newspapers, to our practice of the professions, to government, and to nations. Everything is getting bigger except the individ-

3. New Haven, Yale University Press, 1950.

ual, and he is getting smaller and more insignificant and more dependent on larger social units. Whether we like it or not, this is becoming an administrative society, a planned and controlled society, with ever-increasing concentration of power. This is the day of collectivism and public-opinion polls. It is the day when the individual must be *adjusted to the group*—when he must above all else be sensitive to the feelings and attitudes of others, must get an idea of how others expect him to act, and then react to this.

This is the insecure world which David Riesman has described so well in his book, *The Lonely Crowd*.[3] He pictures man as being no longer "tradition directed" as was primitive man, nor as in Colonial days is he "inner directed" as if by the gyroscope of his own ideals, but today he is "outer directed" as if by radar. He must constantly keep his antenna tuned to the attitudes and reactions of others to him. The shift has been from morals to morale and from self-reliance to dependence on one's peer group. However, the members of one's peer group are each responding to each other. Obviously these shifting sands of public opinion offer no stable values around which life can be consistently integrated and made meaningful. The high-water mark of adjustment in such a society is that the individual be socially accepted and above all else that he appear to be *sincere*.

This is certainly not a favorable environment for the development of steadfast character. It is essentially a neurotic and schizophrenic environment which breeds insecurity.

This socially dependent society also offers an ideal market for the wares of the "huckster," the propagandist, and the demagogue. Lacking a religious interpretation of the divine nature of man, these merchants in mass reaction have sought the least common denominator in human nature and have beamed the movies and newspapers at the ten-year mental level. One wonders if this approach to people does not make them feel that they have been sold short and that they are capable of much better than is expected of

them. Has this demoralizing exposure of the cheapness of our values not intensified our search for something better to believe in?

On top of all these disturbing socioeconomic trends came the war. This certainly was materialism, science, and humanism carried to the logical conclusion. The war made us question our values and our direction. It left us less cocksure that we were right, and more fearful of ourselves as well as of others. It made us fearful of the power which we had gained, and led us to search our soul to determine whether we had the moral strength to assume the leadership role that had been given to us. We have been humbled in our efforts to play god and are about ready to give the job back. Note, however, that this is not a characteristic reaction to war. Typically wars have been followed by a noticeable deterioration of moral standards, of traditional values, and of social institutions.

Perhaps none of these rationalizations for our return to religion is entirely valid. I suspect that the search for some kind of overarching integrative principle or idea is the expression of a normal human need. Certainly history would indicate that man's need for a god is eternal even though it may be more keenly sensed in times of adversity. A religion gives a point of philosophical orientation around which life's experiences can be organized and digested. Without the equivalent, a personality cannot be whole and healthy. Short-term goals which need to be shifted with the changing tide do not serve the same integrative function as do the "skyhooks" which are fastened to eternal values. I do not personally regard the current religious revival as a cultural hangover, nor as a regression. Being a mystic I prefer instead to view the need for such a faith as the spark of the Creator in us to drive us on to achieve His will and our own divine destiny.

Why Monday through Friday?

If we may grant for the moment that modern man *is* searching for deeper meanings in life, we may then ask: What has this to do with industry?

If he needs "skyhooks," let him get them in church, or work out his own salvation. The business leaders of the past insisted that "business is business" and that it had little bearing on the individual's private life and philosophy.

There are several reasons why "skyhooks" must be a primary concern of the business administrator:

☐ For the individual the job is the center of life, and its values must be in harmony with the rest of life if he is to be a whole and healthy personality.

☐ This is an industrial society, and its values tend to become those of the entire culture.

☐ The public is insisting that business leaders are in fact responsible for the general social welfare—that the manager's responsibilities go far beyond those of running the business. They have delegated this responsibility to the business executive whether he wishes to play this role or not.

☐ Even if the administrator insists on a narrow definition of his function as merely the production of goods and services as efficiently as possible, it is nevertheless essential that he take these intangibles into account, since they are the real secrets of motivating an organization.

☐ Besides all this the administrator needs a better set of "skyhooks" himself if he is to carry his ever-increasing load of responsibility without cracking up. The fact that so many administrators are taking time to rationalize, defend, and justify the private enterprise system is an outward indication of this need for more significant meanings.

Anything wrong with capitalism?

We may ask, then: What specifically is wrong with our capitalistic system of private enterprise? What is wrong with production or with trying to improve our present standard of living? What is wrong with a profit, or with private ownership of capital, or with competition? Is this not the true American way of life?

Nothing is necessarily wrong with these values. There are certainly worse motives than the profit motive. A refugee from communism is

reported to have observed: "What a delight to be in the United States, where things are produced and sold with such a nice clean motive as making a profit."

I am not an economist, and it is beyond the scope of this article to attempt a revision of our economic theory. I am tempted, however, to make a couple of observations about these traditional economic concepts:

1. That while the values represented by them are not necessarily wrong, they are certainly pretty thin and do not challenge the best in people.

2. That many of the classical economic assumptions are outmoded and are no longer adequate descriptions of the actual operation of our present-day economy.

For example, the concept of economic man as being motivated by self-interest not only is outmoded by the best current facts of the social sciences, but also fails to appeal to the true nobility of spirit of which we are capable.

The concept of the free and competitive market is a far cry from the highly controlled and regulated economy in which business must operate today. General Motors does not appear to want to put Chrysler out of business, and apparently the union also decided to take the heat off Chrysler rather than to press its economic advantage to the logical conclusion. The assumption that everyone is out to destroy his competitors does not explain the sharing of technology through trade associations and journals. No, we also have tremendous capacity for cooperation when challenged by larger visions. We are daily denying the Darwinian notion of the "survival of the fittest" —which, incidentally, William Graham Sumner, one of the nineteenth-century apologists for our economic system, used for justifying unbridled self-interest and competition.

Certainly the traditional concept of private ownership of capital does not quite correspond to the realities of today's control of large blocks of capital by insurance companies and trusteed funds.

The notion of individual security

through the accumulation of savings has largely given way to the collectivist means of group insurance, company annuities, and Social Security.

The concept that all profits belong to the stockholders is no longer enthusiastically supported by either the government or the unions, since both are claiming an increasing cut.

And so, while we may argue that the system of private enterprise is self-regulatory and therefore offers maximum individual freedom, the simple, cold fact is that it is in ever-increasing degree a managed or controlled economy—partly at the insistence of the voters, but largely as the result of the inevitable economic pressures and the trend toward bigness.[4]

Regardless of the rightness or wrongness of these changes in our system of enterprise, the changes have been considerable, and I doubt that classical economic theory can be used as an adequate rationale of its virtues. I am therefore not particularly optimistic about the efficacy of the current campaign to have businessmen "save the private enterprise system and the American way of life" by engaging in wholesale economic education, much of which is based on outmoded concepts.

Much as economic theory needs revision, I fear that this is not likely to cure our ills. Nor do I believe that profit-sharing or any other device for increasing the workers' cut (desirable as these efforts may be) will give us what we really want. It is, rather, another type of sharing that is needed, a sharing of more worthy objectives, a sharing of the management function, and a sharing of mutual respect and Christian working relationships.

Goals and purposes: What is wrong is more a matter of goals and purposes—of our assumptions about what we are trying to do and how we can dignify and improve ourselves in the doing. There is nothing wrong with production, but we should ask ourselves: *Production for what?* Do we use people for production or produc-

4. See John Kenneth Galbraith, *American Capitalism* (Boston, Houghton Mifflin Company, 1952).

tion for people? How can production be justified if it destroys personality and human values both in the process of its manufacture and by its end use? Clarence B. Randall of Inland Steel, in his book, *A Creed for Free Enterprise*, says:

"We have come to worship production as an end in itself, which of course it is not. It is precisely there that the honest critic of our way of life makes his attack and finds us vulnerable. Surely there must be for each person some ultimate value, some purpose, some mode of self-expression that makes the experience we call life richer and deeper." [5]

So far, so good, Mr. Randall. But now notice how he visualizes industry making its contribution to this worthy objective:

"To produce more and more with less and less effort is merely treading water unless we *thereby release time and energy for the cultivation of the mind and the spirit* and for the achievement of those ends for which Providence placed us on this earth." [6]

Here is the same old dichotomy—work faster and more efficiently so that you can finish your day of drudgery and cultivate your soul on your own time. In fact he says: "A horse with a very evil disposition can nevertheless pull the farmer's plow." No, I am afraid the job *is* the life. *This* is what must be made meaningful. We cannot assume that the end of production justifies the means. What happens to people in the course of producing may be far more important than the end product. Materialism is not a satisfactory "skyhook." People are capable of better and want to do better. (Incidentally, I have the impression that Mr. Randall's practices line up very well with my own point of view even if his words do not.)

Perhaps we should ask: What is the really important difference between Russian communism and our system? Both worship production and are determined to produce more efficiently, and do. Both worship science. Both have tremendously improved the standard of living of their

people. Both share the wealth. Both develop considerable loyalties for their system. (In a mere 40 years since Lenin started the communist revolution a third of the world's people have come to accept its allegiance.) True, in Russia capital is controlled by the state, while here it is theoretically controlled by individuals, although in actual practice, through absentee ownership, it is controlled to a considerable extent by central planning agencies and bureaus, both public and private.

No, the real difference is in the philosophy about people and how they may be used as means to ends. It is a difference in the assumptions made about the origin of rights—whether the individual is endowed with rights by his Creator and yields these only voluntarily to civil authority designated by him, or whether rights originate in force and in the will of the government. Is God a myth, or is He the final and absolute judge to whom we are ultimately responsible? Are all standards of conduct merely man-made and relative, or absolute and eternal? Is man a meaningless happenstance of protoplasm, or is he a divine creation with a purpose, with potential for improvement, and with a special destiny in the overall scheme of things? These are some of the differences—or at least I hope that they still are. And what a difference these intangible, perhaps mythical "skyhooks" make. They are nevertheless the most real and worthwhile and enduring things in the world. The absence of these values permitted the Nazis to "process" people through the gas chambers in order to recover the gold in their teeth.

The administrator contributes

This, then, is part of our general cultural heritage and is passed on to us in many ways. However, it really comes to life in people—in their attitudes, aspirations, and behaviors. And in a managerial society this brings us back to the quality of the individual administrator. He interprets or crystallizes the values and objectives for his group. He sets the climate within which these values either *do* or *do not* become working

realities. He must define the goals and purposes of his group in larger and more meaningful perspective. He integrates the smaller, selfish goals of individuals into larger, more social and spiritual, objectives for the group. He provides the vision without which the people perish. Conflicts are resolved by relating the immediate to the long-range and more enduring values. In fact, we might say this *integrative function* is the core of the administrator's contribution.

The good ones have the mental equipment to understand the business and set sound long-term objectives, but the best ones have in addition the philosophical and character values which help them to relate the overall goals of the enterprise to eternal values. This is precisely the point at which deep-seated religious convictions can serve an integrative function, since they represent the most long-range of all possible goals. [7] Most really great leaders in all fields of human endeavor have been peculiarly sensitive to their historic role in human destiny. Their responsibility and loyalty are to some distant vision which gives calm perspective to the hot issues of the day.

This function of the administrator goes far beyond being a likable personality, or applying correct principles of organization, or being skillful in the so-called techniques of human relations. I am convinced that the difficulties which so many executives have with supervisory relationships cannot be remedied by cultivation of the so-called human relations skills. These difficulties spring, rather, from one's conception of his function or role as a boss, his notion about the origin and nature of his authority over others, the assumptions he makes about people and their worth, and his view of what he and his people are trying to accomplish together. To illustrate:

If, for example, my personal goal is to get ahead in terms of money,

5. Boston, Little, Brown and Company, 1952, p. 16.

6. Ibid.

7. For further elaboration, see Gordon W. Allport, *The Individual and His Religion* (New York, The Macmillan Company, 1953).

position, and power; and if I assume that to achieve this I must best my competitors; that the way to do this is to establish a good production record; that my employees are means to this end; that they are replaceable production units which must be skillfully manipulated; that this can be done by appealing to the lowest form of immediate selfish interest; that the greatest threat to me is that my employees may not fully recognize my authority or accept my leadership—if these are my values, then I am headed for trouble—all supervisory techniques notwithstanding.

I wish I could be quite so positive in painting the picture of the right values and approaches to management. I suspect there are many, many different right answers. No doubt each company or enterprise will have to define its own long-term purposes and develop its own philosophy in terms of its history, traditions, and its real function in our economy. I am also certain that no one philosophy would be equally useful to all managers. The character of an organization is, to a large extent, set by the top man or the top group, and it is inevitable that this be the reflection of the philosophy of these individuals. No one of us can operate with another's philosophy. I have also observed that in most enterprises the basic faith or spirit of the organization is a rather nebulous or undefined something which nevertheless has very profound meaning to the employees.

A successful executive: Recognizing then the futility of advocating any one pattern of values, it occurs to me that it might, however, be suggestive or helpful if I told you something of the philosophy of one extremely successful executive whom I have pumped a good deal on this subject (for he is more inclined to live his values than to talk about them):

As near as I can piece it together, he believes that this world was not an accident but was created by God and that His laws regulate and control the universe and that we are ultimately *responsible to Him.* Man,

as God's supreme creation, is in turn endowed with creative ability. Each individual represents a unique combination of talents and potentials. In addition, man is the only animal endowed with freedom of choice and with a high capacity for making value judgments. With these gifts (of heredity and cultural environment) goes an obligation to give the best possible accounting of one's stewardship in terms of maximum self-development and useful service to one's fellows in the hope that one may live a rich life and be a credit to his Creator.

This executive also assumes that each individual possesses certain God-given rights of self-direction which only *the individual* can voluntarily delegate to others in authority over him, and that this is usually done in the interest of achieving some mutual cooperative good. The executive therefore assumes that his *own* authority as boss over others must be exercised with due regard for the attendant obligations to his employees and to the stockholders who have temporarily and voluntarily yielded their rights in the interest of this common undertaking. (Notice that he does not view his authority as originating with or derived from his immediate superior.) This delegated authority must, of course, be used to advance the common good rather than primarily to achieve the selfish ambitions of the leader at the expense of the led.

He further assumes that the voluntary association of employees in industry is for the purpose of increasing the creativity and productivity of all members of the group and thus of bringing about increased benefits to all who may share in the ultimate use of these goods and services. What is equally important, however, is that in the course of this industrial operation each individual should have an opportunity to develop the maximum potential of his skills and that the working relationships should not destroy the individual's ability to achieve his greatest maturity and richness of experience. As supervisor he must set the working conditions and atmosphere which will make it possible for his employees to achieve

this dual objective of increasing productivity and maximizing self-development.

These goals can best be achieved by giving employees maximum opportunity to exercise their capacity for decision making and judgment within their assigned area of responsibility. The supervisor is then primarily a coach who must instruct, discipline, and motivate all the members of the group, making it possible for each to exercise his special talent in order to maximize the total team contribution. Profits are regarded as a measure of the group's progress toward these goals, and a loss represents not only an improper but even an immoral use of the talents of the group.

There is nothing "soft" about his operation. He sets high quality standards and welcomes stiff competition as an additional challenge to his group. He therefore expects and gets complete cooperation and dedication on the part of everyone. Incidentally, he views the activity of working together in this manner with others as being one of life's most rewarding experiences. He holds that this way of life is something which we have not yet fully learned, but that its achievement is part of our divine destiny. He is firmly convinced that such conscientious efforts *will* be rewarded with success. He manages with a light touch that releases creativity, yet with complete confidence in the outcome.

This is probably a poor attempt at verbalizing the basic philosophy which this man lives so easily and naturally. I hope, however, that it has revealed something of his conception of his role or function as an executive, and his view of what he and his organization are trying to do together. With this account of his values I am sure that you would have no difficulty completing the description of his administrative practices and operating results. They flow naturally from his underlying faith, without benefit of intensive training in the principles and art of administration.

As you would suspect, people like to work for him—or with him. He attracts good talent (which is one of the real secrets of success). Those with shoddy values, selfish ambitions, or character defects do not survive—the organization is self-pruning. Those who remain develop rapidly because they learn to accept responsibility. He not only advocates but practices decentralization and delegation. His employees will admit that they have made mistakes, but usually add with a grin that they try not to make the same one twice. People respond to his leadership because he has faith in them and expects the best in them rather than the worst. He speaks well of the members of his organization, and they appear to be proud of each other and of their record of performance. He takes a keen interest in developing measurements of performance and in bettering previous records or competitive standards. He feels that no one has a right to "louse up a job"—a point on which he feels the stockholders and the Lord are in complete agreement.

While he does not talk much about "employee communications" or stress formal programs of this type, his practice is to spend a large proportion of his time in the field with his operating people rather than in his office. He is "people oriented," and he does a particularly good job of listening. The union committee members have confidence in his fairness, yet do a workmanlike job of bargaining. In administering salaries he seems to be concerned about helping the individual to improve his contribution so that a pay increase can be justified.

In his general behavior he moves without haste or hysteria. He is typically well organized, relaxed, and confident, even under trying circumstances. There is a high degree of consistency in his behavior and in the quality of his decisions because his basic values do not shift. Since he does not operate by expediency, others can depend on him; and this consistency makes for efficiency in the discharge of delegated responsibility. Those operating problems which do come to him for decision seem to move easily and quickly to a conclusion. His long-term values naturally express themselves in well-defined policies, and it is against this frame of reference that the decisions of the moment easily fall into proper perspective.

In policy-level discussions his contributions have a natural quality of objectivity because "self-concern" does not confuse. Others take him at face value because his motives are not suspect. When differences or conflicts do arise, his approach is not that of compromise; rather, he attempts to integrate the partisan views around mutually acceptable longer-range goals. The issues of the moment then seem to dissolve in a discussion of the best means to the achievement of the objective. I have no doubt that he also has some serious problems, but I have tried to give a faithful account of the impression which he creates. There is a *sense of special significance* about his operation which is shared by his associates.

This is the key

It is precisely this "sense of special significance" which is the key to leadership. We all know that there are many different ways of running a successful operation. I am certainly not recommending any particular set of administrative practices—although admittedly some are better than others. Nor am I suggesting that his set of values should be adopted by others, or for that matter could be. What I am saying is that a man's real values have a subtle but inevitable way of being communicated, and they affect the significance of everything he does.

These are the vague intangibles—the "skyhooks"—which are difficult to verbalize but easy to sense and tremendously potent in their influence. They provide a different, invisible, fundamental structure into which the experiences of every day are absorbed and given meaning. They are frequently unverbalized, and in many organizations they defy definition. Yet they are the most real things in the world.

The late Jacob D. Cox, Jr., formerly president of Cleveland Twist Drill Company, told a story that illustrates my point:

Jimmy Green was a new union committee member who stopped in to see Mr. Cox after contract negotiations had been concluded. Jimmy said that every other place he had worked, he had always gone home grouchy; he never wanted to play with the children or take his wife to the movies. And then he said, "But since I have been working here, all that has changed. Now when I come home, the children run to meet me and we have a grand romp together. It is a wonderful difference and I don't know why, but I thought you would like to know." [8]

As Mr. Cox observed, there must be a lot of Jimmy Greens in the world who want an opportunity to take part freely in a cooperative effort that has a moral purpose.

8. *Material Human Progress* (Cleveland, Cleveland Twist Drill Company, 1954), p. 104.

5

THE MANAGEMENT OF IDEAS

Melvin Anshen

Foreword

Current advances in management science stress improved analytical and administrative tools. But these alone will not be enough for survival in the future, because they are geared primarily to improve the efficiency of present operations. The new business leaders will be those who can stretch their minds beyond the management of physical resources. They will have the capacity to conceptualize broad new philosophies of business, and translate their vision into operations. To the traditional skills of managing people, material, machines, and money, they will add a challenging new skill—management of ideas.

A profound change in the main task of top management is emerging as a result of the accelerating dynamics of technologies, markets, information systems, and social expectations of business performance. If this projection is correct, the threat of obsolescence of managers will pass swiftly from today's conversational shocker to tomorrow's operating reality. Executives best prepared to survive this challenge may turn out to be those equipped to think like philosophers —a type of intellectual skill not ordinarily developed in business schools or by the common work experiences of middle management.

The roots of this radical transformation of the general management job can be identified in recent business history:

□ *Resources*—Up to about the last two decades the main task of top management could fairly be described as the efficient administration of physical resources. The focus was essentially short-range and unifunctional, and the dominant decision criteria were economic. The high-est demonstration of management skill was the successful manipulation of revenues and costs in the production and distribution of materials, machines, and products.

□ *People*—Beginning in the 1930's this concern with managing physical things was enlarged by a growing interest in managing people. This was enlargement, rather than change, because the ultimate goal of effective people management was still effective thing management, with top executives extending their grasp over resources by means of their ability to organize and motivate people. The focus of management attention remained within short-term horizons and unifunctional activity.

□ *Money*—After World War II, in a business environment marked by rapid growth in corporate size, product and market diversification, accelerated technological development, and shortened product life cycles, the principal task of top management evolved from concentration on physical and human resources to a major con-

43

cern with money. This shift was accompanied by an extension of planning horizons and a transition from a unifunctional to a multifunctional view of a company's activities.

In contrast to physical resources, money is inherently neutral; to be used it must be transformed into physical and human resources. Money also is flexible through time, that is, capable of expansion and contraction, as well as of rapid shifts in the forms, risks, and costs of financial instruments. These characteristics of neutrality and flexibility encouraged a broader management view that encompassed many functions within a company as well as longer-term planning horizons.

☐ *Ideas*—We are now beginning to sense that a focus on managing money, although broader than the earlier focus on physical and human resources, still fosters a dangerous sort of tunnel vision. The world of management is in a revolutionary phase. Within the company, racing technologies destroy both their own foundations and inter-technological boundaries. Outside the company, the environment is moving faster (in market evolution and consumer behavior), exploding in geographic scope (from nation to world), and reflecting the demands and constraints of a new society in which the traditional role of private business and traditional criteria of management performance are challenged by new concepts and standards.

At the same time, new analytical techniques, largely quantitative and computer-based, are presenting a management opportunity that is unique in at least two important ways. First, they provide an administrative capability without parallel in breadth, depth, and speed. Second, for their full and efficient utilization they press management to establish a unified command over the totality of a business, including the dynamic interface of external environment and internal activities. These changes are defining a novel view of management itself as a universally applicable resource, readily transferred from one business to another, from one industry to another, from one technology to another, from one country to another.

In this emerging management world, what will be the main task of management, common to top-level administrators in all types and sizes of companies? I suggest a combination of spatial and temporal intellectual vision, with the ability to transform vision into operating results through the flexible administration of physical, human, and financial resources in any environment. This might be described as applied conceptualization—or, more simply, as the management of ideas.

Central focus for ideas

Skill in generating and manipulating ideas is precisely the skill of the great philosophers—the ability to universalize from here and now to everywhere and always. If it is true that top executives in the years ahead are going to be tested above all by their ability to manage ideas, then they are going to have to understand what it means to think like philosophers and develop skill in doing it. This has implications for management education, training, and selection, especially at the higher levels of administration. It also carries a substantial threat of obsolescence for managers now holding broad responsibilities whose talent, education, and experience have not equipped them to use their intellects in this manner.

The implications are not limited to the purely intellectual demands placed on general managers. They also extend to corporate purpose, organization, and function. A business devoted to the identification of central ideas and the formulation of strategies for moving swiftly from ideas to operations will differ in structure and activity from a business primarily concerned with management of money, or of physical and human resources.

Management of ideas is a broader concept than either management by objectives or long-range planning. The use of objectives and planning are techniques equally relevant for any major management task, whether it be a focus on physical resources or money, or a principal concern with ideas.

Management of ideas also goes beyond the concept of strategy. Just as there are alternative strategies for attaining an objective, so there are alternative strategies for executing an idea that defines the central purpose of a business. Focusing on the management of ideas contributes to more realistic planning, more appropriate objectives, more relevant strategies.

Ideas for technology

One example of how an idea may be viewed as the central focus for management attention can be found in industries characterized by advanced, dynamic technologies.

Soft answers: In this arena, it is attractively easy to frame a soft answer to the hard question of how to organize resources for maximum effectiveness. A typical soft answer:

"In our fast-moving technological environment, the big winners will be those companies with large investments in research and development, because out of R&D come the new products that capture markets and generate high return on investment. Therefore we should invest every available dollar in R&D."

The inadequacy of this operating design is suggested by the common management complaint in these industries that it is difficult to establish rational control over investment in and performance of R&D, difficult to measure payback on R&D investment, and difficult to concentrate research efforts on projects with high potential payoffs.

Hard answers: However, there are a few companies in high-technology industries in which such complaints rarely arise. These are the companies whose top managers have done the thinking that develops hard, rather than soft, answers. They have observed that a commitment to R&D without a specific central concept for total organization effort is a clumsy, even a meaningless, commitment. But by resolute probing, they have found an opportunity for defining a core idea around which total company effort can be designed. This opportunity can be described in terms of three specific idea options:

1. To mobilize all of a company's resources around the concept of becoming a creative technological leader—the first in the industry to discover, develop, and market new products at the leading edge of moving technology.

2. To organize resources around the central idea of becoming an early imitator and adapter of the successful innovations of the industry's creative leader.

3. To become a low-price mass producer of established products, sacrificing the high margins (and high risks) of innovation for the high volume (and limited risks) of low-price imitation.

Each of these options carries specific implications for the kind of investment in product and market research, as well as for organization structure, information network, scale of activity and risk, and many other aspects of a company's physical, personal, and financial resources. In short, out of each of these idea op-

tions can be derived a total scheme for operating a business. This total scheme will be uniquely determined by the central idea and will represent the top management choice among alternative strategies for executing the idea throughout the business.

Ideas for conglomerates

Another example can be found among diversified or conglomerate companies. Here, too, there have been many soft answers, framed around a generalized acquisition drive. Economic pressures have revealed the inadequacies of this course. In contrast, some managements have exploited opportunities to select as a base for a total enterprise commitment a central idea from several identified options:

1. A structure of unrelated or accidentally related companies anchored to a central core of unusual management competence, both general and functional, available to strengthen the performance of each satellite company.

2. A designed diversification aimed at exploiting complementary technologies, production resources, or market systems.

3. A diversification aimed at balancing high-risk and low-risk ventures, fluctuating and stable industries, and cyclical and seasonal variations.

As with the high-technology idea options, each of the diversification models carries specific implications for every element in a business and for the goals and strategies by which the elements are activated.

Other examples

Still other examples of central ideas may be cited briefly:

○ A shift in the definition of a business from one concerned with the sale of a product to one concerned with the delivery of a complete system of customer values—as in airlines' marketing of packaged vacations, computer manufacturers' marketing of systems to solve customers' information problems, and consumer hard-good companies' marketing of assured lifetime performance of products.

○ The discovery, almost the invention, of new industries—such as environmental hygiene and control, education as a lifespan need, and the profit-oriented performance of traditional public services such as urban redevelopment or even urban creation.

○ The abandonment of accepted notions of industry boundaries—as in the transformation of a steel company into a materials company or of a petroleum company into an energy company.

○ The evolution of "scrambled merchandising" in retail stores which focus on a pattern of consumer needs and buying habits rather than on historic product categories such as groceries or drug products.

Each of these ideas is the energized core of a unique design for a business. The exploitation of each idea requires a comprehensive intellectual grasp of the totality of a business viewed as an interacting system that includes both internal resources and functions and external distribution systems and markets. From such a comprehensive vision will issue a flow of strategic options for products, services, costs, prices, technology, organization structures, responsibilities, information networks, and motivations for all levels of management.

New ways of thinking

Thinking in terms of such ideas, from initial concept through full implementation, is a difficult intellectual task. It is no assignment for second-rate minds, or even for first-rate but narrowly oriented minds. Moreover, it demands the special intellectual ability to visualize the translation of ideas and strategies into controlled operating systems responsive to dynamic change.

The need for these unusual talents is the inevitable outcome of radically new conditions within and outside the corporation. The critical new condition is an acceleration in the rate of change of such magnitude that change itself becomes the central object of management attention. Up to now, with rare exceptions, the administration of change has been handled as a supplement to the administration of established ongoing activities. In this context, the future evolves from the present at a controllable pace, and it is reasonable for managers to concentrate mainly on targets of efficiency and to treat adapting to market challenges as a subsidiary element within a larger administrative responsibility.

Only a few companies have been in a position to report to stockholders such dramatic news as that "50% of our sales in the past year and 75% of our profits were generated by prod-

ucts that we did not handle five years ago." When many companies report such news, or make equally startling observations about short-term penetration of new markets or new technologies (whether from internal development or acquisitions), the fact of change moves to the center of the stage and all else is peripheral.

Preparing for change

At this point, it becomes more important to make correct decisions about the direction, timing, and implementation of change than to attain a high level of efficiency in administering steady-state operations. However, few business organizations have been designed to give primary support to this unfamiliar ordering of goals. In most companies the values, organization, responsibility, control systems, information networks, and performance standards are not well adapted to this requirement.

Most companies, including many with reputations for being well managed, are organized primarily to administer yesterday's ideas. Investments and operations are measured by efficient performance, with relatively short-term targets for achievement, and a primary focus on taut administration of existing resources and markets. This was an appropriate corporate design concept when the rate of changes within and outside the company was slow.

The weakness of such organizations is revealed, however, whenever a new opportunity or a forced adaptation is sensed by a single department. Rapid exploitation of new markets usually increases production costs, and is therefore resisted by managers whose performance will be adversely affected in any shift in ongoing efficient activities. Less common, but equally possible, is resistance from the marketing people to innovation in production technology with its risk of cost, quality, and delivery uncertainties.

But even this view is simplistic. For in spite of the current touted commitment to a marketing orientation in management, the performance record in many companies suggests that leadership by the marketing function frequently generates little more than better adaption of existing products to better defined existing markets. This may be a move in the right direction in the short run. But it is not good enough in a period when new technology may erode established market positions or capture untouched markets "overnight."

Inherent in the concept of core ideas for top

management is a total business orientation, rather than a market-oriented administration (or a technology-oriented or any "other-oriented" administration). A total business orientation views the company as a system of physical, financial, and human resources in dynamic interaction with a changing environment. It views swift response to opportunities and problems as more important for long-run success than efficient control of current operations. It values the future above the present. Such an orientation has revolutionary implications for many management designs and tasks.

New organizational patterns

Consider, as one example, the way companies assign authority and responsibility. Whatever the shape of a company's organization tree, it shares certain characteristics with all organization structures. First among these, and most visible because it is specifically charted, is some type of cluster design that gathers together a prescribed set of related activities. The design may focus on patterns of functions, products, geography, or projects. Whatever the pattern, the task performance is substantially influenced by the prescription of the pattern itself, and the pressures of the perceived reward criteria.

With one exception (the project cluster), all of these cluster patterns inevitably develop a built-in resource and emotional investment in the continuance of the established design. Since there are no defined time limits for the exercise of responsibility within the cluster, the accumulating managerial bias must be toward preservation of existing activities and status.

In such an environment, it would be extraordinary if radical change claimed a dominant share of management attention. Thus we see the common practice of establishing a long-range planning function at a single, usually remote, location in the organization tree, with the resulting problems of working through informal channels to bring ideas about the future into contact with current operations.

In these structures, radical change is painful. It is viewed as disruptive and costly by managers committed to the present and appraised by their administration of the present. In their constrained sighting they are right. They resist change because it is in their perceived economic interest to resist and because change threatens their status and their intellectual and emotional commitments.

This may go a long way toward explaining why so many of the major conceptual innovations—the great new ideas—are introduced and initially exploited by companies other than the corporate giants. (It should be noted, however, that this conclusion has nothing to do with the development and application of technological progress which is one of the prime accomplishments of large research-oriented companies.)

The single organization pattern that is free from this built-in bias is the project cluster. While there may be difficult administrative problems associated with project-oriented structures, they offer the important advantages of tailor-made design to fit unique tasks, flexible resource commitments, defined termination points, and an absence of enduring commitment that encourages resistance to radical innovation.

The project pattern suggests important clues for the characteristics of an organization structure focused on the management of ideas in a dynamic environment. One principal requirement will be unconstrained adaptability to new tasks, with easy transitions across technological, product, and market boundaries. Another will be performance measurement and motivation that give substantial encouragement to future-oriented management thinking. A third will be

an ability to bring multifunctional considerations quickly to bear on opportunities that appear initially in the field of vision of a single function.

All of these requirements suggest a fluid concept of organization structure marked by short-lived, specific-assignment clusters, flexibility in job definitions, and a high degree of vertical and horizontal teamwork. Thus *both* middle and top management must accept and adjust to this fluid concept. This means critical demands on both the quality of managers' intellectual resources and the ways in which managers are motivated to use these resources. None of these demands can be met by fiat. They call for the creation of a new way of life for which many executives are ill-prepared by education and experience.

Information revolution

A further example of revolutionary change in administrative design can be found in the area of information generation and use.

A few words about computers are in order at the outset. The history of computer applications in the 17 years since their introduction to the business market reveals two distinct stages in management concepts of their potential.

1. Initially, most managers viewed computers as electronic clerks. The primary use of computers was therefore in familiar tasks.

2. Recently, a second stage of management thinking can be discerned. This has been marked by a superficial popularization of the concept of the integrated information system which calls on the storage, retrieval, and manipulative capability of large computers to bring the total information requirements of a business within an integrated decision network. (This does not imply a computerized decision system, but simply an organized information system, computer-based, to assist comprehensive human decision making.)

While the notion of the integrated information system has been widely described and explored in technical and management journals, several probes of management practice suggest that few companies have made a sustained attempt to operate in this way, and few managers have any real grasp of what the concept means in either theoretical or operating terms. There is, to be sure, a growing number of fractional, single-function information systems, such as those linking production, inventory, and procurement activities. And there is a growing disposition to talk about comprehensive management information systems. But the operational application is a long way from the discussion,

with many unresolved conceptual and technical problems in between.

It would be a gross misconception to view this gap as the familiar one between software and hardware. The primary task ahead is not to develop programs that will utilize the capabilities of the machines. Rather it is to develop management concepts that define integrated systems. It will then be possible to describe the principal data requirements to make such systems operational, including clear delineation of relationships among the components of a dynamic system responsive to external and internal feedback. The next step will be the design of computer programs to store and manipulate data for management needs.

At present, most top managers have yet to approach even the initial stage of developing basic concepts. The skeptic may be inclined to say: "But this can't be true! Managers are running companies, and this means that they are running systems, with whatever crude tools, including the human brain, they may have at hand." To which the appropriate reply is:

"True enough, managers are running companies. But examination of the typical management decision process reveals that what is happening is in no sense total system analysis. Problems are usually fractionated within the total company system—partly to reduce them to a size and order of simplicity that are manageable with available analytical tools, and partly to follow familiar routines and utilize familiar rules of thumb."

What is defined here is not a technical requirement, but an intellectual requirement. This is essentially a command of logical design. The basic design building blocks are:

1. Identification of critical areas of initiating change that generate effects in one or several operating areas.

2. Rough measures of the magnitudes of the primary cause-effect relationships.

3. Identification of the principal feedbacks.

4. Rough measures of these feedbacks.

For purposes of concept formulation and testing, the degree of precision ordinarily required is modest because this is not primarily a quantitative exercise. One does not need numbers to design a business system. In fact, the truth is quite the reverse. One first needs a concept of a system in order to identify the kinds of numbers needed to work the system.

Furthermore, it is unlikely that any comprehensive business system can be completely quantified in the sense of converting all decision inputs into a set of manipulatable numbers. The objective is limited and practical. It is simply to use both quantitative and qualitative analysis to extend management's decision horizon to the total business viewed as a dynamic system, and thereby to improve the quality of decisions. The improvement will be reflected in the ability to make decisions that are broadly consistent with the basic concept of the business, sensitive to impacts and feedbacks throughout the business, and rapidly and flexibly adaptive to changing conditions within and outside the company.

Focus on the future

A third example of the impact of revolutionary change is the need for upgrading management's ability to forecast the shape of things to come. During the last 20 years economic forecasting has made the transition from favorite parlor game of professional economists to favorite reading matter of professional managers. The prognostications of accredited economic forecasters are a mandatory item on every trade association agenda, while discussions of the economic outlook clog the pages of management magazines.

But economic change is only one of several environmental areas important to managers. Three other areas are equally significant: technological change, social change, and political change. Few companies and few individual managers have addressed themselves in a serious and organized way to the problems of forecasting trends in these areas. Yet changes in the years ahead, coming more rapidly than ever before, will be loaded with opportunities for the forewarned, and with threats for those who have not cast their minds forward and formulated offensive and defensive strategies.

The requirement is for more than a freshened interest in the future. The evolution of economic forecasting to its present significant role in management planning resulted from the invention of sophisticated tools of analysis. One cannot predict economic trends with a useful level of confidence until the significant economic variables have been identified and their interacting dynamics at least roughly measured. Forecasting of technological, social, and political changes (including both trends and rates of movement) will require a comparable intellec-

tual achievement. Large rewards will be realized by organizations that can anticipate developments in these areas with enough confidence to incorporate their forecasts in strategic planning.

Technological forecasting

In the area of technology an essential conceptual adaptation must be to extend management thinking beyond the base to which it is commonly tied, that is, the view that improvements will be regularly generated from developments in the technologies that have been their historical foundation. This is an understandable but limiting and risky framework for forecasting.

Analysis of recent technological advances clearly identifies two related phenomena of great importance to management. One is the application of "foreign" technologies in process and product areas where they have played no significant prior role. The other is the erosion, often the disappearance, of traditional industry and product boundaries. Together, they lay down a requirement that technological forecasting be treated broadly.

It will not be safe for a manager to project the shape of technological changes by extrapolating trends in existing applications. Some of the most significant developments affecting both production and marketing are likely to be spawned within technologies that are not currently applicable in his industry and company.

Technological forecasting of this breadth and sophistication will not progress far without the development of a new kind of professional expertise, comparable to that of professional economists. It will be a prime responsibility of enlightened managers to encourage qualified scientists and engineers to address themselves to the assignment, and to build their own ability to communicate with and guide this new corps of professionals.

In addition, just as the sophisticated manager needs the skill to translate economic forecasts into signals of opportunity and threat for his company's future operations, so will he need a parallel skill to translate technological forecasts into meaningful guides for business strategies. This task cannot safely be left to the technicians. There should be little need to emphasize this warning to managers who have grasped, often after painful experience, the need to guide the work of computer specialists to assure that they mobilize information specifically relevant for management control and decision.

A prime ingredient in translating technological projections into business applications will be a thorough understanding of the difference between technical feasibility and economic feasibility. Technology determines what can be done. Economics determines what will be done. Managers must be familiar with this distinction. Many of today's naive forecasters of the technological outlook who are writing in the popular press certainly are not.

Social forecasting

Forecasting of social trends covers such topics as changing social structure (including racial and ethnic components), evolution of living patterns and related spending patterns, and shifting values and priorities (for example, between work and leisure, between risk assumption and security).

The full implications of the opportunities presented by recent social trends have been grasped by few companies. For instance, managers of a number of financial institutions reveal a persistent preoccupation with superficial economic phenomena of consumers' saving and investment patterns, rather than a probing analysis of the financial service needs of a society marked by widespread affluence, multiple options in discretionary spending, confidence in long-range income security, and rising concern about permanent inflation.

A well-known example of the powerful application of social (appropriately combined with economic) forecasting is the course pursued by Sears, Roebuck and Co. since World War II. The dramatic divergence of this company's performance from that of its direct competitor, Montgomery Ward & Company, Inc., needs no description for a management audience. But the important contribution made by a projection of fundamental social changes and the translation of that forecast into market opportunities deserves to be noted.

Sears made an aggressive exploitation of social perspective through a core institutional idea. The results have been as spectacular as was the comparable grasp of a new business opportunity evoked by socioeconomic change evidenced in the implementation of a core management idea by General Motors under Alfred P. Sloan's direction in the 1920's.

The extension of management's conceptual competence in the area of social dynamics calls for knowledge and perceptiveness that have not been required hitherto. As in the field of technology, managers will be dealing with professional specialists whose work must be directed and interpreted. Competence in doing this will build the confidence to use social projections in designing business strategies that open the way to radical innovations in organization and operations.

Political forecasting

The principal business element in political forecasting is the shifting boundary between the private and public sectors of the economy. Until recently, the prevailing management view of this area was a superficial conclusion that a transfer of activities was occurring from the private to the public sector, directly by intervention or indirectly by control.

Current developments are beginning to suggest that this is a naive judgment. Movement in the opposite direction can also be discerned, for example, in education, research, and construction. New, mixed public-private enterprise forms, such as Comsat, are being invented. More developments of this sort may be anticipated. Moreover, changes in the domain of private enterprise, in pure or mixed form, are not totally a result of decisions taken within government. Business initiative can open the door to private expansion, particularly where the public performance has been lethargic, unimaginative, or grossly inefficient.

The pejorative descriptive phrase, "socialization of American society," indiscriminately applied to developments in such diverse fields as health, insurance, transportation, housing, or even protection of consumer interests, has a dangerous potential for stultifying thinking about the central issues. A more open view might recognize that an industrialized, urbanized, high-technology society, in which a dramatically visible gap appears between the actual and the potential quality of life, is a society ripe for changes in traditional public-private relationships.

The changes may move in either direction: toward public invasion of the private sector or toward private invasion of the public sector. The direction and rate of these changes will be powerfully influenced by managers who can deal confidently with new ideas in areas where businessmen have seldom allowed their minds to be engaged. The political environment, there can be little doubt, will be redesigned. But those who believe that environment is created by forces outside their control will not be in an intellectual position to participate in the redesign. An environment will be imposed on them which, however reluctantly, they will be compelled to accept.

On the positive side, a rising interest and skill in forecasting political relationships will identify opportunities for private enterprise to invent new environmental concepts. Formulating these concepts, and relating them to profitable resource investment, will require an intellectual adventure in the world of ideas such as few managers have so far experienced. Part of the process will surely be fresh definitions of the words "private" and "public," which, as applied to business and government activities, have been largely emptied of meaning by emotional abuse.

As in forecasting social change, it is not easy to perceive shifts in the private-public balance, or potential for inducing shifts by initiatives from the private sector. We lack even the professional discipline to generate the knowledge and develop a reliable analytical base for management thinking. Traditional political science is oriented toward the problems of governing men and the performance of institutions for public legislation and administration. The new issues are closer to those implied by the classic term, "political economy," and involve concepts of social design on the grand scale.

Philosopher-executive

The emerging dominance of ideas as a central concern for top management raises critical questions about the education, selection, and development of candidates for high-level assignments in the years ahead. Neither business school education nor in-company experience is presently structured to emphasize the manager-as-philosopher concept. Rather, the principal thrust in school and company environments is toward new analytic techniques, both quantitative and qualitative, and their application in rational decision making and control.

There is good reason to doubt that students in professional schools are at a stage of their intellectual development where they would benefit from a major emphasis on the role of central ideas in top management responsibilities. Moreover, the relevant technical input to their education is so important and growing so rapidly that any sharp curtailment would constrain their ability to handle management tasks in junior executive positions.

The education of middle-level managers is another matter, however. There are opportunities at this stage to expose selected high-potential executives to the significance of core ideas in the design of long-range corporate strategies and in the adaptation of organization and resources to their implementation. The opportunities arise in planned job experiences and management education programs, both in-house and university. Imaginative action at this level will produce two important benefits. One is the preparation of a cadre of potential top executives for the broad new responsibilities that the future business environment will thrust on them. The other is a new selection criterion for top-level positions, based on specific performance in mid-career assignments where the ability to think conceptually and to relate ideas to applied management can be tested.

Today's development programs give principal emphasis to new techniques for analysis and control in functional areas, and to strategic planning of resource utilization at the general management level. It would be desirable to curtail the technical content to some degree and introduce material on dynamic environmental change (markets, technologies, social, political), on the role and manipulation of ideas, and on the impact of change on corporate strategy.

A related effort to enrich idea-management experience on the job and test executives' abilities would require more opportunities below the top management level for assignments that require imaginative projection, assessment of the total environmental outlook, and relevant strategic decision. Corporations which move in this direction will fortify their management ability to cope powerfully and speedily with a radically new business world.

COPING WITH THE JOB

6

SKILLS OF AN
EFFECTIVE ADMINISTRATOR

Robert L. Katz

Although the selection and training of good administrators is widely recognized as one of American industry's most pressing problems, there is surprisingly little agreement among executives or educators on what makes a good administrator. The executive development programs of some of the nation's leading corporations and colleges reflect a tremendous variation in objectives.

At the root of this difference is industry's search for the traits or attributes which will objectively identify the "ideal executive" who is equipped to cope effectively with any problem in any organization. As one observer of American industry recently noted:

"The assumption that there is an executive type is widely accepted, either openly or implicitly. Yet any executive presumably knows that a company needs all kinds of managers for different levels of jobs. The qualities most needed by a shop superintendent are likely to be quite opposed to those needed by a coordinating vice president of manufacturing. The literature of executive development

is loaded with efforts to define the qualities needed by executives, and by themselves these sound quite rational. Few, for instance, would dispute the fact that a top manager needs good judgment, the ability to make decisions, the ability to win respect of others, and all the other well-worn phrases any management man could mention. But one has only to look at the successful managers in any company to see how enormously their particular qualities vary from any ideal list of executive virtues." [1]

Yet this quest for the executive stereotype has become so intense that many companies, in concentrating on certain specific traits or qualities, stand in danger of losing sight of their real concern: *what a man can accomplish.*

It is the purpose of this article to suggest what may be a more useful approach to the selection and development of administrators. This approach is based not on what good executives *are* (their innate traits and characteristics), but rather on what they *do* (the kinds of skills which they exhibit in carrying out their jobs effectively). As used here, a *skill* implies an ability

AUTHOR'S NOTE: This article is based on a study prepared under a grant from the Alfred P. Sloan Foundation.

[1] Perrin Stryker, "The Growing Pains of Executive Development," *Advanced Management*, August 1954, p. 15.

which can be developed, not necessarily inborn, and which is manifested in performance, not merely in potential. So the principal criterion of skillfulness must be effective action under varying conditions.

This approach suggests that effective administration rests on *three basic developable skills* which obviate the need for identifying specific traits and which may provide a useful way of looking at and understanding the administrative process. This approach is the outgrowth of firsthand observation of executives at work coupled with study of current field research in administration.

In the sections which follow, an attempt will be made to define and demonstrate what these three skills are; to suggest that the relative importance of the three skills varies with the level of administrative responsibility; to present some of the implications of this variation for selection, training, and promotion of executives; and to propose ways of developing these skills.

Three-Skill Approach

It is assumed here that an administrator is one who (a) directs the activities of other persons and (b) undertakes the responsibility for achieving certain objectives through these efforts. Within this definition, successful administration appears to rest on three basic skills, which we will call *technical*, *human*, and *conceptual*. It would be unrealistic to assert that these skills are not interrelated, yet there may be real merit in examining each one separately, and in developing them independently.

Technical Skill

As used here, technical skill implies an understanding of, and proficiency in, a specific kind of activity, particularly one involving methods, processes, procedures, or techniques. It is relatively easy for us to visualize the technical skill of the surgeon, the musician, the accountant, or the engineer when each is performing his own special function. Technical skill involves specialized knowledge, analytical ability within that specialty, and facility in the use of the tools and techniques of the specific discipline.

Of the three skills described in this article, technical skill is perhaps the most familiar because it is the most concrete, and because, in our age of specialization, it is the skill required of the greatest number of people. Most of our vocational and on-the-job training programs are largely concerned with developing this specialized technical skill.

Human Skill

As used here, human skill is the executive's ability to work effectively as a group member and to build cooperative effort within the team he leads. As *technical* skill is primarily concerned with working with "things" (processes or physical objects), so *human* skill is primarily concerned with working with people. This skill is demonstrated in the way the individual perceives (and recognizes the perceptions of) his superiors, equals, and subordinates, and in the way he behaves subsequently.

The person with highly developed human skill is aware of his own attitudes, assumptions, and beliefs about other individuals and groups; he is able to see the usefulness and limitations of these feelings. By accepting the existence of viewpoints, perceptions, and beliefs which are different from his own, he is skillful in understanding what others really mean by their words and behavior. He is equally skillful in communicating to others, in their own contexts, what he means by *his* behavior.

Such a person works to create an atmosphere of approval and security in which subordinates feel free to express themselves without fear of censure or ridicule, by encouraging them to participate in the planning and carrying out of those things which directly affect them. He is sufficiently sensitive to the needs and motivations of others in his organization so that he can judge the possible reactions to, and outcomes of, various courses of action he may undertake. Having this sensitivity, he is able and willing to *act* in a way which takes these perceptions by others into account.

Real skill in working with others must become a natural, continuous activity, since it involves sensitivity not only at times of decision making but also in the day-by-day behavior of the individual. Human skill cannot be a "sometime thing." Techniques cannot be randomly applied, nor can personality traits be put on or removed like an overcoat. Because everything which an executive says and does (or leaves unsaid or undone) has an effect on his associates, his true self will, in time, show through. Thus, to be effective, this skill must be naturally developed and unconsciously, as well as consistently, demonstrated in the individual's every action. It must become an integral part of his whole being.

Because human skill is so vital a part of everything the administrator does, examples of inadequate human skill are easier to describe than are highly skillful performances. Perhaps consideration of an actual situation would serve to clarify what is involved:

When a new conveyor unit was installed in a shoe factory where workers had previously been free to determine their own work rate, the production manager asked the industrial engineer who had designed the conveyor to serve as foreman, even though a qualified foreman was available. The engineer, who reported directly to the production manager, objected, but under pressure he agreed to take the job "until a suitable foreman could be found," even though this was a job of lower status than his present one. Then the following conversation took place:

Production Manager: "I've had a lot of experience with conveyors. I want you to keep this conveyor going at all times except for rest periods, and I want it going at top speed. Get these people thinking in terms of 2 pairs of shoes a minute, 70 dozen pairs a day, 350 dozen pairs a week. They are all experienced operators on their individual jobs, and it's just a matter of getting them to do their jobs in a little different way. I want you to make that base rate of 250 dozen pair a week work!" [Base rate was established at slightly under 75% of the maximum capacity. This base rate was 50% higher than under the old system.]

Engineer: "If I'm going to be foreman of the conveyor unit, I want to do things my way. I've worked on conveyors, and I don't agree with you on first getting people used to a conveyor going at top speed. These people have never seen a conveyor. You'll scare them. I'd like to run the conveyor at one-third speed for a couple of weeks and then gradually increase the speed.

"I think we should discuss setting the base rate [production quota before incentive bonus] on a daily basis instead of a weekly basis. [Workers had previously been paid on a daily straight piecework basis.]

"I'd also suggest setting a daily base rate at 45 or even 40 dozen pair. You have to set a base rate low enough for them to make. Once they know they can make the base rate, they will go after the bonus."

Production Manager: "You do it your way on the speed; but remember it's the results that count. On the base rate, I'm not discussing it with you;

I'm telling you to make the 250 dozen pair a week work. I don't want a daily base rate." [2]

Here is a situation in which the production manager was so preoccupied with getting the physical output that he did not pay attention to the people through whom that output had to be achieved. Notice, first, that he made the engineer who designed the unit serve as foreman, apparently hoping to force the engineer to justify his design by producing the maximum output. However, the production manager was oblivious to (a) the way the engineer perceived this appointment, as a demotion, and (b) the need for the engineer to be able to control the variables if he was to be held responsible for output. Instead the production manager imposed a production standard and refused any changes in the work situation.

Moreover, although this was a radically new situation for the operators, the production manager expected them to produce immediately at well above their previous output — even though the operators had an unfamiliar production system to cope with, the operators had never worked together as a team before, the operators and their new foreman had never worked together before, and the foreman was not in agreement with the production goals or standards. By ignoring all these human factors, the production manager not only placed the engineer in an extremely difficult operating situation but also, by refusing to allow the engineer to "run his own show," discouraged the very assumption of responsibility he had hoped for in making the appointment.

Under these circumstances, it is easy to understand how the relationship between these two men rapidly deteriorated, and how production, after two months' operation, was at only 125 dozen pairs per week (just 75% of what it had been under the old system).

Conceptual Skill

As used here, conceptual skill involves the ability to see the enterprise as a whole; it includes recognizing how the various functions of the organization depend on one another, and how changes in any one part affect all the others; and it extends to visualizing the relationship of the individual business to the industry, the

[2] From a mimeographed case in the files of the Harvard Business School; copyrighted by the President and Fellows of Harvard College.

community, and the political, social, and economic forces of the nation as a whole. Recognizing these relationships and perceiving the significant elements in any situation, the administrator should then be able to act in a way which advances the over-all welfare of the total organization.

Hence, the success of any decision depends on the conceptual skill of the people who make the decision and those who put it into action. When, for example, an important change in marketing policy is made, it is critical that the effects on production, control, finance, research, and the people involved be considered. And it remains critical right down to the last executive who must implement the new policy. If each executive recognizes the over-all relationships and significance of the change, he is almost certain to be more effective in administering it. Consequently the chances for succeeding are greatly increased.

Not only does the effective coordination of the various parts of the business depend on the conceptual skill of the administrators involved, but so also does the whole future direction and tone of the organization. The attitudes of a top executive color the whole character of the organization's response and determine the "corporate personality" which distinguishes one company's ways of doing business from another's. These attitudes are a reflection of the administrator's conceptual skill (referred to by some as his "creative ability") — the way he perceives and responds to the direction in which the business should grow, company objectives and policies, and stockholders' and employees' interests.

Conceptual skill, as defined above, is what **Chester I. Barnard,** former president of the **New Jersey Bell Telephone Company,** implies when he says: ". . . the essential aspect of the [executive] process is the sensing of the organization as a whole and the total situation relevant to it." [8] Examples of inadequate conceptual skill are all around us. Here is one instance:

In a large manufacturing company which had a long tradition of job-shop type operations, primary responsibility for production control had been left to the foremen and other lower-level supervisors. "Village" type operations with small working groups and informal organizations were the rule. A heavy influx of orders following World War II tripled the normal production requirements and severely

[8] *Functions of the Executive* (Cambridge, Harvard University Press, 1948), p. 235.

taxed the whole manufacturing organization. At this point, a new production manager was brought in from outside the company, and he established a wide range of controls and formalized the entire operating structure.

As long as the boom demand lasted, the employees made every effort to conform with the new procedures and environment. But when demand subsided to prewar levels, serious labor relations problems developed, friction was high among department heads, and the company found itself saddled with a heavy indirect labor cost. Management sought to reinstate its old procedures; it fired the production manager and attempted to give greater authority to the foremen once again. However, during the four years of formalized control, the foremen had grown away from their old practices, many had left the company, and adequate replacements had not been developed. Without strong foreman leadership, the traditional job-shop operations proved costly and inefficient.

In this instance, when the new production controls and formalized organizations were introduced, management did not foresee the consequences of this action in the event of a future contraction of business. Later, when conditions changed and it was necessary to pare down operations, management was again unable to recognize the implications of its action and reverted to the old procedures, which, under existing circumstances, were no longer appropriate. This compounded *conceptual* inadequacy left the company at a serious competitive disadvantage.

Because a company's over-all success is dependent on its executives' conceptual skill in establishing and carrying out policy decisions, this skill is the unifying, coordinating ingredient of the administrative process, and of undeniable over-all importance.

Relative Importance

We may notice that, in a very real sense, conceptual skill embodies consideration of both the technical and human aspects of the organization. Yet the concept of *skill,* as an ability to translate knowledge into action, should enable one to distinguish between the three skills of performing the technical activities (technical skill), understanding and motivating individuals and groups (human skill), and coordinating and integrating all the activities and interests of the organization toward a common objective (conceptual skill).

This separation of effective administration into three basic skills is useful primarily for purposes of analysis. In practice, these skills are so closely interrelated that it is difficult to determine where one ends and another begins. However, just because the skills are interrelated does not imply that we cannot get some value from looking at them separately, or by varying their emphasis. In playing golf the action of the hands, wrists, hips, shoulders, arms, and head are all interrelated; yet in improving one's swing it is often valuable to work on one of these elements separately. Also, under different playing conditions the relative importance of these elements varies. Similarly, although all three are of importance at every level of administration, the technical, human, and conceptual skills of the administrator vary in relative importance at different levels of responsibility.

At Lower Levels

Technical skill is responsible for many of the great advances of modern industry. It is indispensable to efficient operation. Yet it has greatest importance at the lower levels of administration. As the administrator moves further and further from the actual physical operation, this need for technical skill becomes less important, provided he has skilled subordinates and can help them solve their own problems. At the top, technical skill may be almost nonexistent, and the executive may still be able to perform effectively if his human and conceptual skills are highly developed. For example:

In one large capital-goods producing company, the controller was called on to replace the manufacturing vice president who had been stricken suddenly with a severe illness. The controller had no previous production experience, but he had been with the company for more than 20 years and knew many of the key production personnel intimately. By setting up an advisory staff, and by delegating an unusual amount of authority to his department heads, he was able to devote himself to coordination of the various functions. By so doing, he produced a highly efficient team. The results were lower costs, greater productivity, and higher morale than the production division had ever before experienced. Management had gambled that this man's ability to work with people

was more important than his lack of a technical production background, and the gamble paid off.

Other examples are evident all around us. We are all familiar with those "professional managers" who are becoming the prototypes of our modern executive world. These men shift with great ease, and with no apparent loss in effectiveness, from one industry to another. Their human and conceptual skills seem to make up for their unfamiliarity with the new job's technical aspects.

At Every Level

Human skill, the ability to work with others, is essential to effective administration at every level. One recent research study has shown that human skill is of paramount importance at the foreman level, pointing out that the chief function of the foreman as an administrator is to attain collaboration of people in the work group.[4] Another study reinforces this finding and extends it to the middle-management group, adding that the administrator should be primarily concerned with facilitating communication in the organization.[5] And still another study, concerned primarily with top management, underscores the need for self-awareness and sensitivity to human relationships by executives at that level.[6] These findings would tend to indicate that human skill is of great importance at every administrative level, but notice the difference in emphasis.

Human skill seems to be most important at lower levels, where the number of direct contacts between administrators and subordinates is greatest. As we go higher and higher in the administrative echelons, the number and frequency of these personal contacts decrease, and the need for human skill becomes proportionately, although probably not absolutely, less. At the same time, conceptual skill becomes increasingly more important with the need for policy decisions and broad-scale action. The human skill of dealing with individuals then becomes subordinate to the conceptual skill of integrating group interests and activities into a coordinated whole.

In fact, a recent research study by Professor Chris Argyris of Yale University has given us

[4] A. Zaleznik, *Foreman Training in a Growing Enterprise* (Boston, Division of Research, Harvard Business School, 1951).

[5] Harriet O. Ronken and Paul R. Lawrence, *Adminis-*

tering Changes (Boston, Division of Research, Harvard Business School, 1952).

[6] Edmund P. Learned, David H. Ulrich, and Donald R. Booz, *Executive Action* (Boston, Division of Research, Harvard Business School, 1950).

the example of an extremely effective plant manager who, although possessing little human skill as defined here, was nonetheless very successful:

This manager, the head of a largely autonomous division, made his supervisors, through the effects of his strong personality and the "pressure" he applied, highly dependent on him for most of their "rewards, penalties, authority, perpetuation, communication, and identification."

As a result, the supervisors spent much of their time competing with one another for the manager's favor. They told him only the things they thought he wanted to hear, and spent much time trying to find out his desires. They depended on him to set their objectives and to show them how to reach them. Because the manager was inconsistent and unpredictable in his behavior, the supervisors were insecure and continually engaged in interdepartmental squabbles which they tried to keep hidden from the manager.

Clearly, human skill as defined here, was lacking. Yet, by the evaluation of his superiors and by his results in increasing efficiency and raising profits and morale, this manager was exceedingly effective. Professor Argyris suggests that employees in modern industrial organizations tend to have a "built-in" sense of dependence on superiors which capable and alert men can turn to advantage.[7]

In the context of the three-skill approach, it seems that this manager was able to capitalize on this dependence because he recognized the interrelationships of all the activities under his control, identified himself with the organization, and sublimated the individual interests of his subordinates to *his* (the organization's) interest, set his goals realistically, and showed his subordinates how to reach these goals. This would seem to be an excellent example of a situation in which strong conceptual skill more than compensated for a lack of human skill.

At the Top Level

Conceptual skill, as indicated in the preceding sections, becomes increasingly critical in more responsible executive positions where its effects are maximized and most easily observed. In fact, recent research findings lead to the conclusion that at the top level of administration this conceptual skill becomes the most important ability of all. As Herman W. Steinkraus, president of Bridgeport Brass Company, said:

"One of the most important lessons which I learned on this job [the presidency] is the importance of coordinating the various departments into an effective team, and, secondly, to recognize the shifting emphasis from time to time of the relative importance of various departments to the business."[8]

It would appear, then, that at lower levels of administrative responsibility, the principal need is for technical and human skills. At higher levels, technical skill becomes relatively less important while the need for conceptual skill increases rapidly. At the top level of an organization, conceptual skill becomes the most important skill of all for successful administration. A chief executive may lack technical or human skills and still be effective if he has subordinates who have strong abilities in these directions. But if his conceptual skill is weak, the success of the whole organization may be jeopardized.

Implications for Action

This three-skill approach implies that significant benefits may result from redefining the objectives of executive development programs, from reconsidering the placement of executives in organizations, and from revising procedures for testing and selecting prospective executives.

Executive Development

Many executive development programs may be failing to achieve satisfactory results because of their inability to foster the growth of these administrative skills. Programs which concentrate on the mere imparting of information or the cultivation of a specific trait would seem to be largely unproductive in enhancing the administrative skills of candidates.

A strictly informative program was described to me recently by an officer and director of a large corporation who had been responsible for the executive development activities of his company, as follows:

"What we try to do is to get our promising young men together with some of our senior executives in regular meetings each month. Then we give the young fellows a chance to ask questions to let them find out about the company's history and how and why we've done things in the past."

---

[7] *Executive Leadership* (New York, Harper & Brothers, 1953); see also "Leadership Pattern in the Plant," HBR, January–February 1953, p. 63.

[8] "What Should a President Do?" *Dun's Review*, August 1951, p. 21.

It was not surprising that neither the senior executives nor the young men felt this program was improving their administrative abilities.

The futility of pursuing specific traits becomes apparent when we consider the responses of an administrator in a number of different situations. In coping with these varied conditions, he may appear to demonstrate one trait in one instance — e.g., dominance when dealing with subordinates — and the directly opposite trait under another set of circumstances — e.g., submissiveness when dealing with superiors. Yet in each instance he may be acting appropriately to achieve the best results. Which, then, can we identify as a desirable characteristic? Here is a further example of this dilemma:

A Pacific Coast sales manager had a reputation for decisiveness and positive action. Yet when he was required to name an assistant to understudy his job from among several well-qualified subordinates, he deliberately avoided making a decision. His associates were quick to observe what appeared to be obvious indecisiveness.

But after several months had passed, it became clear that the sales manager had very unobtrusively been giving the various salesmen opportunities to demonstrate their attitudes and feelings. As a result, he was able to identify strong sentiments for one man whose subsequent promotion was enthusiastically accepted by the entire group.

In this instance, the sales manager's skillful performance was improperly interpreted as "indecisiveness." Their concern with irrelevant traits led his associates to overlook the adequacy of his performance. Would it not have been more appropriate to conclude that his human skill in working with others enabled him to adapt effectively to the requirements of a new situation?

Cases such as these would indicate that it is more useful to judge an administrator on the results of his performance than on his apparent traits. Skills are easier to identify than are traits and are less likely to be misinterpreted. Furthermore, skills offer a more directly applicable frame of reference for executive development, since any improvement in an administrator's skills must necessarily result in more effective performance.

Still another danger in many existing executive development programs lies in the unqualified enthusiasm with which some companies

and colleges have embraced courses in "human relations." There would seem to be two inherent pitfalls here: (1) Human relations courses might only be imparting information or specific techniques, rather than developing the individual's human skill. (2) Even if individual development does take place, some companies, by placing all of their emphasis on human skill, may be completely overlooking the training requirements for top positions. They may run the risk of producing men with highly developed human skill who lack the conceptual ability to be effective top-level administrators.

It would appear important, then, that the training of a candidate for an administrative position be directed at the development of those skills which are most needed at the level of responsibility for which he is being considered.

Executive Placement

This three-skill concept suggests immediate possibilities for the creating of management teams of individuals with complementary skills. For example, one medium-size midwestern distributing organization has as president a man of unusual conceptual ability but extremely limited human skill. However, he has two vice presidents with exceptional human skill. These three men make up an executive committee which has been outstandingly successful, the skills of each member making up for deficiencies of the others. Perhaps the plan of two-man complementary conference leadership proposed by Robert F. Bales, in which the one leader maintains "task leadership" while the other provides "social leadership," might also be an example in point.[9]

Executive Selection

In trying to predetermine a prospective candidate's abilities on a job, much use is being made these days of various kinds of testing devices. Executives are being tested for everything from "decisiveness" to "conformity." These tests, as a recent article in *Fortune* points out, have achieved some highly questionable results when applied to performance on the job.[10] Would it not be much more productive to be concerned with skills of doing rather than with a number of traits which do not guarantee performance?

This three-skill approach makes trait testing unnecessary and substitutes for it procedures

[9] "In Conference," HBR, March–April 1954, p. 44.

[10] William H. Whyte, Jr., "The Fallacies of 'Personality' Testing," *Fortune*, September 1954, p. 117.

which examine a man's ability to cope with the actual problems and situations he will find on his job. These procedures, which indicate what a man can *do* in specific situations, are the same for selection and for measuring development. They will be described in the section on developing executive skills which follows.

This approach suggests that executives should *not* be chosen on the basis of their apparent possession of a number of behavior characteristics or traits, but on the basis of their possession of the requisite skills for the specific level of responsibility involved.

Developing the Skills

For years many people have contended that leadership ability is inherent in certain chosen individuals. We talk of "born leaders," "born executives," "born salesmen." It is undoubtedly true that certain people, naturally or innately, possess greater aptitude or ability in certain skills. But research in psychology and physiology would also indicate, first, that those having strong aptitudes and abilities can improve their skill through practice and training, and, secondly, that even those lacking the natural ability can improve their performance and effectiveness.

The *skill* conception of administration suggests that we may hope to improve our administrative effectiveness and to develop better administrators for the future. This skill conception implies *learning by doing*. Different people learn in different ways, but skills are developed through practice and through relating learning to one's own personal experience and background. If well done, training in these basic administrative skills should develop executive abilities more surely and more rapidly than through unorganized experience. What, then, are some of the ways in which this training can be conducted?

Technical Skill

Development of technical skill has received great attention for many years by industry and educational institutions alike, and much progress has been made. Sound grounding in the principles, structures, and processes of the individual specialty, coupled with actual practice

and experience during which the individual is watched and helped by a superior, appear to be most effective. In view of the vast amount of work which has been done in training people in the technical skills, it would seem unnecessary in this article to suggest more.

Human Skill

Human skill, however, has been much less understood, and only recently has systematic progress been made in developing it. Many different approaches to the development of human skill are being pursued by various universities and professional men today. These are rooted in such disciplines as psychology, sociology, and anthropology.

Some of these approaches find their application in "applied psychology," "human engineering," and a host of other manifestations requiring technical specialists to help the businessman with his human problems. As a practical matter, however, the executive must develop his own human skill, rather than lean on the advice of others. To be effective, he must develop his own personal point of view toward human activity, so that he will (a) recognize the feelings and sentiments which he brings to a situation; (b) have an attitude about his own experiences which will enable him to re-evaluate and learn from them; (c) develop ability in understanding what others by their actions and words (explicit or implicit) are trying to communicate to him; and (d) develop ability in successfully communicating his ideas and attitudes to others.[11]

This human skill can be developed by some individuals without formalized training. Others can be individually aided by their immediate superiors as an integral part of the "coaching" process to be described later. This aid depends for effectiveness, obviously, on the extent to which the superior possesses the human skill.

For larger groups, the use of case problems coupled with impromptu role playing can be very effective. This training can be established on a formal or informal basis, but it requires a skilled instructor and organized sequence of activities.[12] It affords as good an approximation to reality as can be provided on a continuing classroom basis and offers an opportunity for critical reflection not often found in actual prac-

[11] For a further discussion of this point, see F. J. Roethlisberger, "Training Supervisors in Human Relations," HBR, September 1951, p. 47.

[12] See, for example, A. Winn, "Training in Administration and Human Relations," *Personnel,* September 1953, p. 139; see also, Kenneth R. Andrews, "Executive Training by the Case Method," HBR, September 1951, p. 58.

tice. An important part of the procedure is the self-examination of the trainee's own concepts and values, which may enable him to develop more useful attitudes about himself and about others. With the change in attitude, hopefully, there may also come some active skill in dealing with human problems.

Human skill has also been tested in the classroom, within reasonable limits, by a series of analyses of detailed accounts of actual situations involving administrative action, together with a number of role-playing opportunities in which the individual is required to carry out the details of the action he has proposed. In this way an individual's understanding of the total situation and his own personal ability to do something about it can be evaluated.

On the job, there should be frequent opportunities for a superior to observe an individual's ability to work effectively with others. These may appear to be highly subjective evaluations and to depend for validity on the human skill of the rater. But does not every promotion, in the last analysis, depend on someone's subjective judgment? And should this subjectivity be berated, or should we make a greater effort to develop people within our organizations with the human skill to make such judgments effectively?

Conceptual Skill

Conceptual skill, like human skill, has not been very widely understood. A number of methods have been tried to aid in developing this ability, with varying success. Some of the best results have always been achieved through the "coaching" of subordinates by superiors.[13] This is no new idea. It implies that one of the key responsibilities of the executive is to help his subordinates to develop their administrative potentials. One way a superior can help "coach" his subordinate is by assigning a particular responsibility, and then responding with searching questions or opinions, rather than giving answers, whenever the subordinate seeks help. When Benjamin F. Fairless, now chairman of the board of the United States Steel Corporation, was president of the corporation, he described his coaching activities as follows:

"When one of my vice presidents or the head of one of our operating companies comes to me for instructions, I generally counter by asking him questions. First thing I know, he has told me how to solve the problem himself." [14]

Obviously, this is an ideal and wholly natural procedure for administrative training, and applies to the development of technical and human skill, as well as to that of conceptual skill. However, its success must necessarily rest on the abilities and willingness of the superior to help the subordinate.

Another excellent way to develop conceptual skill is through trading jobs, that is, by moving promising young men through different functions of the business but at the same level of responsibility. This gives the man the chance literally to "be in the other fellow's shoes."

Other possibilities include: special assignments, particularly the kind which involve inter-departmental problems; and management boards, such as the McCormick Multiple Management plan, in which junior executives serve as advisers to top management on policy matters.

For larger groups, the kind of case-problems course described above, only using cases involving broad management policy and interdepartmental coordination, may be useful. Courses of this kind, often called "General Management" or "Business Policy," are becoming increasingly prevalent.

In the classroom, conceptual skill has also been evaluated with reasonable effectiveness by presenting a series of detailed descriptions of specific complex situations. In these the individual being tested is asked to set forth a course of action which responds to the underlying forces operating in each situation and which considers the implications of this action on the various functions and parts of the organization and its total environment.

On the job, the alert supervisor should find frequent opportunities to observe the extent to which the individual is able to relate himself and his job to the other functions and operations of the company.

Like human skill, conceptual skill, too, must become a natural part of the executive's make-up. Different methods may be indicated for developing different people, by virtue of their backgrounds, attitudes, and experience. But in every case that method should be chosen which will enable the executive to develop his own

---

[13] For a more complete development of the concept of "coaching," see Myles L. Mace, *The Growth and Development of Executives* (Boston, Division of Research, Har-vard Business School, 1950).

[14] "What Should a President Do?" *Dun's Review*, July 1951, p. 14.

personal skill in visualizing the enterprise as a whole and in coordinating and integrating its various parts."

Conclusion

The purpose of this article has been to show that effective administration depends on three basic personal skills, which have been called *technical*, *human*, and *conceptual*. The administrator needs: (a) sufficient technical skill to accomplish the mechanics of the particular job for which he is responsible; (b) sufficient human skill in working with others to be an effective group member and to be able to build cooperative effort within the team he leads; (c) sufficient conceptual skill to recognize the interrelationships of the various factors involved in his situation, which will lead him to take that action which achieves the maximum good for the total organization.

The relative importance of these three skills seems to vary with the level of administrative responsibility. At lower levels, the major need is for technical and human skills. At higher levels, the administrator's effectiveness depends largely on human and conceptual skills. At the top, conceptual skill becomes the most important of all for successful administration.

This three-skill approach emphasizes that good administrators are not necessarily born; they may be developed. It transcends the need to identify specific traits in an effort to provide a more useful way of looking at the administrative process. By helping to identify the skills most needed at various levels of responsibility, it may prove useful in the selection, training, and promotion of executives.

7

CLUES FOR SUCCESS
IN THE PRESIDENT'S JOB

Joseph C. Bailey

Is it the role of a company president to do what other members of his organization do not do, cannot do, or should not do? Does he have a special function, or does he merely do *more* of the same things others do — on a far bigger and broader scale? Is there a common denominator among those who successfully handle the "toughest problems" of their organizations that cuts across industries, companies, types of organizations, and even cultures? Must the ability to find solutions to such problems be a requirement of the president's job, inevitable to his role? Is there some largely concealed aspect of his job that is worthy of a serious research undertaking?

The answers to these questions, based on my current sample of company presidents (see the box on page 66), are decidedly in the affirmative. Yes, there does seem to be a common de-

AUTHOR'S NOTE: This article is based on an investigation supported by the Division of Research, Harvard Business School. For the data on which it rests, I am gratefully indebted to the many executives who so freely made their experiences available. I owe much also to help given from time to time by Professors Bertrand Fox, F. J. Roethlisberger, and Renato Tagiuri of the Harvard Business School; Professor Abraham H. Maslow of Brandeis University; and Professor Warren G. Bennis of Massachusetts Institute of Technology.

[1] Cambridge, Massachusetts, Harvard University Press, 1938, Chapter 17.

nominator. There do seem to be clear reasons why the organization's toughest problems demand — and *must* receive — the top man's exclusive attention. Moreover, there seem to be utterly understandable reasons why these problems often remain shrouded in silence and secrecy. And finally, there seems to me clearly to be a challenge for a major research effort of a most difficult and sophisticated character.

The single-common-demoninator clue which I have elected to pursue in my current inquiry is one that was alluded to in the "conflict of codes" concept presented by Chester I. Barnard in *The Functions of the Executive*.[1] Essentially, this concept claims that in every formally organized cooperative human activity there will arise from time to time inevitable and inescapable conflict between the codes that control the conduct of different individuals and the groups who are contributing to the overall cooperative purpose.

At the very apex of the executive responsibility, Barnard puts the burden of resolving the recurring conflict of codes that will inevitably arise in every formal organization. He sees this task as the key to successful leadership, and acutely so for the role of the top man. He further contends that the solution to such problems has to be the "creation of a higher moral

The provisional clues for success discussed here are drawn from a sample skewed by accident of selection toward a group of two dozen company presidents. I say "accident of selection" advisedly. When I began my current inquiry two years ago, I sent out a large number of letters to those I knew to be involved in or close to the president's problems. I told them I would appreciate an opportunity to hear from the president himself some examples of what he had found to be his toughest problems, what made them so, and how he had handled them. I received far more responses than I could reply to, let alone interview. From the most accessible, I selected randomly a dozen presidents whose companies varied in size from quite small to exceedingly large and from close family ownerships to multinational corporate ventures. Another dozen presidents were chosen as they were made available by introduction from friends.

In all instances, I sought appointments with top executives who gave the most unqualified, unhesitant assent. I did so, frankly, because that promised to economize my time; but — as it worked out later — I discovered I had unwittingly selected a sample of the top men who were more self-confident and more successful in coping with their toughest problems.

My findings from this limited sample reaffirm, and never stand at variance with, a far larger number of confidential disclosures (many unsought, but gladly accepted) that I have received during four and a half decades of teaching as well as management experiences of my own. These voluntary disclosures have totaled a hundred that I can easily identify and perhaps an equal number of others I cannot identify so positively. — *The Author*

code" — one that will encompass and reconcile at a higher and more embracing level the interests and values that come into unanticipated, yet still legitimate, conflict as the organization goes about pursuit of its ever-evolving goals.

Clues for Success

This view of the importance and the difficulties of the creative art and skills required in successfully handling serious conflict of codes is offered here because my long experience with such problems, as well as my current inquiry, seems to confirm it.

Should it stand confirmed, then it follows that the hidden key to success in the president's role of final and ultimate decision maker for his organization may rest more on his capabilities in this limited area than in any other single segment of his total presidential task. And should that prove to be the case, then it further follows that this is a less urgent inquiry than the one inevitably linked with it, to wit: What kinds of behavior, and what attitudes, values, skills, and training are characteristic of those chief executives who do relatively better than their peers in handling "conflict" issues? Can any uniformities be discerned among them, or among their problem-handling attributes, that may provide provisional clues for their relatively greater success?

There do seem to be some. In fact, I feel rather certain that there are even though the ones I shall present in this article may turn out to be merely a first approximation of those that

are truly indispensable. It is much too soon at this juncture, and my present sample of top men is much too limited, to be confident that anything more than clues for further exploration have made an appearance.

Yet the frequent recurrence of some uncommon patterns of behavior, accompanied and supported by some key values and attitudes the presidents hold toward their jobs and themselves, stand out in sharp contrast to those of a large number of their peers. In my experience, the latter generally have greater difficulties with their toughest problems, are less self-confident of a healing solution, and are clearly more inclined both to minimize the seriousness of and to postpone, ignore, or evade (rather than deliberately and consciously confront) their problems.

It must be kept in mind, then, that the uniformities discussed here are drawn from a random sample of presidents who have learned somehow, somewhere, to do relatively better than their peers with the toughest problems that beset their jobs.

Management of Stress

Of all the individual uniformities common to top men, the most immediately self-evident is their ability to cope with stress. They all have learned to live — and for most of the time alone — with heavy stress. They have learned how to control it, contain it, channel it, offset it, or simply "lock the door" on it, while they rest and refresh themselves to resume their quest for an alternative that will acceptably resolve the conflict of codes.

The practices, devices, habits, and mental and emotional points of view that are utilized in coping with heavy stress are seemingly infinite in their variety and ingenuity. They are strongly influenced by the temperament, the background, and the idiosyncrasies of each individual executive. Yet behind all this seeming diversity is an implicit — and frequently quite explicit — acknowledgement that unless heavy stress is "managed" — that is, held within some tolerable limit — it can quickly become unmanageable, inducing panic and collapse of promising remedies.

To cope with stress, some top executives deliberately turn to a strikingly different kind of problem and immerse themselves thoroughly in it for a few hours. Or they sometimes return to their offices at unconventional hours — late at night or early in the morning — when the building is deserted and they can isolate themselves and think. Often they carefully compose a memorandum to themselves stating the problem as bluntly and concisely as possible and indicating what an adequate solution will require. This practice has a dual purpose:

(1) It forces out the plainest possible statement of the problem and its desired solution. This, when well done, enables them to "forget" the problem or, more accurately, to force it down to the level of their subconscious for attention there.

(2) It forces them to do all they can with the problem at the intellectual level and to signify this to their nervous systems by drafting the most up-to-date résumé of the situation that they can then prepare.

In either case they rid themselves of a persistent nagging from their minds and nerves and win a respite which they can use to renew themselves before resuming the search and struggle.

Further along on the spectrum above, or on one like it, some of these men occasionally seem to find the means to tap serendipity. After prolonged and intensive struggle with the issues at conflict, suddenly they take off for a distant region and a sport or pleasure (such as fishing for rare and prized species or elk hunting high in the Sierras) that is a keen joy in life to them. After two or three weeks out of all old ruts and routines, removed physically and emotionally as far as they can get, they sometimes discover — perhaps on the journey home — that the answer comes to them. They know that this prac-

tice is not surefire; but when they are "at wit's end," there is little to lose and, maybe, an inspiration to gain.

One president I talked with secured such a gain on the morning of the day I saw him. Over his wife's demur, he rose at four o'clock, took a long horseback ride in the mountain foothills near his home, and returned jubilantly with the reconciling solution to a problem that had vexed him for months. It was a deep-seated and unyielding conflict of codes that had nearly brought open warfare among members of his board, various groups of stockholders, and a large number of civic leaders whose communities' welfare seemed to them to be involved. He made that story the subject of his toughest-problem narrative.

Self-Expendable Attitude

Another recurring uniformity of belief and behavior among these men is their readiness to view themselves as "expendable." Because this attitude is so clearly the ultimate device employed in standing — and in *withstanding* — stress, it could have been placed under the success clue just discussed. Yet, because of its decisive importance, I have chosen to present it separately.

The readiness to put their jobs on the line over an issue they deem fundamental to their organization's long-range welfare is perhaps the simplest touchstone by which the more successful company presidents are distinguishable.

Sometimes it is utilized directly, virtually in the form of an ultimatum: "If continued, our labor relations policy will incur liquidation or bankruptcy in less than five years. It must be revised and reformulated radically, even at the risk of an immediate strike. Either our current policy goes, or I go."

Far more often, the readiness of the president to put his job on the line is merely latent in crisis situations. Nonetheless, it is clearly present and perceived by those who deal with him on these peak decisions. And it *is* present because when the top man does his utmost in working out a resolution to his conflict issues, he is the one prepared to undertake its implementation and abide by the consequences. No man can do more than shoulder that decisive responsibility — and the moment sometimes comes when a vote of confidence is called for.

Men less sure of themselves — those lacking the opportunity to practice and achieve some preliminary successes with such problems or those unable to face with equanimity the loss or surrender of their job with its power, prominence, and inward gratification — are generally tempted to rationalize away the importance of making such an ultimate decision and to minimize the hazards that they hope to be able to postpone or evade. They find it uncomfortable to view themselves as expendable and to contemplate the disquieting prospect of having to renew their careers in other environments where they might not regain such organizational eminence.

Psychological forces, deeply hidden yet very powerful, are so obviously involved in this ability to view oneself as expendable in the role of president that it is only necessary to call attention to the uniformity with which I find it present among my interviewees. (I leave its further explanation to those better equipped to interpret its psychic importance.) Organizationally, however, its value to a president when he is confronted alone with heavy stress is unmistakable. For him it is the ultimate safety valve, and I think it enables him to labor at his critical decision making well shielded from fears and anxieties about his personal fate. That bridge he has crossed beforehand.

That most of these top men recognize the value of this ability to view themselves as expendable usually comes out when I ask them whom they look to for approval, approbation, or understanding once a serious crisis has been satisfactorily surmounted. Reference groups frequently mentioned include: members of the board, the business community (watching from the sidelines), members of their own executive organization, the investment community (frequently privy to the severity and seriousness of some of these crises), and their whole organization as a total system cognizant in some degree of what has been afoot.

Surprisingly, a near majority of the top men in my sample — after some quiet reflection on my query — named none of the reference groups above. The answer simply was something like this: "Me. I must satisfy myself, above all, that I have done the best I can do. When I can do that, anything else or anyone's approval is pleasant, but superfluous."

When I questioned the top men who named other groups first about the importance of self-approval, it was instantly accepted as being so self-evident that each had taken for granted that I understood its priority and its indispensability to his view of his role in the organization.

Capacity to Concentrate

Another factor, closely related to the one just given, appears with sufficient frequency that I believe it to be a uniformity also. Sometimes it is mentioned early in the interviews, when the presidents feel that a brief résumé of the assignments given them as they rose through the ranks is relevant. Sometimes it is supplied later, when I request a recapitulation of their advancement by rank and increasing responsibility.

Beginning usually with their very first task after entering the organization, they reveal a capacity to immerse themselves with so much zest and with such an uncommon self-forgetfulness in the job assigned that it is completed ahead of schedule — and completed so well that another and a more demanding one is promptly supplied. Not only are these assignments expected, but so are the rewards: more work and more responsibility!

These top executives seem to have risen faster than their peers (and faster than is customary) principally because of a demonstrated capacity or appetite for exacting assignments into which they plunge *for the sake of the challenge* rather than for an opportunity to get ahead of their competitors. None of these men are naive about organizational politics; yet it is displaced — both as a major preoccupation in their minds and as a diversion to their energies — by their preference to get a job well done ahead of anything else. This trait of deep absorption in the task at hand creates, in a manner of speaking, a pull upward in the nature of assignments to ever-increasing responsibilities.

From listening carefully to these executives' stories, by studying the details written down later, and by occasionally hearing about some of them from other people who know them personally, I have formed the opinion that not many of these top men invest much of their time or thought in the race of "getting to the top." They get there, but rather as an afterthought, as it were, or as something secondary and extrinsic to doing well the job at hand. (With several of the men interviewed, I gained the impression that their job as president had come as something of a surprise at the time.)

This ability of the more successful men to concentrate deeply on each day's work not only serves to conserve time and energy that other contenders invest in clique activities, power plays, empire-building pursuits, and so on, but it leaves them largely free of the leftover resentments from old feuds and battle scars that handicap those unsuccessful candidates when the president's position becomes vacant at a time all are ready for consideration. In some cases it may tip the scales in their favor because they are less beholden to others for their advancement; in other cases, the deciding factor may be that they are more acceptable to more of their future subordinates than are their "rivals" who have made numerous enemies on *their* way up.

Influence of 'Model'

In my early interviews with top men, it often happened that a leading second executive was soon brought into the conversation and reappeared repeatedly as the discussions unfolded. Although seldom involved directly in the specific cases being presented, he was pictured as being of dominant importance in the president's organization career.

He usually was about 30 years older than the speaker, and most often their acquaintance began soon after the younger man first entered the company and was assigned to the older man's organizational unit. Typically, the rank of the elder man at the time of first meeting was general manager or division vice president. Again, typically, the older man went on to become president, then chairman, and only recently retired or died.

Positive Pattern. I now have come to expect this "model" background figure to appear in my interviews, and in nearly every case he does so.

He frequently threatens to run away with the "case" at hand because the narrator's enthusiasm about him is so evident, as is his admiration and gratitude. It is common to hear a president say, "You should have known *him*; he was the best executive I've ever known." Or, "He brought me up; he taught me the ropes." Or, "He gave me the chance to show what I could do." Or, "He really made this company." The speaker sometimes has difficulty in returning to the thread of the narrative he is relating and does so with regret and visible reluctance because he plainly feels we are dropping a more engrossing topic — namely, the personality and behavior of the man who "taught me all I know about this job I've got."

A father figure? Probably, as far as that tired phrase can carry us toward any agreed-on significance. At another level of discourse, however, the part this older individual has played in helping his young associate to form, to work out, and to *practice* his own patterns of organizational behavior is unmistakable. Aside from their expressions of admiration, 90% of the material my narrators supply about their older sponsor (tutor? coach? mentor?) are concrete illustrations of *his* organizational behavior that was exceptionally skillful as to morale-building, performance-producing, conflict-reducing, and so forth. And his were the patterns on which the younger man consciously chose to model his own developing organizational behavior. Whatever else the older man may be, he is clearly a model the young associate eagerly copies and to whom he renders tribute and gives predominant credit for most of his accomplishments.

Negative Figure. The very few top men who fail to introduce their model immediately, later invariably bring into their stories a similar background figure who seems to serve the same need in a reverse manner. For want of a better phrase, I have come to see this older man in the same way many presidents do — as an anti-model.

He is usually introduced not only later on in these discourses, but in a different fashion, such as: "Do you know anything about So-and-so, an earlier predecessor of mine? I ask because he was quite well known in his day." From this opening, they then characterize So-and-so as the chief executive who "brought this organization to the brink of ruin" because "he made *all* the decisions." Or, "He trusted no one but himself; he just couldn't delegate." Or, "You couldn't talk to him because he wouldn't listen." Or, he was "arbitrary," "insensitive," "ruthless," "vindictive," "obstinate," "vain."

The refrain about the anti-model is unvarying: "I watched every move he made because I couldn't believe what I saw. I asked myself, doesn't he know what damaging and costly results that move he is making (illustrated with a concrete example of his predecessor's behavior) will have on the people in this organization, or doesn't he care? How could a man be so stupid about organizational matters and ever get to be president?" (In one of these cases, the individual in question had bought control of the company with an enormous fortune made in stock market operations; in another, he had been ensconced through a famous family's influence.)

The lessons these top men draw from their anti-models are vivid and explicit: "I made up my mind that should I ever be a president, I would do exactly the opposite of X, and I could not lose!" Or, "I could hardly wait for a chance to replace him and try to undo the damage he had done." Or, "I wanted to try and see if we could ever catch up with all the opportunities he let slip by."

Again, whether anti-father figure or not, his every move was followed with minute vigilance by his anti-acolytes; his policies and managerial practices were daily scrutinized, analyzed, and criticized by an intent observer who was driven to declare — at least to himself and to a confidant or two from time to time — what he would do differently as the top executive, and in what specific ways the organization would be better, and why. Such resistance to, and disapproval of, the organizational behavior of Mr. Anti produced for these top men nearly the same first-hand knowledge-in-detail about administration-in-detail that was acquired by their counterparts under more agreeable (but scarcely more instructive) circumstances.

Other Attributes

Beyond these four uniformities, there seem to be some others, perhaps of equal or greater relevance. One of these might be the value the presidents clearly attach to having a temperamental opposite — some person available and near their level in the organization — who is a formidable and constructive critic or skeptic on whom they can test out their schemes for innovation. Such loyal opposition is encouraged and rewarded because "he's saved us from some God-awful blunders"; or because "if he can punch holes in it that I can't overcome, I usually drop it."

Most of the other attributes I have discerned, in addition to those I have given as examples, do not recur as frequently or have not been articulated as unmistakably. They must wait for the collection of more data from more top men, although I am inclined now to believe that, fully pursued, enough separate individual uniformities will disclose themselves to reappear as linked indissolubly together in patterns of mutually reinforcing uniformities common

to top executives of the caliber I have had the good fortune to listen to.

Innate or Acquired?

The age-old issue of nature versus nurture presents itself at this point. How do men such as these get to be what they are? What aspects of their organizational behavior is learned behavior? What portion rests on natural endowments? How much of it stems from, let us say, a quarter-century of career training opportunities *before* taking over the top job? How much of it is role-induced *after* assuming the presidential task? How much of their fitness for that role was actually present well before they even entered their organizations? Does the constant daily testing on the various jobs they hold tend to sift out and to favor those with some inherent aptitude for the top organizational job?

Literature Inconclusive

Definitive answers to this long-standing issue still elude us. Since even a little light thereon is better than no light at all, readers who share my involvement in this pursuit may welcome a few further comments from the literature now accumulating rapidly on creativity and creative people. I, myself, ventured into this area some time past to see what others have found pertinent to the question of how these men "get that way." To what extent can the relatively better performance of some presidents be traced to their career training? To what extent must it be ascribed to a fortuitous combination of factors, some of them genetic and hence beyond our present ability to duplicate and transmit to others? Specifically, I wanted to find out what the chances are that a sizable segment of top men could have been — and *now* can be — better equipped by experience, training, or any kind of help to deal more constructively and creatively with the conflict of codes inherited with their office.

The views of writers on this topic range the spectrum from a few who hold that "they are born that way" to a larger number who feel that creativity is present as a variable in all healthy humans and can be strongly developed through the efforts of others if such "training" is understood to be the total influence exerted 24 hours a day by all other individuals on the subject in question. This view, of course, identifies education as an individual's total life experience and, for our purposes, begs the issue. In the center of this spectrum of views as to training are found the majority — those who are in doubt or decline to offer an opinion.

My present view is that since the question is currently beyond our reach to settle with certainty, we should follow the lead given us by those who hold that more creativity is available if we seek it. Not *all* creativity. And maybe not creativity for *all*. But more creativity for most of us *if* we take a culture-wide view of what an individual's total life experience actually does — and does not — "teach" us. This view has been strongly reinforced by my sample of some of the better top men, all of whom insist on pounding home the value and indispensability of (a) the training they received over 25 or 30 years of managing, and (b) having a model figure to emulate — or to repudiate — in terms of specific day-in, day-out episodes of organizational behavior.

Training for 'Comers'

If additional data support my present surmise that the attributes I find are indeed uniformities-in-common, then it seems to me that it should be possible to devise tests or screening procedures to locate more quickly and more accurately individuals who possess, or are busy developing, the traits most often associated with the behavior of the more successful presidents. If the improvement in selectivity were to be no more than 5% to 10%, the larger yield would still be an enormous benefit. The most direct beneficiaries, naturally, would be the individuals possessing or acquiring the cluster of special talents required for the president's role.

Of course, other individuals intensely pursuing the job, but plainly lacking some of the essential traits, would also gain by having their drives redirected away from reasonably certain frustration and defeat toward goals more compatible with their capabilities. Their organizations would so palpably gain from better placement of executives for tasks to which their behavior patterns point that the savings from futility, frayed nerves, loss of forward movement, and so on, would simply be monumental. And the general society, in which these corporations' activities occupy an ever-increasing importance, would be the gainer by finding its affairs more often in the most competent hands.

The opportunities to improve, enlarge, and

hasten the better training of more promising candidates would multiply the same benefits indicated above. Consider, for example, the manifold ways in which any total organization would flourish if the potential presidential timber within its ranks could be tentatively identified and placed under the skillful and nurturing supervision of some excelling "model" such as most of my sample presidents have had the supreme good fortune to attract! At the very least, another 5% to 10% improvement over our current trial-and-error methods would be another huge source of gain at trifling cost.

Aid for Incumbents

Returning to the present, I feel an obligation to call attention to the crushing character of the burdens — whose weight is often grossly underestimated or is airily dismissed as being overcompensated — the more successful presidents assume on behalf of the whole organization and indirectly on behalf of society-at-large. It does not reduce the seriousness of the point I am making to reply that many of these presidents actually relish opportunities to wrestle with seemingly insoluble problems. I know they do. I am glad they do. But I seriously want to see a far greater number of their peers feel the same way, and this brings me to the very point I most wish to make.

These top men face their most stressful, most important organizational problems alone — too much alone with respect to their own health and/or optimum task performance. And, in my opinion, needlessly too much alone.

They need, most of all, the vast relief of someone to talk with. They need to share, at least in part, the stress — to explore and clarify it, and to speed up the process of identifying the key issues from the more clamorous ones. In short, they need someone to aid them in expediting their search for the jugular.

They do not need a prop, a substitute problem-solver, or a pinch-hitter. They do not need an expert or other specialist in some given area for a problem that embraces a conflict of codes issue; there are no specialists in an area where each problem seldom has an applicable precedent. They do not need either a yes-man or a no-man. Preferably, they need most a non-involved alter ego who can share their diagnostic search for the core problem — one who can stimulate the seeking for creative alternatives, but who resolutely leaves the ultimate decision to the top man for the simple and all-sufficient reason that he can never share the costs and risks of implementation.

The top executives most in need of the kind of help so roughly outlined are not the relatively more successful presidents that I know. (Being what they are, these successful men would probably be the first to use such expediting assistance!) Rather, the top men most in need of assistance are those whose batting averages are currently at the midpoint. Aid just a few times at critical junctures could possibly tip the scales favorably and put them — and their self-confidence — on a more equal footing with the fortunate sample of company presidents I have come to know.

Conclusion

Where have we gotten to? How can this limited first step of inquiry be summed up? I shall attempt to do this by enumerating the four essential things that I feel I have learned from this preliminary reconnaissance.

1. *Presidents do have to face problems for their organizations that other executives do not — and cannot — handle.* This is a matter of necessity, not of choice. It comes affixed to their role of final decison maker and cannot be evaded. Nor can it be delegated, at least as a totality, although portions — especially some of the technical and financial aspects — can be assigned for study and analysis.

On this part of my query, I feel reasonably confident that further research will confirm and not significantly modify the position stated.

2. *Problems that presidents must handle force their way upward because their resolution demands an ultimate "yes" or "no."* They demand the attention of the man whose authority is the widest and whose responsibility is the broadest in acting for the organization as a whole. These problems demand not only the ultimate in authority, but also the ultimate in overall ability because they are the most fraught with risks to the system. They compel admission to where "the buck stops."

Beyond their potential threat, these problems generally are also confusing in their complexity — cutting across all formal organization structures and frequently being intertwined with unheard-of nonorganizational elements of decisive importance. They are obscure as well as complex; one or more facets that are only dimly glimpsed, or even hidden, may conceal the core issue or contain the king pin to releasing the whole log jam.

Complicated, obscure, freighted with risk, attended by a welter of strong contradictory individual feelings of anger, frustration, anxiety, and fear, it is small wonder that these problems get passed rapidly upward ("Let him solve *this* one! Isn't that his job?").

This part of my quest seems rather clearly established too; namely, that the toughest, most unprecedented, most embracing, and touchiest problems in all organizations unfailingly make their way to the presidential desk. And they rightly are the top man's problems because that *is* his job — to handle the problems that no one else is sufficiently empowered to cope with and and to handle these alone, somehow, or see his influence slowly dwindle.

3. *Conflict of codes — and the necessity of reconciling it through the creation of a higher, more embracing code — is inevitably present in every formal organization.* Since this is the interpretation and judgment of only one person, its merit must remain indeterminate pending the accumulation of a much broader sample, but more especially its verification by other investigators and methods.

4. *The patterns of organizational behavior disclosed by the data secured thus far strike me strongly with numerous parallels to the behavior of creative people encountered in the literature.* For those who may wish to look at some of the parallels involved, I suggest for a starter, Abraham H. Maslow's unconventional book, *Eupsychian Management.*[2] His long-pursued interest in those whom he labels "superior people" leads him to identify many of their traits and characteristics as the necessary attributes to make such people outstanding candidates for leadership and management. There is, in fact, a close fit between the uniformities I find common to my subjects and those he ascribes to the superior people. I offer this reference to Maslow's work chiefly to promote — and perhaps to provoke — relevant speculation as to where and how we can increase our supply of such people or, more exactly, the creative behavior they display.

[2] Homewood, Illinois, Richard D. Irwin and Dorsey Press, Inc., 1965.

8

POWER AND POLITICS
IN ORGANIZATIONAL LIFE

Abraham Zaleznik

Foreword

The competition for power is characteristic of all political structures. And, whatever else they may be, business organizations are political structures in that they provide both a base for the development of executive careers and a platform for the expression of individual interests and motives. People in positions of authority, however, "differ from 'ordinary' humans," says this author, "in that they have the capacity to impose their personal defenses onto the stage of corporate life. Fortunately, the relationships are susceptible to intelligent management," and it is to the nature of this intelligence that the discussion is devoted.

There are few business activities more prone to a credibility gap than the way in which executives approach organizational life. A sense of disbelief occurs when managers purport to make decisions in rationalistic terms while most observers and participants know that personalities and politics play a significant if not an overriding role. Where does the error lie? In the theory which insists that decisions should be rationalistic and nonpersonal? Or in the practice which treats business organizations as political structures?

Whatever else organizations may be (problem-solving instruments, sociotechnical systems, reward systems, and so on), they are political structures. This means that organizations operate by distributing authority and setting a stage for the exercise of power. It is no wonder, therefore, that individuals who are highly motivated to secure and use power find a familiar and hospitable environment in business.

At the same time, executives are reluctant to acknowledge the place of power both in individual motivation and in organizational relationships. Somehow, power and politics are dirty words. And in linking these words to the play of personalities in organizations, some managers withdraw into the safety of organizational logics.

As I shall suggest in this article, frank recognition of the importance of personality factors and a sensitive use of the strengths and limitations of people in decisions on power distributions can improve the quality of organizational life.

Political pyramid

Organizations provide a power base for individuals. From a purely economic standpoint, organizations exist to create a surplus of income over costs by meeting needs in the marketplace. But organizations also are political structures which provide opportunities for people to develop careers and therefore provide platforms for the expression of individual interests and motives. The development of careers, particularly at high managerial and professional levels, depends on accumulation of power as the vehicle for transforming individual interests into activities which influence other people.

Scarcity & competition

A political pyramid exists when people compete for power in an economy of scarcity. In other words, people cannot get the power they want just for the asking. Instead, they have to enter into the decisions on how to distribute authority in a particular formal organization structure. Scarcity of power arises under two sets of conditions:

1. Where individuals gain power in absolute terms at someone else's expense.

2. Where there is a gain comparatively—not literally at someone else's expense—resulting in a relative shift in the distribution of power.

1. See my article, "The Management of Disappointment," HBR November-December 1967, p. 59.

In either case, the psychology of scarcity and comparison takes over. The human being tends to make comparisons as a basis for his sense of self-esteem. He may compare himself with other people and decide that his absolute loss or the shift in proportional shares of authority reflects an attrition in his power base. He may also compare his position relative to others against a personal standard and feel a sense of loss. This tendency to compare is deeply ingrained in people, especially since they experience early in life the effects of comparisons in the family where—in an absolute sense—time and attention, if not love and affection, go to the most dependent member.

Corporate acquisitions and mergers illustrate the effects of both types of comparisons. In the case of one merger, the president of the acquired company resigned rather than accept the relative displacement in rank which occurred when he no longer could act as a chief executive officer. Two vice presidents vied for the position of executive vice president. Because of their conflicting ambitions, the expedient of making them equals drove the competition underground, but not for long. The vice president with the weaker power base soon resigned in the face of his inability to consolidate a workable definition of his responsibilities. His departure resulted in increased power for the remaining vice president and the gradual elimination of "rival camps" which had been covertly identified with the main contenders for power.

The fact that organizations are pyramids produces a scarcity of positions the higher one moves in the hierarchy. This scarcity, coupled with inequalities, certainly needs to be recognized. While it may be humane and socially desirable to say that people are different rather than unequal in their potential, nevertheless executive talent is in short supply. The end result should be to move the more able people into the top positions and to accord them the pay, responsibility, and authority to match their potential.

On the other side, the strong desires of equally able people for the few top positions available means that someone will either have to face the realization of unfulfilled ambition or have to shift his interest to another organization.[1]

Constituents & clients

Besides the conditions of scarcity and competition, politics in organizations grows out of the existence of constituencies. A superior may be content himself with shifts in the allocation of resources and consequently power, but he represents subordinates who, for their own reasons, may be unhappy with the changes. These subordinates affirm and support their boss. They can also withdraw affirmation and support, and consequently isolate the superior with all the painful consequences this entails.

While appointments to positions come from above, affirmation of position comes from be-

low. The only difference between party and organizational politics is in the subtlety of the voting procedure. Consider:

□ In a large consumer products corporation, one division received almost no capital funds for expansion while another division, which had developed a new marketing approach for products common to both, expanded dramatically. The head of the static division found his power diminished considerably, as reflected in how seriously his subordinates took his efforts at influence (e.g., in programs to increase the profit return from existing volume).

He initiated one program after another with little support from subordinates because he could not make a claim for capital funds. The flow of capital funds in this corporation provided a measure of power gains and losses in both an absolute and a relative sense.

Power & action

Still another factor which heightens the competition for power that is characteristic of all political structures is the incessant need to use

whatever power one possesses. Corporations have an implicit "banking" system in power transactions. The initial "capitalization" which makes up an individual's power base consists of three elements:

1. The quantity of formal authority vested in his position relative to other positions.

2. The authority vested in his expertise and reputation for competence (a factor weighted by how important the expertise is for the growth areas of the corporation as against the historically stable areas of its business).

3. The attractiveness of his personality to others (a combination of respect for him as well as liking, although these two sources of attraction are often in conflict).

This capitalization of power reflects the total esteem with which others regard the individual. By a process which is still not too clear, the individual internalizes all of the sources of power capital in a manner parallel to the way he develops a sense of self-esteem. The individual knows he has power, assesses it realistically, and is willing to risk his personal esteem to influence others.

A critical element here is the risk in the uses of power. The individual must perform *and* get results. If he fails to do either, an attrition occurs in his power base in direct proportion to the doubts other people entertained in their earlier appraisals of him.

What occurs here is an erosion of confidence which ultimately leads the individual to doubt himself and undermines the psychological work which led him in the first place to internalize authority as a prelude to action. (While, as I have suggested, the psychological work that an individual goes through to consolidate his esteem capital is a crucial aspect of power relations, I shall have to reserve careful examination of this problem until a later date. The objective now is to examine from a political framework the problems of organizational life.)

What distinguishes alterations in the authority structure from other types of organizational change is their direct confrontation with the political character of corporate life. Such confrontations are real manipulations of power as compared with the indirect approaches which play on ideologies and attitudes. In the first case, the potency and reality of shifts in authority have an instantaneous effect on what people do, how they interact, and how they think about themselves. In the second case, the shifts in attitude are often based on the willingness of people to respond the way authority figures want them to; ordinarily, however, these shifts in attitude are but temporary expressions of compliance.

One of the most common errors executives make is to confuse compliance with commitment. Compliance is an attitude of acceptance when a directive from an authority figure asks for a change in an individual's position, activities, or ideas. The individual complies or "goes along" usually because he is indifferent to the scope of the directive and the changes it proposes. If compliance occurs out of indifference, then one can predict little difficulty in translating the intent of directives into actual implementation.[2]

Commitment, on the other hand, represents a strong motivation on the part of an individual to adopt or resist the intent of a directive. If the individual commits himself to a change, then he will use his ingenuity to interpret and implement the change in such a way as to assure its success. If he decides to fight or block the change, the individual may act as if he complies but reserve other times and places to negate the effects of directives. For example:

□ In one large company, the top management met regularly for purposes of organizational planning. The executives responsible for implementing planning decisions could usually be counted on to carry them out when they had fought hard and openly in the course of reaching such decisions. When they seemed to accept a decision, giving all signs of compliance, the decision usually ended up as a notation in the minutes. Surface compliance occurred most frequently when problems involved loyalties to subordinates.

In one instance, a division head agreed to accept a highly regarded executive from another division to meet a serious manpower shortage in his organization. When the time came to effect the transfer, however, this division general manager refused, with some justification, on the grounds that bringing someone in from outside would demoralize his staff. He used compliance initially to respond to the problem of "family" loyalties to which he felt committed. Needless to say, the existence of these loyalties was the major problem to be faced in carrying out organizational planning.

Compliance as a tactic to avoid changes and commitment as an expression of strong motiva-

tion in dealing with organizational problems are in turn related to how individuals define their interests. In the power relations among executives, the so-called areas of common interest are usually reserved for the banalities of human relationships. The more significant areas of attention usually force conflicts of interest, especially competition for power, to the surface.

Interest conflicts

Organizations demand, on the one hand, cooperative endeavor and commitment to common purposes. The realities of experience in organizations, on the other hand, show that conflicts of interest exist among people who ultimately share a common fate and are supposed to work together. What makes business more political and less ideological and rationalistic is the overriding importance of conflicts of interest.

If an individual (or group) is told that his job scope is reduced in either absolute or proportional terms for *the good of the corporation,* he faces a conflict. Should he acquiesce for the idea of common good or fight in the service of his self-interest? Any rational man will fight (how constructively depends on the absence of neurotic conflicts and on ego strength). His willingness to fight increases as he comes to realize the intangible nature of what people think is good for the organization. And, in point of fact, his willingness may serve the interests of corporate purpose by highlighting issues and stimulating careful thinking before the reaching of final decisions.

Secondary effects

Conflicts of interest in the competition for resources are easily recognized, as for example, in capital budgeting or in allocating money for research and development. But these conflicts can be subjected to bargaining procedures which all parties to the competition validate by their participation.

The secondary effects of bargaining do involve organizational and power issues. However, the fact that these power issues *follow* debate on economic problems rather than *lead* it creates a manifest content which can be objectified much more readily than in areas where the pri-

2. See Chester Barnard, *The Function of the Executive* (Cambridge. Harvard University Press, 1938), p. 167.

mary considerations are the distributions of authority.

In such cases, which include developing a new formal organization structure, management succession, promotions, corporate mergers, and entry of new executives, the conflicts of interest are severe and direct simply because there are no objective measures of right or wrong courses of action. The critical question which has to be answered in specific actions is: Who gets power and position? This involves particular people with their strengths and weaknesses and a specific historical context in which actions are understood in symbolic as well as rational terms. To illustrate:

☐ A large corporation, General Motors in fact, inadvertently confirmed what every seasoned executive knows: that coalitions of power to overcome feelings of rivalry and the play of personal ambitions are fragile solutions. The appointment of Edward Cole to the presidency followed by Semon Knudsen's resignation shattered the illusion that the rational processes in business stand apart or even dominate the human emotions and ties that bind men to one another. If any corporation prides itself on rationality, General Motors is it. To have to experience so publicly the inference that major corporate life, particularly at the executive levels, is not so rational after all, can be damaging to the sense of security people get from belief in an idea as it is embodied in a corporate image.

The fact that Knudsen subsequently was discharged from the presidency of Ford (an event I shall discuss later in this article) suggests that personalities and the politics of corporations are less aberrations and more conditions of life in large organizations.

But just as General Motors wants to maintain an image, many executives prefer to ignore what this illustration suggests: that organizations are political structures which feed on the psychology of comparison. To know something about the psychology of comparison takes us into the theory of self-esteem in both its conscious manifestations and its unconscious origins. Besides possibly enlightening us in general and giving a more realistic picture of people and organizations, there are some practical benefits in such knowledge. These benefits include:

○ Increased freedom to act more directly; instead of trying to "get around" a problem, one can meet it.

○ Greater objectivity about people's strengths

and limitations, and, therefore, the ability to use them more honestly as well as effectively.

○ More effective planning in organizational design and in distribution of authority; instead of searching for the "one best solution" in organization structure, one accepts a range of alternatives and then gives priority to the personal or emotional concerns that inhibit action.

Power relations

Organizational life within a political frame is a series of contradictions. It is an exercise in rationality, but its energy comes from the ideas in the minds of power figures the content of which, as well as their origins, are only dimly perceived. It deals with sources of authority and their distribution; yet it depends in the first place on the existence of a balance of power in the hands of an individual who initiates actions and gets results. It has many rituals associated with it, such as participation, democratization, and the sharing of power; yet the real outcome is the consolidation of power around a central figure to whom other individuals make emotional attachments.

Faulty coalitions

The formal organization structure implements a coalition among key executives. The forms differ, and the psychological significance of various coalitions also differs. But no organization can function without a consolidation of power in the relationship of a central figure with his select group. The coalition need not exist between the chief executive and his immediate subordinates or staff. It may indeed bypass the second level as in the case of Presidents of the United States who do not build confident relationships within their cabinets, but instead rely on members of the executive staff or on selected individuals outside the formal apparatus.

The failure to establish a coalition within the executive structure of an organization can result in severe problems, such as paralysis in the form of inability to make decisions and to evaluate performance, and in-fighting and overt rivalry within the executive group.

When a coalition fails to develop, the first place to look for causes is the chief executive and his problems in creating confident relationships. The causes are many and complex, but they usually hinge around the nature of the chief executive's defenses and what he needs to avoid as a means of alleviating stress. For example:

□ The "palace revolt," which led to Semon Knudsen's departure from Ford Motor Company, is an illustration of the failure in the formation of a coalition. While it is true that Henry Ford II named Knudsen president of the company, Knudsen's ultimate power as a newcomer to an established power structure depended on forming an alliance. The particular individual with whom an alliance seemed crucial was Lee Iacocca. For some reason, Knudsen and Iacocca competed for power and influence instead of using cooperatively a power base to which both contributed as is the case with most workable coalitions. In the absence of a coalition, the alternate postures of rivalry and battle for control erupted. Ford ultimately responded by weighing his power with one side over the other.

As I have indicated, it is not at all clear why in Knudsen's case the coalition failed to develop. But in any failure the place to look is in the personalities of the main actors and in the nature of their defenses which make certain coalitions improbable no matter how strongly other realities indicate their necessity.

But defensiveness on the part of a chief executive can also result in building an unrealistic and unworkable coalition, with the self-enforced isolation which is its consequence. One of the most frequently encountered defensive maneuvers which leads to the formation of unrealistic coalitions or to the isolation of the chief executive is the fear of rivalry.

A realistic coalition matches formal authority and competence with the emotional commitments necessary to establish and maintain the coalition. The fear of rivals on the part of chief executives, or the jealousy on the part of subordinates of the chief executive's power, can at the extreme result in paranoid distortions. People become suspicious of one another, and through selective perceptions and projections of their own fantasies create a world of plots and counterplots.

The displacement of personal concerns onto substantive material in decision making is potentially the most dangerous form of defensiveness. The need for defenses arises because people become anxious about the significance of evaluations within existing power coalitions. But perhaps even more basic is the fear and the rivalry to which all coalitions are susceptible

given the nature of investments people make in power relations. While it is easy to dismiss emotional reactions like these as neurotic distortions, their prevalence and impact deserve careful attention in all phases of organizational life.

Unconscious collusions

All individuals and consequently groups experience areas of stress which mobilize defenses. The fact that coalitions embody defensive maneuvers on those occasions where stress goes beyond the usual level of tolerance is not surprising. An even more serious problem, however, occurs when the main force that binds men in a structure is the need to defend against or to act out the conflicts which individuals cannot tolerate alone.

Where coalitions represent the aggregation of power with conscious intention of using the abilities of members for constructive purposes, collusions represent predominance of unconscious conflict and defensive behavior. In organizational life, the presence of collusions and their causes often becomes the knot which has to be unraveled before any changes can be implemented.

The collusion of latent interests among executives can become the central theme and sustaining force of an organization structure of top management. For a collusion to take hold, the conflicts of the "power figure" have to be communicated and sensed by others as an overriding need which seeks active expression in the form of a theme. The themes vary just as do the structures which make a collusion. Thus one common theme is the need to control; another is the need to be admired and idealized; and still another is the need to find a scapegoat to attack in response to frustrations in solving problems.

If people could hold on to and keep within themselves areas of personal conflict, there would be far fewer collusions in organizational life. But it is part of the human condition for conflicts and needs to take over life situations. As a result, we find numerous instances of collusions controlling the behavior of executives. To illustrate:

□ A multidivisional corporation found itself with a revolution on its hands. The president was sensitive to the opinions of a few outside board members representing important stockholder interests. He was so concerned that he would be criticized by these board members, he demanded from vice presidents full information on their activities and complete loyalty to him. Over a period of years, he moved divisional chief executives to corporate headquarters so he could assure himself of their loyalty. Other executives joined in to gratify the president's need for control and loyalty.

The result of this collusion, however, was to create a schism between headquarters and field operations. Some of the staff members in the field managed to inform the board members of the lack of attention to and understanding of field problems. Discontent grew to such an extent that the board placed the president on early retirement.

Subsequently, the new president, with the support of the board, decentralized authority and appointed new division heads who were to make their offices in divisional headquarters with full authority to manage their respective organizations. One of the lingering problems of the new president was to dissolve the collusion at headquarters without wholesale firing of vice presidents.

Just as power distributions are central to the tasks of organizational planning, so the conservation of power is often the underlying function of collusions. Thus:

☐ A manufacturing vice president of a medium-sized company witnessed over a period of 15 years a procession of changes in top management and ownership. He had managed to retain his job because he made himself indispensable in the management of the factory.

To each new top management, he stressed the importance of "home rule" as a means of assuring loyalty and performance in the plant. He also tacitly encouraged each supervisor to go along with whatever cliques happened to form and dominate the shop floor.

However, over time a gradual loss of competitive position, coupled with open conflict among cliques in the form of union disputes, led to the dismissal of the vice president. None of his successors could reassert control over the shop, and the company eventually moved or liquidated many of the operations in this plant.

'Life dramas'

Faulty coalitions and unconscious collusions, as I have illustrated, can result from the defensive needs of a chief executive. These needs, which often appear as a demand on others to bolster the self-esteem of the chief executive, are tolerated to a remarkable degree and persist for a long time before harmful effects become apparent to outside stockholders, bankers, or boards of directors which ultimately control the distributions of power in organizations. Occasionally, corporations undergo critical conflicts in organizational politics which cannot be ignored in the conscious deliberations which affect how power gets distributed or used.

Intertwined with the various expressions of power conflicts in organizations are three underlying "life dramas" deserving careful attention:

The *first* portrays stripping the powers of a *parental figure.*

The *second* portrays the predominance of *paranoid thinking*, where distortions of reality result from the surfacing of conflicts which formerly had been contained in collusions.

The *third* portrays a *ritualistic ceremonial* in which real power issues are submerged or isolated in compulsive behavior but at the cost of real problem solving and work.

Parental figure

The chief executive in a business, along with the heads of states, religious bodies, and social movements, becomes an object for other people. The term "object" should be understood, in a psychological sense, as a person who is the recipient of strong emotional attachments from others. It is obvious that a chief executive is the *object* because he controls so many of the levers which ultimately direct the flow of rewards and punishments. But there is something to say beyond this obvious calculation of rewards and punishments as the basis for the emotional attachments between leader and led as *object* and *subject.*

Where a leader displays unusual attributes in his intuitive gifts, cultivated abilities, or deeper personal qualities, his fate as the *object* is governed by powerful emotions. I hesitate to use the word "charismatic" to describe such a leader, partially because it suggests a mystique but also because, in its reference to the "great" man as charismatic leader, it expands to superhuman proportions what really belongs to the psychology of everyday life.

What makes for strong emotional attachments is as much in the need of the *subject* as in the qualities of the *object.* In other words, the personalities of leaders take on proportions which meet what subordinates need and even demand. If leaders in fact respond with the special charisma that is often invested in them at the outset, then they are parties to a self-fulfilling prophecy. Of course, the qualities demanded have to be present in some nascent form ready to emerge as soon as the emotional currents become real in authority relationships.

The emotional attachments I am referring to usually contain mixtures of positive and negative feelings. If the current were only of one kind, such as either admiration or hostility, then the authority relationship would be simpler to describe as well as to manage. All too often, the way positive feelings blend into the negative sets off secondary currents of emotion which intensify the relationships.

On the one side, subordinates cannot help but have fantasies of what they would do if they held the No. 1 position. Such fantasies, besides providing fleeting pleasures and helping one to regulate his ambitions, also provide channels for imaginative and constructive approaches to solving problems. It is only a short step from imagining what one would do as chief executive to explaining to the real chief executive the ideas which have been distilled from this flight into fantasy. If the chief executive senses envy in back of the thoughts, he may become frightened and choke off ideas which can be used quite constructively.

Critical episode: But suppose a situation arises where not one but several subordinates enjoy the same fantasy of being No. 1? Suppose also that subordinates feel deprived in their relationship with the chief executive? Suppose finally that facing the organization there are substantive problems which are more or less out of control. With these three conditions, and depending on the severity of the real problems besetting the enterprise, the stage is set for a collusion which, when acted out, becomes a critical episode of displacing the parental figure. To demonstrate:

☐ In November 1967, the directors of the Interpublic Group, a $700 million complex in advertising and public relations, moved for the resignation of the leader and chief executive officer, Marion Harper, Jr. Briefly, Harper had managed over a period of 18 years to build the world's largest conglomerate in market services, advertising, and information on the base of a personally successful agency career. In expanding from this base, Harper made acquisitions, started new companies, and widened his orbit into international branches and companies.

As often happens, the innovator and creative person is careless in controlling what he has built so that financial problems become evident. In Harper's case, he appeared either unwilling or unable to recognize the seriousness of his financial problems and, in particular, the significance of allowing cash balances to go below the minimum required in agreements with lending institutions.

Harper seemed careless in another, even more telling, way. Instead of developing a strong coalition among his executive group, he relied on individual ties to him in which he clearly dominated the relationship. If any of the executives "crossed" him, Harper would exile the offender to one of the "remote" branches or place him on partial retirement.

When the financial problems became critical, the aggrieved executives who had once been dependent on Harper and then cast out, formed their own coalition, and managed to garner the votes necessary to, in effect, fire the head man. Although little information is available on the aftermath of this palace revolution, the new coalition had its own problems—which, one would reasonably judge, included contentions for power.

A cynic viewing this illustration of the demise of a parental figure could conclude that if one seeks to maintain power by dominance, then one had best go all the way. This means that to take some but not all of the power away from rebellious sons sets the stage for a cabal among the deprived. With a score to settle, they await only the right circumstances to move in and depose the aggressor.

While this cynical view has its own appeal, it ignores the deeper issues of why otherwise brilliant men fail to recognize the realistic needs for coalitions in the relationships of superior and subordinates. To answer this question, we would need to understand how powerful people operate with massive blind spots which limit vision and the ability to maneuver in the face of realistic problems.

The one purpose that coalitions serve is to guard against the effects of blind spots, since it is seldom the case that two people have identical limitations in their vision and ability to respond. The need to control and dominate in a personalistic sense is perhaps the most serious of all possible blind spots which can affect a chief executive, because he makes it difficult for people to help him, while creating grievances which sooner or later lead to attacks on him.

The unseating of a chief executive by a coalition of subordinates seldom reduces the emotional charge built up in the uncertain attachments to the ousted leader. A new head man has to emerge and establish a confident coalition. Until the contentions for power subside and the guilt reactions attached to deposing the leader dissolve, individuals remain vulnerable to their own blind spots and unconscious reactions to striving for power.

The references to a parental figure in the preceding discussion may appear to exaggerate the meaning of power conflicts. In whatever ways it exaggerates, it also condenses a variety of truths about coalitions among executives. The chief executive is the central *object* in a coalition because he occupies a position analogous to parents in the family. He is at the nucleus of a political structure whose prototype is the family in which jealousy, envy, love, and hate find original impetus and expression.

It would be a gross error to assume that in making an analogy between the family and formal organizations the parental role is strictly paternal. There are also characteristics of the mother figure in certain types of chief executives and combinations of mother-father in the formation of executive coalitions.

Chief executives can also suffer from depersonalization in their roles and as a result become emotionally cold and detached. The causes of depersonalization are complex but, in brief, have some connections to the narrow definitions of rationality which exclude the importance of emotions in guiding communication as well as thought.

For the purpose of interpreting how defensive styles affect the behavior of leaders, there is some truth to the suggestion that the neutrality and lack of warmth characteristic of some leaders is a result of an ingrained fear of becoming the *object* for other people—for to become the *object* arouses fears that subordinates will become envious and compete for power.

Paranoid thinking

This is a form of distortion in ideas and perception to which all human beings are susceptible from time to time. For those individuals who are concerned in their work with the consolidation and uses of power, the experience with sus-piciousness, the attribution of bad motives to others, jealousy, and anxiety (characteristics of paranoid thinking), may be more than a passing state of mind.

In fact, such ideas and fantasies may indeed be communicated to others and may even be the main force which binds men into collusions. Organizational life is particularly vulnerable to the effects of paranoid thinking because it stimulates comparisons while it evokes anticipations of added power or fears of diminished power.

To complicate matters even more and to suggest just how ambiguous organizational decisions become, there may be some truth and substance in back of the suspicions, distrust, and jealousies which enflame thinking. Personality conflicts do affect decisions in allocating authority and responsibility, and an individual may not be distorting at all to sense that he had been excluded or denied an ambition based on some undercurrents in his relationships with others. To call these sensitivities paranoid thinking may itself be a gross distortion. But no matter how real the events, the paranoid potential is still high as a fallout of organizational life.

Paranoid thinking goes beyond suspiciousness, distrust, and jealousy. It may take the form of grandiose ideas and overestimation of one's power and control. This form of distortion leads to swings in mood from elation to despair, from a sense of omnipotence to helplessness. Again, when acted out, the search for complete control produces the tragedies which the initial distortions attempt to overcome. The tragedy of Jimmy Hoffa is a good case in point. Consider:

☐ From all indications, Hoffa performed brilliantly as president of the teamsters' union. He was a superb organizer and bargainer, and in many ways a highly moral and even prudish man. There is little evidence to support allegations that he used his office to enrich himself.

Hoffa's troubles stemmed from his angry reactions when he could not get his way in managing the union's pension fund and from his relations with the government. In overestimating his power, Hoffa fell victim to the illusion that no controls outside himself could channel his actions. At this writing, Hoffa is serving a sentence in Lewisburg Penitentiary, having been found guilty of tampering with a jury.

It is interesting to note that Hoffa's successor delegated considerable authority to regional officers, a step that removed him from direct comparisons with Hoffa and served to cement a coalition of top officers in the teamsters.

Executives, too, can be victims of their successes just as much as of their failures. If past successes lead to the false sense of omnipotence which goes unchecked in, say, the executive's control of the board of directors, then he and his organization become the victims of changing times and competitive pressures along with the weakening in perception and reasoning which often accompanies aging.

One could speculate with some reason that paranoid distortions are the direct result of senility and the inability to accept the fact of death. While intellectually aware of the inevitability of death, gifted executives can sometimes not accept emotionally the ultimate in the limitations of power. The disintegration of personality in the conflict between the head and the heart is what we come to recognize as the paranoid potential in all forms of our collective relations.

Ritualistic ceremonial

Any collective experience, such as organizational life with its capacity for charging the atmosphere in the imagery of power conflicts, can fall victim to rigidities. The rigidities I have in mind consist mainly of the formation and elaboration of structures, procedures, and other ceremonials which create the illusion of solving problems but in reality only give people something to act on to discharge valuable energies.

The best example of a ritualistic approach to real problems is the ever-ready solution of bringing people together in a committee on the naive grounds that the exchange of ideas is bound to produce a solution. There are even fads and fashions to ritualism as in the sudden appearance of favorite words like "brainstorming" or "synergism."

It is not that bringing people together to discuss problems is bad. Instead, it is the naive faith which accompanies such proposals, ultimately deflecting attention from where it properly belongs. Thus:

□ In one research organization, professionals faced severe problems arising from personal jealousies as well as differences of opinion on the correct goals and content for the research program. Someone would periodically suggest that the problems could not be solved unless people came together, preferably for a weekend away from the job, to share ideas and really get down to the "nitty-gritty" of the problem. (It is interesting to note that no one ever defines the "nitty-gritty.") The group would indeed follow such suggestions and typically end the weekend with a feeling of euphoria brought on by considerable drinking and a sumptuous meal.

The most concrete proposal for action was in the idea that the basic problem stemmed from the organization's increased size so that people no longer knew one another and their work. The solution which appeared, only shortly to disappear, was to publish a laboratory newsletter that would keep people abreast of their colleagues' newest ideas.

In a more general vein, ritualism can be invoked to deal with any real or fancied danger, with uncertainty, ambivalent attitudes, or a sense of personal helplessness. Rituals are used even in the attempt to manipulate people. That power relations in organizations should become a fertile field for ritualism should not surprise anyone.

As I have tried to indicate, the problems of organizational life involve the dangers associated with losses of power; the uncertainties are legion especially in the recognition that there is no one best way to organize and distribute power, and yet any individual must make a commitment to some form of organization.

Ambivalent attitudes, such as the simultaneous experience of love and hate, are also associated with authority relationships, particularly in how superior-subordinate become the subject and object for the expression of dependency reactions. In addition, the sense of helplessness is particularly sensitized in the events which project gains and losses in power and status.

Finally, superior and subordinate in any power structure are constantly tempted to manipulate each other as a way of gaining control over one's environment, and the more so when there is a lack of confidence and credibility in the organization's efforts to solve problems in realistic ways.

The negative effects of ritualism are precisely in the expenditure of energy to carry out the rituals and also in the childlike expectation that the magic formulas of organizational life substitute for diagnosing and solving real problems. When the heads of organizations are unsure of the bases for the exercise of power and become defensive, the easy solution is to play for time by invoking rituals which may temporarily relieve anxiety.

Similarly, when executives fail to understand the structure and potential of the power coalitions they establish (either consciously or unconsciously), they increasingly rely on rituals to deflect attention away from their responsibilities. And, when leaders are timid men incapable of initiating or responding, the spontaneous reaction is to use people to act out rituals. Usually, the content and symbolism in the rituals provide important clues about the underlying defensiveness of the executive.

Obsessional leaders: The gravitational pull to ceremonials and magic is irresistible. In positions of power, obsessional leaders use in their public performances the mechanisms of defense which originate in their private conflicts. These defenses include hyper-rationality, the isolation of thought and feeling, reactive behavior in turning anger into moral righteousness, and passive control of other people as well as their own thought processes.

Very frequently, particularly in this day and age of psychologizing conflict, obsessive leaders "get religion" and try to convert others into some new state of mind. The use of sensitivity training with its attachment to "openness" and "leveling" in power relations seems to be the current favorite.

What these leaders do not readily understand is the fallacy of imposing a total solution for the problem of power relations where reality dictates at best the possibility of only partial and transient solutions. To force openness through the use of group pressure in T-groups and to expect to sustain this pressure in everyday life is to be supremely ritualistic. People intelligently resist saying everything they think to other people because they somehow have a deep recognition that this route leads to becoming over-extended emotionally and, ultimately, to sadistic relationships.

Intelligent uses of power: The choice fortunately is not between ritualistic civility and naive openness in human relationships, particularly where power is concerned. In between is the choice of defining those partial problems which can be solved and through which bright people can learn something about the intelligent uses of power.

We should not lose sight of the basic lesson that people in positions of power differ from "ordinary" human beings mainly in their capacity to impose their personal defenses onto the stage of corporate life. Fortunately, the relationships are susceptible to intelligent management,

and it is to the nature of this intelligence that I wish to address the conclusion of this article.

Coming full circle

The main job of organizational life, whether it concerns developing a new political pyramid, making new appointments to executive positions, or undergoing management succession at top levels, is to bring talented individuals into location for the legitimate uses of power. This is bound to be a highly charged event in corporate relationships because of the real changes in power distributions and the emotional reactions people experience along with the incremental gains and losses of power.

The demand, on the one hand, is for objectivity in assessing people and needs (as opposed to pseudorationality and rationalizing). This objectivity, on the other hand, has to be salvaged from the impact of psychological stresses which impel people to act out fantasies associated with power conflicts. The stresses of change in power relations tend to increase defensiveness to which counterreactions of rationalizing and of myth-making serve no enduring purpose except perhaps to drive underground the concerns which make people react defensively in the first place.

Stylistic biases

Thought and action in the politics of organizational life are subject to the two kinds of errors commonly found in practical life: the errors of omission and those of commission. It is both what people do and what they neglect to do that result in the negative effects of action outweighing the positive. But besides the specific errors of omission and commission (the tactical aspects of action), there are also the more strategic aspects which have to be evaluated. The strategic aspects deal both with the corporate aims and objectives and with the style of the leaders who initiate change.

In general, leaders approach change with certain stylistic biases over which they may not have too much control. There is a preferred approach to power problems which derives from the personality of the leader and his defenses as well as from the realities of the situation. Of particular importance as stylistic biases are the preferences for partial, as contrasted with total, approaches and the preferences for substance over form.

Partial vs. total: The partial approaches attempt to define and segregate problems which become amenable to solution by directive, negotiation, consensus, and compromise.

The total approaches usually escalate the issues in power relations so that implicitly people act as though it were necessary to undergo major conversions. The conversions can be directed toward personality structure, ideals, and beliefs, or toward values which are themselves connected to important aspects of personal experience.

When conversions become the end products of change, then one usually finds the sensitization of concerns over such matters as who dominates and who submits, who controls and who is being controlled, who is accepted and who is rejected. The aftermath of these concerns is the heightening of fantasy and defense at the expense of reality.

It may come as something of a disappointment to readers who are favorably disposed to psychology to consider the possibility that while organizations do have an impact on the attitudes of their constituent members, they cannot change personality structures or carry out therapeutic procedures. People may become more effective while working in certain kinds of organizations, but only when effectiveness is not dependent on the solution of neurotic conflict.

The advocates of total approaches seem to miss this point in their eagerness to convert people and organizations from one set of ideals to another. It becomes a good deal wiser, if these propositions are true, to scale down and make concrete the objectives that one is seeking to achieve.

A good illustration is in the attention given to decentralization of authority. Decentralization can be viewed in the image of conversion to certain ideals about who should have power and how this power should be used responsibly, or through an analytical approach to decide selectively where power is ill-placed and ill-used and to work on change at these locations. In other words, the theory of the partial approach to organizations asserts priorities and depends on good diagnostic observation and thought.

Substance vs. form: Leaders can also present a stylistic bias in their preference for substance or form. Substance, in the language of organizations, is the detail of goals and performance—that is, who has to do what with whom to meet specific objectives. Form directs attention to the relationship of "who to whom" and attempts to achieve goals by specifying how the people should act in relation to each other.

There is no way in which matters of form can be divorced from substance. But students of organization should at least be clear that attention to form *ahead of* substance threatens a person's sense of what is reasonable in undertaking actions. Attention to form may also present an implicit attack on one's conception of his independence and freedom from constraint.

Making form secondary to substance has another virtue: it can secure agreement on priorities without the need of predetermining who will have to give way in the ultimate give-and-take of the negotiations that must precede decisions on organization structure.

The two dimensions of bias, shown in the *Exhibit I* matrix, along with the four cells which result, clarify different executive approaches to

Exhibit I. Cognitive management styles in organizational life

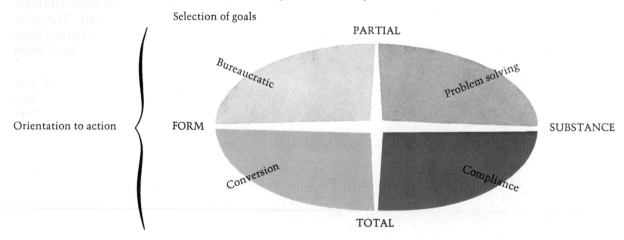

power. The two dimensions define the executive's cognitive biases in: (1) selection of goals (partial vs. total), and (2) orientation toward action (form vs. substance).

In the *bureaucratic* approach—that is, partial goals and attachment to form as a mode of acting—the emphasis is on procedure and the establishment of precedent and rule to control the uses of power.

The appeal of this approach is its promise of certainty in corporate relationships and in the depersonalization of power. The weaknesses of the bureaucratic approach are too familiar to need detailing here. Its major defect, however, is its inability to separate the vital from the trivial. It more easily commands energy over irrelevant issues because the latent function of the bureaucratic approach is to bypass conflict.

My contention here is that few important problems can be attended to without conflict of ideas and interests. Eventually organizations become stagnant because the bureaucratic approaches seldom bring together power and the vital issues which together make organizations dynamic.

The *conversion* approach (total-form) is notable through the human relations and sensitivity training movements as well as ideological programs, such as the Scanlon Plan and other forms of participative management. The popularity of "management by objectives" bears some scrutiny as a conversion movement directed toward power figures.

Another "total" approach which differs from conversion in its emphasis on substance is *compliance* with the directives of the powerful leader. This is the arena of the authoritarian personality (in both the leader, who has the power, and in the led, who seek submission), for whom personal power gets expressed in some higher goal that makes it possible for ends to justify means. The ideals may, for example, be race, as with dictator Adolf Hitler, or religion, as with Father Charles Coughlin, a dictator-type of the depression. In business, the illustrations are of a technological variety as with Frederick Winslow Taylor's "scientific management" and Henry Ford's automobile and assembly line.

Almost any technology can assume the proportions of the total approach if it is advanced by a charismatic leader and has deep emotional appeal. This explains the popularity of "management information systems," "value analysis," and "program planning and budgeting" which lead to a belief that the system itself is based on

order, rationality, and control; therefore, the belief in turn helps to counteract the fears of chaos and lack of control which make people willing to demand total dependence and compliance in power relations. The effects of this fear on how people seek to arrange power relations in business, government, and the community cannot be overestimated.

Problem-solving approach

It should be perfectly obvious by now that my favored approach to organizational life combines the biases in *Exhibit I* of the partial substantive quadrant which I have designated "problem solving." From observation of competent business executives, we know it is precisely their ability to define problems worthy of thought and action and to use their organization to evolve solutions which characterize their style.

The contrary notion that executives are primarily caretakers, mediators, and seekers of consensus is more a myth than an accurate portrayal of how the competent ones attach themselves to power. To have power and not direct it to some substantive end that can be attained in the real world is to waste energy. The difficulties with the problem-solving approach are in risking power in favor of a substantive goal.

While there are no absolute right answers in problem solving, there are ways of evaluating the correctness of a program and plan. With a favorable average, the executive finds his power base enhanced and his ability to take risks increased.

The problem-solving approach to organization structure operates according to certain premises:

1. That organization structure is an instrument rather than an end. This means that a structure should be established or modified quickly instead of stringing out deliberations as though there actually exists a best and single solution for the problem of allocating power.

2. That organization structure can be changed but should not be tinkered with. This means that members of an executive organization can rely on a structure and can implement it without the uncertainty which comes from the constant modification of the organization chart.

3. That organization structure expresses the working coalition attached to the chief executive. In other words, the coalition has to be established de facto for the structure to mean anything. If the structure is out of line with the coalition, there will be an erosion of power and

effectiveness. If no coalition exists in the minds of participants, putting it on paper in the form of an organization chart is nothing more than an academic exercise and a confusing one at that.

4. That organization structure represents a blend of people and job definitions, but the priority is in describing the structure to accommodate competent people. The reason for this priority lies in the fact that competent executives are hard to find. Therefore, as an action principle, one should ensure the effective uses of the scarcest resources rather than conform to some ideal version of power relations.

5. That organization structure is a product of negotiation and compromise among executives who hold semiautonomous power bases. The more the power base of an executive is his demonstrated competence, the greater his autonomy of power and therefore capacity to determine the outcome in the allocations of power.

The basic criticism of the problem-solving approach is in the danger of defining issues narrowly and ultimately undermining the moral-ethical basis of leadership. This criticism is valid, but as with so many problems in practical affairs, it can be overcome only by leaders who can see beyond the limits of immediate contingencies. In fact, I have tried to show throughout this article how the limitations of leaders, in both their cognitive and their emotional capacities, become the causes of power problems.

We have therefore come full circle in this analysis: because power problems are the effects of personality on structure, the solutions demand thinking which is free from the disabilities of emotional conflicts. This insight is often the margin between enduring with what exists or taking those modest steps which align competence with institutional authority in the service of human needs.

9

WHAT KILLED BOB LYONS?

Harry Levinson

Those who knew Bob Lyons thought extremely well of him. He was a highly successful executive who held an important position in a large company. As his superiors saw him, he was aggressive, with a knack for getting things done through other people. He worked hard and set a vigorous pace. He drove himself relentlessly. In less than ten years with his company, he had moved through several positions of responsibility.

Lyons had always been a good athlete. He was proud of his skill in swimming, hunting, golf, and tennis. In his college days he had lettered in football and baseball. On weekends he preferred to undertake rebuilding and repairing projects around the house, or to hunt, interspersing other sports for a change of pace. He was usually engaged, it seemed, in hard, physical work.

His life was not all work, however. He was active in his church and in the Boy Scouts. His wife delighted in entertaining and in being with other people, so their social life was a round of many parties and social activities. They shared much of their life with their three children.

Early in the spring of his ninth year with the company, Bob Lyons spoke with the vice president to whom he reported. "Things are a little quiet around here," he said. "Most of the big projects are over. The new building is finished, and we have a lot of things on the ball which four years ago were all fouled up. I don't like this idea of just riding a desk and looking out the window. I like action."

About a month later, Lyons was assigned ad-

ditional responsibilities. He rushed into them with his usual vigor. Once again he seemed to be buoyant and cheerful. After six months on the assignment, Lyons had the project rolling smoothly. Again he spoke to his vice president, reporting that he was out of projects. The vice president, pleased with Lyons' performance, told him that he had earned the right to do a little dreaming and planning; and, furthermore, dreaming and planning were a necessary part of the position he now held, toward which he had aspired for so long. Bob Lyons listened as his boss spoke, but it was plain to the vice president that the answer did not satisfy him.

About three months after this meeting, the vice president began to notice that replies to his memos and inquiries were not coming back from Lyons with their usual rapidity. He noticed also that Lyons was developing a tendency to put things off, a most unusual behavior pattern for him. He observed that Lyons became easily angered and disturbed over minor difficulties which previously had not irritated him at all.

Bob Lyons then became involved in a conflict with two other executives over a policy issue. Such conflicts were not unusual in the organization since, inevitably, there were varying points of view on many issues. The conflict was not a personal one, but it did require intervention from higher management before a solution could be reached. In the process of resolving the conflict, Lyons' point of view prevailed on some questions, but not on others.

AUTHOR'S NOTE: I wish to express my appreciation to Mrs. Helen Friend, Dr. Roy W. Menninger, and Dr. Joseph Satten, for critical reading of the manuscript and many useful suggestions.

A few weeks after this conflict had been resolved, Lyons went to the vice president's office. He wanted to have a long private talk, he said. His first words were, "I'm losing my grip. The old steam is gone. I've had diarrhea for four weeks and several times in the past three weeks I've lost my breakfast. I'm worried and yet I don't know what about. I feel that some people have lost confidence in me."

He talked with his boss for an hour and a half. The vice president recounted his achievements in the company to reassure him. He then asked if Lyons thought he should see a doctor. Lyons agreed that he should and, in the presence of the vice president, called his family doctor for an appointment. By this time the vice president was very much concerned. He called Mrs. Lyons and arranged to meet her for lunch the next day. She reported that, in addition to his other symptoms, her husband had difficulty sleeping. She was relieved that the vice president had called her because she was beginning to become worried and had herself planned to call the vice president. Both were now alarmed. They decided that they should get Lyons into a hospital rather than wait for the doctor's appointment which was still a week off.

The next day Lyons was taken to the hospital. Meanwhile, with Mrs. Lyons' permission, the vice president reported to the family doctor Lyons' recent job behavior and the nature of their conversations. When the vice president had finished, the doctor concluded, "All he needs is a good rest. We don't want to tell him that it may be mental or nervous." The vice president replied that he didn't know what the cause was, but he knew Bob Lyons needed help quickly.

During five days in the hospital, Lyons was subjected to extensive laboratory tests. The vice president visited him daily. He seemed to welcome the rest and the sedation at night. He said he was eating and sleeping much better. He talked about company problems, though he did not speak spontaneously without encouragement. While Lyons was out of the room, another executive who shared his hospital room confided to the vice president that he was worried about Lyons. "He seems to be so morose and depressed that I'm afraid he's losing his mind," the executive said.

By this time the president of the company, who had been kept informed, was also becoming concerned. He had talked to a psychiatrist and planned to talk to Lyons about psychiatric treatment if his doctor did not suggest it. Meanwhile, Lyons was discharged from the hospital as being without physical illness, and his doctor recommended a vacation. Lyons then remained at home for several days where he was again visited by the vice president. He and his wife took a trip to visit friends. He was then ready to come back to work, but the president suggested that he take another week off. The president also suggested that they visit together when Lyons returned.

A few days later, the president telephoned Lyons' home. Mrs. Lyons could not find him to answer the telephone. After 15 minutes she still had not found him and called the vice president about her concern. By the time the vice president arrived at the Lyons home, the police were already there. Bob Lyons had committed suicide.

Why Did It Happen?

This tragic story is not an unusual one. Probably no other single emotional problem is as disturbing to those who must live with it as is suicide. No doubt Bob Lyons' colleagues and superiors suffered almost as much anguish as his family did. The president and vice president were concerned long afterward. They wondered if, despite their conscientious efforts, they had in some way been at fault or if they could have prevented it. Neither his family nor his colleagues could understand why it happened. It made no sense to them that a successful man in the prime of his life, like Lyons, should destroy himself.

Lyons' problem may have been extreme, but similar problems are not rare in business and industry. Executives, managers, supervisors, industrial physicians, and — to a lesser extent — all employees frequently must cope with emotional problems on the job. Many problems are of lesser proportion than Lyons' was, but all have four factors in common:

• They are painful both for the person who suffers from them and for those who must deal with him.

• They are usually destructive to both the sufferer and the organization.

• The origins of the problem are almost always more complex than either of the parties realizes; and only infrequently are even the precipitating events clear.

• Rarely does the person responsible for dealing with the on-the-job problem know what he should do about it.

As a result, few businesses have ways of dealing with these matters even reasonably well, and management actions tend to range from abrupt firing to hostile discipline to, in some instances, procrastination which goes on for years. Often there is a vacillating series of management efforts, accompanied by feelings of guilt, failure, and anger on the part of those who must make the managerial decisions. Emotional problems, then, are contagious. The disturbance suffered by one person has its effects on the emotions of others.

Was It Hereditary?

How can we understand what happened to Bob Lyons and the ways his problem relates to problems with which all of us must deal? The customary commonsense reasons fail us. He had no serious illness. He did not fail in his business activity. There was no indication of difficulty in his family life. The course of the story told by the vice president is too consistent to attribute his death to an accident or to chance. Then, what was responsible?

Heredity? Can we say he inherited a tendency to suicide? Man inherits certain capacities and traits, but these are essentially physiological. He inherits the color of his eyes, the size of his nose, and other physical features. He inherits certain sensory and motor capacities. That is, he will be able to see, hear, or feel physical stimuli — color, sound, warmth — more or less keenly. Newborn infants in a hospital nursery will vary widely in their response to such stimuli. Some are calm and placid; an attendant could drop a metal tray with a clang, but these children would continue to sleep. Others, however, would be startled and awake crying.

The reasons for these differences in reaction are obscure. We have some clues from recent experiments with white rats. When pregnant rats are placed in crowded cages or in other situations where they experience stress, this stress apparently produces biochemical imbalances in the mothers which affect the rat fetuses. When the baby rats are born, they have greater anxiety and greater difficulty in adapting to the external world than rats whose mothers were not subjected to such stress. Among human beings, the mother's diet, the illnesses she has during pregnancy, and her general physical condition have their effects on the human fetus.

Something Physical?

Apparently man also inherits the capacity to coordinate his muscles with greater or lesser efficiency. If a person inherits excellent coordination potential and develops it, he may ultimately become a good athlete or a good musician. If he inherits a better than usual capacity for abstracting sights and sounds, he may have the makings of an artist. Man does not inherit athletic or artistic skill, but some men and women inherit such a high level of sensitivity and physiological harmony that they seem to have a "natural bent" toward certain talents.

Some apparently are born with greater general intelligence; therefore, they have the potential for dealing with their environments with better reasoning power and more effective judgment. Others have more specialized capacities: the ability to abstract ideas readily, the ability to remember well, and so on. Such differences, which in some instances appear at birth, bring about different kinds of interactions with the environment. The irritable infant will have quite a different relationship with his mother than will the placid child. The child who walks and talks early comes into contact sooner with a wider range of experiences than does another child in the same general environment, in whom these skills develop later.

Heredity, then, to a large extent determines what a person will be, in the sense that all of us have to be two-armed, ten-fingered, two-legged men or women, short or tall, intelligent or unintelligent, and with different thresholds of our various senses. Each person is different in the combination of endowments that he has and in the degree to which they enable him to cope with life's stresses.

While hereditary factors predispose man to behave in gross, or general, ways, they have little direct effect on his specific behavior. Because of the high level of development of the frontal lobes of his brain, man is capable of both abstract and reflective thinking. He is also capable of a wide range of emotions, particularly feelings about himself in relation to other people. These capacities for thought and feeling make man extremely responsive to many nuances of environmental stimulation. They also make it possible for him to initiate a wide range of actions in keeping with his thoughts and feelings, as well as in response to his environment, particularly to the other people in it.

Family Influence?

Another environmental factor which has an important influence on behavior is the extremely long period, particularly in Western cultures, during which the human child is dependent upon his parents. The intimacy of these relationships and the many social pressures which are transmitted through the parents to the children make family influences extremely important in guiding and controlling behavior. The extended period of dependency also presents a psychological problem because each person must then resolve the conflict between his wishes to retain the pleasures of dependency and his desire to become an independent adult. No one ever completely gives up the former or completely obtains the latter.

Each seeks some way of being interdependent with others that enables him to depend on others without losing his pride — because they in turn depend on him. Each person has dependency needs to varying degrees, the extent depending on how well each one has resolved this problem for himself. Some who have not resolved it well will always be more dependent than others. Some have resolved it reasonably well and can accept whatever dependency needs they have. Some have rejected or denied such needs and will have nothing to do with situations in which they might have to depend on others.

So, too, different companies will require different degrees of dependency in their employees. People who remain in a stable public utility company for a long time will be more dependent on their company for their security than will itinerant salesmen who sell magazines on commission. The fact that such a range of possibilities is available for fulfilling such needs at work is one of the health-giving aspects of work in business organizations.

Something Inside Him

Thus, we cannot, after this, very well say that Bob Lyons committed suicide because of heredity. We might be able to say hereditary factors, interacting with environmental factors, led to his death, but in our present state of knowledge it would be extremely difficult to demonstrate a hereditary predisposition which contributed to his self-destruction. Of necessity, we must call on more purely psychological factors for an explanation. In a way, when people, in despair over accounting for why someone like Bob Lyons would kill himself, cry out, "There must have been something odd inside of him that drove him into doing it," they are partially right. Inside all of us are many emotional drives that seem odd when we do not understand them.

For an approach toward understanding, let us return for a moment to the first paragraph of his superiors' description of Lyons. There we find these phrases: "highly successful," "aggressive," "a knack for getting things done through other people," "worked hard," "set a vigorous pace," and "drove himself relentlessly." These phrases speak of drive or energy. The subsequent two paragraphs describe other ways in which he discharged his energy. Some of these ways were highly useful to himself, his company, his family, and his friends. Others had a destructive potential: "He drove himself relentlessly." In fact, his difficulties seemed to begin when he could no longer drive himself on his job.

Warring Drives

The theories of Sigmund Freud help us understand the importance of such drives. According to Freud, there are two constantly operating psychological drives in the personality. One is a *constructive drive* and the other a *destructive drive*. Just as there are always processes of growth and destruction in all biological matter, anabolism and catabolism, so there are similar processes in the personality. These drives constitute the basic, primitive, energy sources for the personality.

The constructive drive (sometimes referred to as the *libido*) is the source of feelings of love, creativity, and psychological growth. The destructive drive gives rise to feelings of anger and hostility to others. The twin forces are variously referred to as Love and Hate, in terms of Greek mythology as Eros and Thanatos, or Sex and Aggression. (When used in this way, both the terms sex and aggression have a far broader meaning than they do in ordinary usage.)

A major psychological task for every human being is to so fuse these drives that the constructive drive tempers, guides, and controls the destructive drive and that the energy from both sources may thus be used in his own self-interest and that of society. If we speak of the destructive drive as the aggressive drive (recognizing that we are using the word aggressive according to its dictionary meaning and not as synonymous with assertion as in ordinary usage), we can say that it is far better for a person to use his aggressive drive, tempered by larger amounts of the constructive drive, in the pursuit of a career, the creation of a family, and in business competition than in destroying others as might be the case if the drives were not adequately fused.

Perhaps an analogy will help. Think of an automobile engine. A mixture of gasoline and air serves as the energy source. If there is too much gasoline, the engine will flood. If there is too much air, then it will sputter and die. With the right blend or fusion of fuel, and particularly with considerably more gasoline than air, which is then channeled through a mechanical structure, the automobile engine can serve a useful purpose.

Channeling the Drives

In Bob Lyons' case we saw that much of his constructive and aggressive energy, and more of the former than the latter, was well fused and channeled into his work, his relationships with his family, and service to his community. In some ways his constructive drive was less dominant, for he drove himself, as the vice president put it, "relentlessly."

The two drives are included in a part of the personality (a set of functions, not a physical thing) to which Freud gave the name "id," the Latin neuter for "it." In addition to the two basic drives, the id also includes many memories and experiences which the person can no longer recall.

The brain acts like a vast tape recorder. Theoretically, a person should be able to recall all of the experiences and feelings about those experiences he has had. We know that under hypnosis, in psychoanalysis, and under the influence of some drugs, a person can recall many of them. He could not do so before, no matter how hard he tried. Many of these memories, feelings, and impulses (impulses are derivatives of drives) are *repressed* or buried in the id, but they are still "alive," because they would be expressed, as we shall see later, if there were not adequate controls. For the id cares little about restraint; it operates on the pleasure principle: "I want what I want when I want it."

Repression, incidentally, is the process of "forgetting" or of making unconscious certain kinds of experiences and information which may be too troublesome or painful to handle on a conscious level. Here is how repression may have worked in Bob Lyons' case:

To judge from his behavior, he may have learned in his childhood that the only way to obtain love from his parents was by good performance. If high performance was the price of love, Lyons may well have resented his parents' attitude. But since such a conscious feeling of anger toward his parents would have been painful to live with, it was repressed. Lyons was no longer aware of his anger toward them, but it remained with him. The id, being unconscious, has no sense of time; it is inconsistent, contradictory, and not amenable to logic or persuasion. Thus, the early experiences that caused Bob Lyons' feelings of resentment were still "alive" and painful in his id.

In speaking of the drives, we have said that psychological growth and survival require more of the constructive drive, implying that there are differences in the amount of drive energy. We assume that there are differences among people in how much drive energy they have. We don't know how these differences come about, nor do we have any satisfactory way of specifying amount other than grossly and comparatively. We do know, however, that warm, affectionate relationships, especially those between mother and child, give added strength to the constructive drive, while those in which the child experiences severe frustration and hostility from others stimulate more aggression in the child. In a general way, the same is true of adults: the relationships and experiences which provide affection and gratification bring out the good side of people, while those which precipitate frustration and anger bring out the bad side of people.

Something Outside Him

Not only did Bob Lyons (as do all of us) have the major psychological task of balancing or fusing his constructive and aggressive drives, but he also had to discharge these drives in socially acceptable ways only. It might have been permissible in more primitive times to hit a man on the head and take his wife, but it is no longer so. There are stringent cultural controls on how love and aggression may be expressed.

These controls on how we may express our basic drives vary from culture to culture, even

Handling the Constructive Drive

In this article, because we are focusing on Bob Lyons' case, we are looking at ways in which the ego deals with the *aggressive* drive by calling into play certain defense mechanisms in order to maintain its equilibrium. But the ego also must deal with the *constructive* drive in order to maintain the proper balance. We see how it might handle sexual stimulation by control and refinement, or even denial, of the impulse. Other examples illustrate how the same mechanisms that are used to cope with the aggressive drive apply themselves to handling constructive drives and, in so doing, often cause us distress as well as relief:

1. *Fusion of Drives.* Fused with the aggressive drive, and dominant over it, the constructive drive is directed toward appropriate targets in intimate relationships with one's family, the solution of work and family problems, citizenship activities, and so on. Idealistic love without an aggressive component might lead to merely fantasied images of a sweetheart rather than marriage, or a person might dream about job success rather than take action toward it.

2. *Displacement to Less Appropriate Targets.* Like the aggressive drive, the constructive drive may be deflected from appropriate targets. Homosexuality is one such phenomenon whose dynamics are too complex for discussion here. In brief, the homosexual cannot establish adequate and satisfying relationships with those of the opposite sex. Instead, he uses the mechanism of substitution and builds up extended rationalizations to appease his superego.

Some people can invest themselves in causes, but not really in other people. Some lavish great affection on animals or houses or hobbies at the expense of personal relationships. Some adults can have affectionate relationships only with young children, but cannot tolerate other adults. These targets provide useful channels for love, but not the fully satisfying wide range of relationships enjoyed by most mature adults.

3. *Containment.* Some people, for complicated reasons, learned that it was psychologically safe not to express affection and have repressed their affectionate feelings. These people we know colloquially as "cold fish," people seemingly without emotion. They may be highly intellectual or great professional successes, but they have divorced compassion from judgment and feeling from reasoning. Others are known as ruthlessly efficient. They keep their emotions tightly controlled and their feelings of love deeply buried within themselves.

4. *Displacement Onto the Self.* Children rejected by their parents learn bitterly that it is too painful to try to love other people because they will not return love. In adult life, such people become highly self-centered. In conversation they are constantly talking about themselves. They give overmeticulous attention to their appearance, and revel in self-display. They tend to seek out activities which provide public adulation, and become extremely unhappy when they cannot get it. We find such people unpleasant to deal with because they are unable to give anything of themselves to someone else. Often they exploit others for their own gain. Because they cannot love others, they have almost no real friends and often are unable to sustain their marriages.

For these people much of the constructive drive is displaced onto themselves because environmental forces have made identification and introjection difficult, thereby impairing the possibility of relationships with other people. The early conflicts, now repressed, still exist unconsciously for the person. With its memories of early pain, the ego will not open itself again to the possibilities of rejection and narrowly constricts the constructive drive to a limited target to protect itself. Because of the limited range of attachments their egos permit, such people do not really enjoy life, despite what appears to others to be an extremely sparkling series of social adventures.

Each person must have a certain amount of self-love if he is to have self-respect. Overweening egocentricity, however, is ultimately destructive because of the absence of gratification, because of the pain caused other people, and because it diverts energy from social contributions the person could make.

An extreme form of egocentricity is hypochondriasis. Some people invest all of their energy in themselves in an extremely distorted way by being preoccupied with their own bodies. They are never free of aches and pains, often spend years and untold dollars "doctoring." They sacrifice most of life's pleasures to nurse their fancied ills, undeterred by repeated medical reports that show there is no need for surgery or that they do not have cancer, and the like. In some respects, such people commit slow suicide as they cut themselves off more and more from the outside world. In some cases, such persons will even allow one or more limbs to atrophy from disuse because they claim it is too painful to walk or to move.

from one social class to another; but they are transmitted through parents and other authority figures to children. Early in the child's development, the parents control and direct him. They permit some forms of behavior but prohibit others. As the child grows older, he incorporates into his own personality what his parents have taught him. He will incorporate these rules and values most effectively if he feels an affectionate bond with the parents and wants to be like them. This is one of the reasons the parent-child relationship is so important and why it should be one which enables the child to feel happy and secure.

Various values and rules can be "pounded into" the child, but these tend not to be genuinely his. He lives by them only as long as external pressures require him to, and abandons them when the external pressures diminish. Some parents who try to force piety and goodness into their children are dismayed to find them neither pious nor good when they grow up.

Still, Small Voice

When the child develops a conscience, he becomes self-governing. In Freudian terms, he has developed a *superego*. The superego is made up of four parts: (1) the values of the culture as transmitted through parents, teachers, friends, scoutmasters, ministers, and so on; (2) rules, prohibitions, and taboos; (3) an ego ideal — the image of ourselves at our future best which we never fully attain and as a result of which we are perennially discontented with ourselves; and (4) a police-judging or self-critical function.

Some theorists separate the superego and the conscience. They limit the superego to the values and the ego ideal (Parts 1 and 3 above), and refer to the rules (Part 2) and the self-critical function (Part 4) as the conscience. While that distinction is important scientifically, for our purposes we can ignore it. We will consider the conscience to be a part of the superego and include all four factors in the superego, as above.

The superego begins to develop in the child the first time the words "no" or "don't" enter his small world. Its general form tends to be established by the time the child enters elementary school, although it becomes further refined and expanded as a person grows up. Some features of the superego, developed early in life, are not conscious. The person is no longer aware of why he must live by certain rules and values; he knows only that if he does not do so, he feels uncomfortable or experiences anxiety. Some children, for example, feel that they must be the best in their class. They may not know why they feel they must, but if they are not always successful, they feel they are no good.

Conscience & Culture

Because the superego is acquired from the culture in which a person lives (principally through the medium of his parents and later by incorporating the values, rules, and ideals of others he respects), it is reinforced by the culture. One's superego may keep him from stealing, for example, but there are also social penalties for stealing. Cultural changes may, in turn, bring about some changes in the superego, particularly in those aspects of the superego which are conscious. Thus, every older generation contends that every younger generation is going to the dogs. While certain basic values and rules endure, others change with time. This is also why many parents are so concerned about where the family lives and about the beliefs and attitudes of their children's teachers and friends.

Among the directions that the superego provides are those which have to do with how the constructive and aggressive drives may be directed, how a person may love and how he may hate (and under what circumstances), and what kind of an adult person he should be. A man may love his parents but in a way different from the way he loves his wife. He may not, in Western cultures, love another woman as he loves his wife. In Italy and Spain he may express affection to other men by embracing them, but not in the United States. He may express his anger verbally, but not in physical attack. He may direct some of his aggressive drive in work, sports, and community activities, but not comfortably in those areas which are commonly regarded as feminine.

There are many variations among families and subcultures which become part of the superegos of people in those groups. Among middle-class American families there is a heavy emphasis on achievement, on cleanliness, on good manners, on hard work, and on the avoidance of open expressions of hostility. Lower class families, particularly those at the lowest socioeconomic levels, are not particularly concerned about these values. Some fundamentalist religious groups prohibit drinking and dancing. Some groups teach their children they are sinful by nature, others that almost anything they want to do is acceptable.

"Know Then Thyself"

How one looks upon himself, or his self-image, is related to the superego. One measure of self-evaluation is the disparity between the ego ideal and how one perceives himself at present. When one is depreciated by people who are important to him, this reinforces the critical aspects of the superego and lowers self-esteem. When self-esteem is enhanced, however, this counteracts the criticism of the superego and neutralizes some of the aggressive drive, thus stimulating the person to an expanded, more confident view of himself and his capacities.

It has been said that no wound is as painful as that inflicted by the superego. When a man behaves in ways not in keeping with the values and rules he has made a part of himself or when, in his judgment, he falls too short of his ego ideal, the superego induces a feeling of guilt. For most of us guilt feelings are so strong and so painful that we try to make up for violations of the superego by some form of atonement. The religious concept of penance is a recognition of this phenomenon. Restitution is another way to relieve guilt feelings. It is not unusual to see newspaper articles about people who have anonymously sent money to the government because they cheated on their taxes years before. Government officials speak of this as "conscience money."

Because the development of the superego begins early and the child is not in a position to judge rationally the relative importance of some of the rules he is taught, it is easy for the child to learn to judge himself more harshly than he should. With his limited capacity to reason, he may hold himself to blame for events he had nothing to do with. For example, suppose a two-year-old child is severely hurt in a fall. His four-year-old brother, who must inevitably have some feelings of hostility and rivalry toward the younger child, may come to feel he is responsible for the fall. As a matter of fact, he had nothing to do with the fall, but for a small child the wish is often tantamount to the act. To wish the younger child to be destroyed may be the same to a four-year-old as actually having pushed him. He may then harbor irrational guilt feelings for many years thereafter, completely unaware that he has such feelings or how they came about.

Since there is love and hate in every relationship, children have considerable hostility toward, as well as affection for, their parents. Usually young children do not understand that their hostile feelings are not "bad" and that parents will not be destroyed merely because their children have such feelings. As a result, most of us carry a considerable load of irrational guilt feelings. One of the major tasks in some forms of psychological treatment for people who are emotionally disturbed is to make such irrational unconscious feelings conscious so their irrationality may be recognized and they will no longer plague the person.

The Balance Wheel

The superego, then, becomes a built-in governor, as it were. It is the internalized civilizing agent. Without it, there would be no continuing self-guide to behavior. The superego is an auto-

matic protective device. Because of it some issues are never raised; we never even ask: "Should I or should I not steal?" As a guide to behavior it makes for stability and consistency of performance.

If, however, the values and rules which the child is taught are inconsistent, then the superego will be inconsistent. If there are too many, too strict rules, then the superego becomes a harsh taskmaster, either constricting too narrowly the way a person can behave or burdening him excessively with feelings of guilt and demanding constant atonement. But even without punishment or strict rules, a tyrannical superego can develop — if performance is the basis for obtaining love and there are unrealistic expectations of extremely high performance. In such a case, there tends to be a quality of drivenness to much of the person's behavior. He has a feeling that there is so much that he ought to do or must do as contrasted with so much he would enjoy doing. Unless he is constantly doing what he feels he ought to do, then he feels uncomfortable, not knowing either why he ought to be doing or why he feels uncomfortable if he is not doing. Lyons, for example, not only drove himself relentlessly, but also usually had to be working hard.

We have seen so far that the constructive and aggressive drives, which continuously seek discharge, are major motivating forces in the personality. The superego, with its capacity to induce guilt feelings, not only defines acceptable ways in which the drives may be discharged but also serves as a motivating force.

Home & Job

Not everything we do, of course, is completely influenced by our emotional drives. Our environment plays its part and should be considered in our attempt to understand Bob Lyons' suicide. For, in addition to the task of balancing or fusing our drives in keeping with the strictures of the superego, we do have to deal with our external environment. At times, this environment is a source of affection, support, and security. The infant in his mother's arms, a woman in a happy marriage, a man enjoying himself among his friends, a man building a business, a minister serving his congregation, all draw emotional nourishment from the environment. Such nourishment strengthens the constructive forces of the personality.

Looked at closely, *needs for status and esteem*

are essentially needs for love and affection. Each person, no matter how old or jaded, wants to be held in esteem by some others. Few can survive long without giving and receiving love, though often these expressions are thoroughly disguised, even from the self. Status needs have to do with the constructive forces of the personality as we have described them here. When one seeks symbols of status, he simply searches for concrete indications that some others do or will hold him in esteem. One way to describe status needs is to say that the person needs infusions of love and of gratification to foster his own strength.

However, the environment may also stimulate aggression: anger and jealousy, exploitation, competition for various advantages, economic reverses, wars, and so on. Every person has to deal with the realities of his environment — whether with the necessities of earning a living, the frustration of an unsolved problem, the achievement of personal goals, the development of satisfying relationships with other people, or something else. We saw that Lyons was actively involved with all of these things in his environment.

Ego & Reality

Now we have spoken of three sets of forces — id drives, the superego, and the environment — each interacting with the others, which must be kept in sufficient balance or equilibrium so that a person can function effectively. Some mechanism is required to do the balancing task, to serve as the executive part of the personality. Such a component of personality must fuse the drives, control their discharge in keeping with the conditions set by the superego, and act upon the environment. Freud gave the name *ego* to this set of functions. We tend to speak of the ego as a thing; actually, the term is merely a short way of describing *the organized executive functions of the personality, those functions that have to do with self-control and with testing reality.*

The ego includes such mental functions as recall, perception, judgment, attention, and conceptual or abstract thinking — those aspects of the personality which enable the individual to receive, organize, interpret, and act upon stimuli or psychological and physiological data. The ego develops (except in those who are mentally retarded) as the person grows. Like a computer, the ego acquires and stores information in the form of memory images, particularly information and experiences which previously have led to successful solution of problems. When an impulse arises from one of the drives, the ego contains the impulse until, in effect, it has checked with the superego and has determined what the consequences of acting on the impulse will be.

The impulse may have to be fully contained, or expressed in some modified fashion to meet both the conditions of the superego and the demands of the environment. The ego presumably checks its memory images to find acceptable ways of refining and discharging the impulse. When the ego can do this well, we speak of a strong ego or of psychological maturity. When it cannot do so adequately, we say a person does not have adequate strength or that he is immature. *The ego acts on the basis of what is called the reality principle*: "What are the long-run consequences of this behavior?"

The process of checking the memory images and organizing a response is what we know as thinking. Thinking is trial action or "dry run," as it were. Sometimes it goes on consciously, but much of the time it is an unconscious process. Thinking serves to delay impulses until they can be discharged in the most satisfactory way the person knows how. When a person acts impulsively in minor ways, for instance, in being inconsiderate of another person, we commonly speak of such behavior as "thoughtless."

The ego, operating on the reality principle and obeying the superego, must contain, refine, or redirect id impulses so that the integrity of the personality is preserved. The ego is constantly concerned with the cost and consequences of any action. In other words, the ego is concerned with psychological economy.

Beleaguered Ego

This task puts the ego in a difficult position. This system of psychological functions is always a buffer between the other systems, the id and the superego, and also between them and the forces of the environment. The ego, then, is always under psychological pressure. To carry on its integrating function well requires considerable strength. Strength comes from several sources: the basic inherited capacities, experiences of love and gratification which enhance the constructive forces, the development of skills and abilities which help it master the environment, and the physical health of the person.

The ego may be weakened through physical injury or illness — a brain tumor, a debilitating sickness — or by having to devote too much of its energy to repressing or otherwise coping with severe multiple or chronic emotional pressures.

The ego cannot deal with all of the stimuli which impinge upon it. It is constantly being bombarded with all kinds of data. It would be swamped if it tried to deal with all of the information it had, in the form of both past experiences and present ones. It must be selective in what it will deal with. Some data are therefore passed directly on to the id. The ego is never consciously aware of them. Furthermore, it has not been able to successfully resolve all of its psychological problems, some of which are extremely painful. With these it acts on the thesis, "If you can't lick it, forget it." These problems are repressed, or pushed down into the id. The little boy who erroneously thought he hurt his brother, then repressed his guilt feelings, is a case in point.

Perhaps some other examples will help us to understand these processes better:

◀ Suppose someone walking along the street sees a new car parked at the curb. He has an impulse to take the car and, acting on the impulse, drives it off. We say he acted impulsively, by which we mean he was governed by an impulse from the id and not by rational considerations. To put it another way, we might say that the ego was weak, that it did not anticipate the consequences of the act and control the impulse. The price paid for acting on the impulse, perhaps a jail term, is a high one for what little momentary pleasure might have been gained. We say such a person is immature, meaning that his ego is not sufficiently developed to enable him to act in a wiser and less costly way.

◀ A store manager might also be said not to have good judgment if he bought items without thinking through their marketing possibilities or merely because he liked the salesman who sold them. This is another form of impulsiveness or immaturity. Marketing men count on the irrational impulsiveness in all of us by creating in supermarkets such a vast array of stimuli to our desires for pleasure that the ego does not function quite as well as it might. Impulse buying results — unless the ego is bolstered by additional support in the form of a shopping list and a budget.

◀ Here is a more personal example. If you observe young children, you see that they live extremely active lives. They have many pleasant moments and some painful ones. They remember experiences from day to day and recall exciting events like a trip to the zoo with great relish. Now try to remember your own early childhood experiences, especially those which occurred before you were four or five. Probably you will be able to recall few in any detail, if you can recall any at all. Many other experiences of childhood, adolescence, and even adulthood are beyond voluntary recall. Yet under hypnosis they could be recalled. This information, much of it not immediately necessary to solve today's problems, is stored in the id.

Memory traces of some of these experiences, which might help us solve problems, are stored in the ego, though even they are usually not conscious. A person may be surprised to find himself at home, having driven from work while preoccupied with a problem, without ever having noticed the turns, stop lights, or other cars. Obviously, he used many cues and did many specific things to get home safely, though he did so without being aware of what he was doing.

◀ A final example illustrates the way the ego deals with impulses from the id. Suppose an attractive secretary comes to work in a new dress whose lines are calculated to stimulate the interest of men — in short, to stimulate the sexual impulse. When this impulse reaches the ego of one of the men in the office, the ego, acting within the limits set by the superego ("Look, but don't touch"), and its judgment of the consequences of giving vent to the impulse ("You'll destroy your reputation"), will control and refine the impulse. The man may then comment, "That's a pretty dress" — a highly attenuated derivative of the original impulse. Another man with a more rigid superego might never notice the dress. His superego would protect him by automatically prohibiting the ego from being sensitive to such a stimulus.

Ego's Assistants

If the ego has the job of first balancing the forces from the id, the superego, and the environment, and then of mediating and synchronizing them into a system which operates relatively smoothly, it requires the assistance of two kinds of psychological devices to make its work possible. Thus:

1. It needs *anxiety* to serve as an alarm system to alert it to possible dangers to its equilibrium.

2. It must have *defense mechanisms* which can be called into play, triggered by the alarm system; these will help it either to fend off the possible threats or to counteract them.

Anxiety's Purpose

The alarm-triggering system called anxiety is what we are conscious of whenever we are afraid of something. It is a feeling of unease or tension. But there is a much more subtle and complex phenomenon of anxiety which operates spontaneously and unconsciously whenever the ego is threatened. Being unaware of its operation, we may not know consciously why we are restless, tense, or upset. Bob Lyons, we recall, was worried but he did not know why. We have all experienced his anxiety. A feeling of tension and restlessness that one person picks up from another is very common. Sensing that the other person is upset makes us feel uneasy for reasons which are not very clear to us. We do not consciously decide that we are threatened, but we feel we "can't relax," that we must be on guard.

Perhaps the work of unconscious anxiety may be likened to a gyroscope on a ship or an airplane. The gyroscope must sense the imbalance of the ship or plane as a result of waves, currents, or storms. It must then set into motion counteracting forces to regain the vehicle's balance. This analogy highlights something else for us: *There is no state of placid emotional stability, just as there is never a smooth ocean or an atmosphere devoid of air currents. There is no peace of mind short of the grave. Everyone is always engaged in maintaining his psychological equilibrium.* Even when a person is asleep, his dreaming is an effort to resolve psychological problems, to discharge tension, and to maintain sleep. The workings of unconscious anxiety may be seen in a number of different ways:

⁋ Suppose a three-year-old child, drinking milk from a glass, bites and shatters the edge of the glass. The glass cuts the child's lip, which bleeds profusely. Striving to remain calm, the mother places a compress under the lip and stops the bleeding. But she does not know whether the child has swallowed any of the glass and, therefore, what she should do next. She asks the child if he has swallowed glass. He says he has not. To be certain, she asks again, saying, "Please tell me if you have, because if you have, you might have a tummyache and we don't want you to have a tummyache." At this point the child says he *has* swallowed some glass. Now the mother does not know whether he has or has not.

Before the mother can decide that she had better take the child to the hospital, he begins to quiver as he might shake from the cold. This shaking is involuntary. Though the child has no conscious concept of the possible fatal danger of swallowing glass, and though the mother has tried to remain calm, unconsciously the child has sensed the inherent threat in the situation. Automatically, emergency physiological and biochemical processes are called into play to cope with the danger. It is the effects of these we see in the shaking. The manner and attitude of the hospital physician assure the child that there is no threat and gradually the shaking subsides.

⁋ Adults may have the same experience in many different ways. Suppose you are driving your car down the street and a youngster dashes out from between parked cars into the path of yours. You immediately slam on the brakes. For a moment you do not know whether you have hit the child. When you get out of the car, you see that you have not; but you find yourself shaking, your heart beating rapidly, your skin perspiring. You did not consciously cause any of these things to happen. The threat to your equilibrium, constituting a stress, aroused anxiety, which in turn mobilized your resources for dealing with the emergency. A similar experience is a commonplace among athletes. Some of them experience such psychological tension before competitive events that they cannot eat; if they do, they throw up.

Here we are speaking of conscious anxiety at one level. We are aware of certain threats and react to them. But at another, unconscious level, our reaction is disproportionate to the event. There is no objective reason for the driver to continue to be anxious when he discovers that he has not hit the child. The overt threat is past. Yet he may continue to shake for hours and may even dream about the event to the point of having nightmares. It is understandable that the athlete would want to win the game for conscious reasons. Why the competition should cause him such violent physical reaction is a more complex and obscure problem. He himself does not know why he must go to such extremes of defensive mobilization that his body cannot tolerate food. Unconscious anxiety is at work.

Ego Defenses

If we are to penetrate deeply enough into Bob Lyons' reasons for suicide, we must go beyond admitting that he was undoubtedly anxious and under stress. We need to see why his ego was not sufficiently protected from such a completely destructive attack — why the defense mechanisms mentioned earlier as one of the ego's assistants did not enable him to overcome his anxiety.

There are a number of personality mechanisms which operate automatically to help the ego maintain or regain its equilibrium. These mechanisms may be viewed as falling into three broad classes:

(1) One group has to do with shaping or forming the personality. Included in this category is *identification*, the process of behaving like someone else. A man identifies himself with his boss when he dresses or speaks as his boss does. Women identify themselves with a leading movie star when they adopt her hair style. Another device, *introjection*, is a stronger form of identification, although the line between them is hazy. When one introjects the mannerisms or attitudes of another, he makes these firmly a part of himself. We speak of introjecting the values of the parents and thereby of becoming a "chip off the old block."

(2) Another group of mechanisms are universally used devices which are required to control, guide, refine, and channel the basic drives or impulses from the id. We have already talked about *repression*. Another mechanism, *sublimation*, is the process by which basic drives are refined and directed into acceptable channels. Lyons, for example, sublimated much of his aggressive drive in his work.

(3) A third group of mechanisms is made up of temporary devices which are called into play automatically when there is some threat to the personality.

Denial, a form of repression, is one of these devices, and can be clarified by an example.

Suppose a plant superintendent has five years to go to retirement and his boss suggests that he pick a successor and train him. But our plant superintendent does not select a successor, despite repeated requests from the boss. He cannot "hear" what the boss is saying. He may be forced to select such a man. When the time for retirement arrives, he may then say to his boss that the boss really did not intend to retire him. He cannot believe the boss will compel him to leave. This behavior reflects a denial of the reality of the situation because the ego has difficulty accepting what it regards to be a loss of love (status, esteem, etc.).

Rationalization is another temporary mechanism that all of us use from time to time. In fact, as the following example shows, it provides the subject matter for comedy!

A man's wife suggests that it is time to get a new car because theirs is already eight years old and getting shabby. At first, acting under the influence of the superego, the man doubts if he needs a new car. He cannot justify it to himself. To buy one without an adequate reason would be a waste of money for him. "You're too mature to be so extravagant and to fall for style," his superego says. The guilt aroused by the thought of buying a new car gives rise to anxiety, and the idea is rejected to appease the superego. The old car still runs well, he says; it gives no trouble, and a new one would be expensive. Soon we see him in an automobile showroom. "Just looking," he tells the salesman. "He thinks he's found a sucker," he chuckles to himself to avoid the condemnation of the superego. Next, however, he begins to complain to his wife and his friends that the old car will soon need repairs, that it will never be worth more on a trade-in. Before long he has developed a complete rationale for buying the new car, and has convinced himself to do so.

Projection, another temporary mechanism, is the process of attributing one's own feelings to someone else. If, for example, one can project hostility onto someone else ("He's mad at me; he's out to get me"), then one can justify to his superego his hostility toward the other person ("It's all right for me to get him first").

Idealization is the process of putting a halo around someone else and thereby being unable to see his faults. This process is seen most vividly in people who are in love or who have identified strongly with political leaders. It enhances the image of the idealized person as a source of strength and gratification.

Reaction formation is a formidable term for the process of doing the opposite of what one wants to do to avoid the threat of giving rein to impulses. Some people become so frightened of their own aggressive impulses that they act in an extremely meek and mild manner, avoiding all suggestion of aggression.

Another important mechanism is *substitution*, or displacement. This is the process in which the ego, unable to direct impulses to the appropriate target, directs them to a substitute target. In a benign way, this is what happens when a person devotes much of his affection to pets or to his work if, for whatever reasons, he does not have satisfactory ways of giving his affection to other people. More destructive displacement occurs when a person seeks substitute targets for his aggression. Unable to express his anger at his boss to the boss, a man may displace it onto the working conditions or wages. He may even unwittingly carry it home and criticize his wife or his children. This is the mechanism which is behind scapegoating and prejudice. Not only does displacement of this kind hurt others; worse yet, it doesn't contribute to the solution of the real problem.

Compensation is still another mechanism, and often a highly constructive one. This is the process of developing talents and skills to make up for one's deficiencies, or of undertaking activities and relationships to regain lost gratification. In certain respects, compensation and substitution are, of course, closely related.

The Defensive Process

These mechanisms need not be elaborated further here. Our answer to why Bob Lyons killed himself has necessarily been delayed long enough. Now we see the point, however. When the ego is threatened in some fashion, anxiety spontaneously and unconsciously triggers off mechanisms to counteract the threat. If there are too many emergencies for the personality, it may then overuse these mechanisms, and this in turn will seriously distort the person's view of reality, or cripple him psychologically. To identify with those one respects is fine; to imitate them slavishly is to lose one's individuality. It is one thing to rationalize occasionally, as we all do, but another to base judgments consistently on rationalizations. At times all of us project our own feelings, but we would be sick indeed if we felt most of the time that everyone else had it in for us.

By and large, self-fulfillment has to do with the ego's capacity to function as effectively as it can. When emotional conflicts can be diminished, when the need for defensiveness can be decreased, the energy which ordinarily maintained the defenses is freed for more useful activity. In a sense, the effect is to remove some of the brakes from the psychological wheels. Furthermore, when, as threats are removed, the defenses need no longer be used, one perceives reality more accurately. He then can relate to other people more reasonably and can communicate more clearly. A psychological blossoming-out can occur. When such balancing fails to take place, the ego is overwhelmed for the time being. In Bob Lyons' case, he acted to relieve his emotional pain and killed himself before equilibrium could be restored in a less destructive way. Since this balancing process is the ultimate key to an understanding of Lyons' act, let us make sure we understand how it works and then apply our knowledge directly to Bob Lyons' case:

Fusion of drives toward appropriate target — Suppose a man is called into his boss's office and his boss criticizes him harshly for something he did not do. The ideally healthy man, if he exists, will listen calmly to what his boss has to say and, in good control of his rising aggressive impulse, might well reply, "Boss, I'm sorry that such a mis-

take has happened. I had nothing to do with that particular activity, but perhaps I can help you figure out a way to keep the same mistake from happening again." His boss, also brimming with good mental health, might then respond, "I'm sorry that I criticized you unfairly. I would appreciate your giving me a hand on this." Together they direct their energies toward the solution of the problem.

Displacement to less appropriate target — But take a similar situation where, however, the man knows his boss will brook no contradiction or is so emotionally overwrought that there is little point in trying to be reasonable with him. This man may fume with anger at the unjust attack, but control his impulse to strike back at the boss. His reality-testing ego tells him that such action won't help the situation at all. He takes the criticism, anticipating a better solution when the boss cools off. Nevertheless, he is angry for being unjustly criticized, and there has been no opportunity to discharge his aroused aggressive impulse in an appropriate way toward the solution of the problem.

Because in this situation it seems so rational to control one's impulse (i.e., the boss is upset and there's no point in discussing it with him now), the ego finds this secondary anger an inappropriate feeling to allow into consciousness. The more primitive secondary anger is then repressed. When the employee goes bowling that night, he gets particular pleasure from knocking the pins down, without knowing why. Unconsciously he is using bowling to drain off his excess aggression. Such a displacement is a partially constructive way of discharging aggression: it hurts no one, it provides gratification. However, it does not contribute directly to resolving the problem itself, presuming that some further action toward solution might be required.

Containment of drives — Suppose that another man finds himself in the same situation. This man has learned in the course of growing up that it is not permissible to express one's aggression directly to authority figures. Being human, he has aggressive impulses, but also, having a severe superego, he feels guilty about them and goes to great lengths to repress them. When the boss criticizes him and his aggressive impulse is stimulated, repression automatically sets in and the impulse is controlled without his being aware of it. However, it is so controlled that he can't speak up to contribute to the solution of the problem.

Because this man constantly maintains a high degree of control to meet the demands of his superego, he is already in a potentially more explosive situation, ready to defend himself from the slightest possible threat. If he has to contain more of his anger within himself, we have a situation which is much like rising steam pressure in a boiler. If this situation is repetitive or chronic, the mobilization and remobilization of defenses almost requires of the ego that it be in a steady emergency state. The alarm bells are ringing most of the time. This kind of reaction strains the ego's resources and is particularly wearing physiologically because each psychological response to stress is accompanied by physiological mobilization, too.

The result is psychosomatic symptoms. The body is literally damaged by its own fluids, leading to ulcers, hypertension, and similar phenomena. This experience is commonly recognized in the phrase, "stewing in one's own juice." Clinical data seem to show that there are reasons why one particular organ is the site for a psychosomatic symptom, but often these reasons are obscure.

Displacement onto the self —Take still another man. This one also has learned that aggression should not be expressed to others, and he cannot do so without feelings of guilt. In fact, his superego won't tolerate much hostility on his part, so he lives constantly with feelings of guilt. The guilt, in turn, makes him feel inadequate as his superego repeatedly berates him for his hostility. No matter how nice, by means of reaction formation, he may try to be, he can't satisfy his superego. Somehow, he himself always seems to be at fault. With such a rigid, punitive superego, this man under the same kind of attack may then respond by saying, "I guess you're right. I'm always wrong; it's my fault. I never seem to do things right." He may also then have a mild depression. Depression is always an indication of anger with one's self, originating from anger toward another, and reflects the attack of the superego on the ego. The aggression is displaced from the appropriate target back onto the self and results in a form of self-blame and self-punishment.

Another form of self-attack or self-punishment is seen in many accidents. Most accidents are not actually accidents in the sense that they occur by chance, but are unconscious modes of self-punishment. The "forgetting" to turn the motor switch off before repairing the machine or not seeing or hearing possible threats frequently are indications that denial or repression has been operating in order to permit the person to hurt himself to appease his own superego. In extreme form, this self-directed aggression is the mechanism behind suicide, and now we are prepared to see what happened to Bob Lyons.

The Reason Why

Driven by an extremely severe superego, Bob Lyons sublimated his drives successfully in his work as long as he could work hard. There was

an ego-superego-id environment equilibrium, although only a tenuous one. By driving himself, he could appease the relentless pressure of his superego.

Such a superego, however, is never satisfied. Its demands arise from unconscious sources, which, because they are unconscious, probably have existed from early childhood and are to a large extent irrational. If they were not irrational, their terms could be met.

Whenever he reached a goal toward which he had aspired, Lyons got no satisfaction from it, for his superego still drove him. And when he could no longer work as hard as he had, this for him was an environmental deprivation. He could no longer earn love by performing well. His superego became more relentless. The vacation, with no demands on him at all, simply added to his guilt, his feelings of unworthiness and inadequacy. With sublimations and displacements reduced, given the kind of superego he had, his aggressive drive had only his ego as a major target.

And at that moment, the only way that Bob Lyons knew to appease his superego was to kill himself.

Had his superego been developed differently, Lyons might have achieved as he did because of ego reasons (the pleasure and gratification he got from his work), with a mild assist from the superego to do well. When his superego developed so strongly, probably because of a heavy burden of hostility in childhood for which he felt irrationally guilty for a lifetime, there was no real pleasure in what he did and nothing more than temporary gratification. The relentless driving of himself was a form of self-sacrifice, just as are alcoholism, most accidents, repeated failures on the job, presenting the worst side of one's self to others, and some forms of crime.

We should recognize that there is a bit of this phenomenon in all of us, just as we can see something of ourselves at times in each of the preceding three examples. The ancient observation that "man is his own worst enemy" is testimony to the self-destructive potential in each person. Bob Lyons differed from the rest of us only in degree, and only because of a combination of forces at a given point which precipitated his death. A change in any single force might conceivably have prevented it: more and harder work, psychiatric treatment, no vacation to add to the feelings of guilt and uselessness, or open recognition by his physician of the seriousness of mental illness.

Groping for Shadows

But how would his physician or his friends have recognized early symptoms of Bob Lyons' illness? It would not have been easy. We cannot put an ego under a microscope or locate the id in any part of the body. These are simply names given to what seem to be systems of forces operating in the personality. We cannot see repression — it is only a name for the observation that some things are forgotten and can be recalled only under certain circumstances. The same is true when we speak of something being unconscious. It is not relegated to a given physical organ or place. One is merely not able to call it into consciousness.

If the ego has a constant balancing task and calls certain mechanisms into play to carry it out, being concerned with psychological economy, the ego will develop preferred mechanisms, preferred because they work best consistently. These become the established personality traits. As individuals we make our preferred modes of adjustment those ways of behaving which are most comfortable (least anxiety-arousing) to us.

The consistent modes of adjustment, the personality traits, become the hallmarks by which we are known to others. Even physical styles of behavior become part of this system. If we hear on the telephone a voice that we recognize, we can place it with a name. If we meet a friend we have not seen in ten years, we will observe that he seems to be the same as he always was — he talks, reacts, thinks in much the same way. Some are hail-fellow-well-met gregarious types, others more diffident and conservative. Each has his own preferred modes of adjustment, his preferred way of consistently maintaining equilibrium.

Given these entrenched modes of adaptation, even clinical psychologists and psychiatrists are unlikely to make *radical* changes in people, although they can often help alter certain forces so that people can behave more healthily than they did previously. The alteration of internal forces (ego-superego-id) is the job of the clinician. The layman often can make a contribution to the alteration of external forces (ego-environment). Even minor changes of the balance of forces can make significant differences in how people feel, think, and behave.

The very fact that people do not radically change their styles of behavior makes it possible to detect signs of emotional stress. Given certain characteristic modes of adaptation in the form of personality traits, once a person experiences some kind of emotional stress, he is likely first to make greater use of those mechanisms which worked best for him before. The first sign of stress is that a person seems to be conspicuously more like he always was. If he ordinarily is a quiet man, under stress he may become withdrawn. If he is like Lyons, his first reaction may well be to try to work harder.

Secondly, if this first line of defense does not work too well (or if the stress is too severe or chronic for that method alone), we will begin to see the appearance of inefficient functioning — vague fears, inability to concentrate, compulsions to do certain things, increasing irritability, and declining work performance. We will also see the results of physiological defensive efforts. We saw in Lyons' case that tension, jitteriness, and inability to hold food or to sleep all accompanied his psychological stress. The whole organism — physiological and psychological — was involved in the struggle.

Psychological and physiological symptoms are ways of "binding" or attempting to control the anxiety. They are ways of trying to do something about a problem, however ineffective they may be. And they are the best ways of dealing with that problem that the person has available to him at the moment, though better ways of coping may be apparent to others who do not have his psychological makeup. That's why it is dangerous to try to remove symptoms. Instead, it is wiser to resolve the underlying problem.

Thirdly, if neither of these types of defenses can contain the anxiety, we may see sharp changes in personality. The person no longer behaves as he did before. Lyons felt himself to be falling apart, unable to work as he did previously. A neat person may become slovenly, an efficient one alcoholic. Radical changes in personality indicate severe illness which usually requires hospitalization.

Conspicuous change in behavior indicates that the ego is no longer able to maintain effective control. If a person is so upset that he hears voices or sees things which do not exist, previously unconscious thoughts and feelings are breaking through. Obviously irrational behavior indicates the same thing. There is a loss of contact with reality, seriously impaired judgment, and an inability to be responsible for oneself. In such a state, Bob Lyons committed suicide.

Conclusion

Now that we *think* we understand why Bob Lyons killed himself, it is important that two cautions be raised.

About Ourselves

First, the reader newly exposed to psychoanalytic theory invariably falls victim to what may be called the freshman medical student's syndrome: he gets every symptom in the book. Everything to which this article refers, the average reader will be able to see in himself. As we were discussing Lyons, we were talking about human beings and human motivation; so it was inevitable that we ended up talking about ourselves. We must recognize this tendency to read ourselves into these pages, and compensate for this by consciously trying to maintain an objective distance from the material.

At the same time, does this very experience not make it clear to us that everyone has the continuing task of maintaining an equilibrium? At any given time any one of us may be listing to starboard a little, or trying to keep from being buffeted about by a sudden storm. Despite these pressures, we must nevertheless move forward, correcting for the list as best we can, or conserving our strength to ride out the storm. Each will defend himself the best way he knows how. As he does so, the more energy he must devote to defense, the less he will have available for forward movement.

Each of us at one time or another, therefore, will be emotionally disturbed or upset. For a few hours, a few days, a few weeks, we may be irritable or angry ("I got up on the wrong side of the bed"), or blue ("I'm feeling low today"), or hypersensitive. When we feel these ways, when we are having difficulty maintaining an equilibrium, for that brief period of time we are emotionally disturbed. We cannot work as well as we usually do. It is more difficult for us to sustain our relationships with other people. We

may feel hopeless or helpless. We're just not ourselves.

But just because we are mildly emotionally disturbed does not mean we need professional help or hospitalization. A cold is a minor form of upper respiratory infection, the extreme of which is pneumonia. If one has a cold, that does not mean he will have pneumonia. Even if he does get pneumonia, with present treatment methods most people recover, and the same is true of mental illness. The difference between the mild and the severe is one of degree, not of kind. It is just more of the same thing.

Because each of us is human and no one of us has had either perfect heredity or perfect environment, each of us has his weak spots. When the balance of forces is such that there is stress where we are weak, we will have difficulty. The incidence of mental illness, then, is not one out of twenty or some other proportionate statistic. Rather it is one out of one!

What We Can Do

The second caution has to do with the limitations of this exposition and the reader's preparation for understanding it. This necessarily has been a highly condensed version of some aspects of psychoanalytic theory. Many important aspects of the theory have been omitted and others have been presented without the many qualifications a serious scientific presentation would require. The reader should therefore look upon what is presented only as an introduction to better understanding of problems. He should be careful about overgeneralization and should studiously avoid using jargon or interpreting people's behavior to them.

Unless he observes these limitations, the layman will be unable to help anyone. Within these limitations, however, a businessman can render extremely important help to others in his company — and to himself. Specifically, he can recognize that:

• *All* behavior is motivated, much of it by thoughts and feelings of which the person himself is not aware. Behavior does not occur by chance.

• At any one time each person is doing the best he can, as a result of the multiple forces which bring about any given behavior. A change in the forces is required to bring about a change in behavior.

• Love neutralizes aggression and diminishes hostility. "A soft word turneth away wrath," says the old aphorism. This does not mean maudlin expressions, but actions which reflect esteem and regard for the other person as a human being. The most useful demonstration of affection is support which takes the form of:

— *Understanding* that the pain of emotional distress is real. It will not go away by wishing it away, by dismissing it as "all in your head," or by urging the person to "forget it," "snap out of it," or to "take a vacation."

— *Listening* if the person brings his problem to you, or if it so impairs his work that you must call his work performance to his attention. Listening permits him to define his problem more clearly and thereby to examine courses of action. Acting constructively to solve a problem is the best way the ego has to maintain the fusion of drives in dealing with reality. Listening, by providing some relief for the distressed person, already brings about some alteration in the balance of forces.

If you listen, however, you must clearly rec-ognize your limitations: (1) you can offer only emergency help; (2) you cannot hold yourself *responsible* for other people's personal problems, some of which would defy the most competent specialist.

— *Referring* the troubled person to profes-sional sources of help if the problem is more than a temporary one, or if the person is severely upset. Every organization should have channels for referral. If a person who has responsibil-ity for other people has no formal organizational channels for referral, he would do well to estab-lish contact with a psychiatrist, a clinical psy-chologist, or a community mental health agency. He will then have professional sources of guid-ance available when problems arise.

Finally, we can maintain a watchful, but not morbid, eye on ourselves. If we find that we are having difficulties which interfere with our work or with gratifying relationships with other people, then we should be wise enough to seek professional help.

Readings Suggested by the Author

Charles Brenner, *An Elementary Textbook of Psychoanalysis* (New York, International Universities Press, Inc., 1955).

O. Spurgeon English and G. H. J. Pearson, *Emotional Problems of Living* (New York, W. W. Norton & Company, Inc., 1955).

Anna Freud, *The Ego and the Mechanisms of Defense* (New York, International Univer-sities Press, Inc., 1946).

Calvin S. Hall, *A Primer of Freudian Psychology* (New York, The World Publishing Company, 1954).

Karl A. Menninger, *Man Against Himself* (New York, Harcourt, Brace & Co., 1938).

William C. Menninger and Harry Levinson, *Human Understanding in Industry* (Chicago, Science Research Associates, Inc., 1956).

Fritz Redlich and June Bingham, *The Inside Story* (New York, Alfred A. Knopf, Inc., 1953).

10

MANAGEMENT EVOLUTION
IN THE QUANTITATIVE WORLD

Robert F. Vandell

Foreword

Management has let two genies out of their bottles: one is quantitative analysis, the other electronic data processing. In combination, these constitute powerful servants—so powerful, in fact, that management must undergo some radical changes if it wants to master them fully. This article sketches the shape these changes will take and sets forth some guidelines man-agers can use in preparing themselves for an altered business environment. As the author points out, the evolution of management techniques is bound to suffer sharp discontinuities over the next decade unless the managers themselves make a concerted effort to understand what the roles of these servants ought to be.

"Electronic data processing is about to precipitate a management revolution." This prediction is neither new nor startling—if anything, this early promise of the computer sciences now seems overdue. In many companies the revolutionary impact that quantitative methods and EDP were expected to have are not yet clearly evident; and in a good many instances the glowing forecasts of a few years ago only emphasize how little real progress seems to have been made in this area to date.

This appearance is deceptive, however, because it overlooks the fact that a solid foundation has now been laid for some remarkably fast and profound changes in the years immediately ahead. Over the next 10 to 15 years, new-found opportunities for rapid quantitative analysis will shorten the decision-making cycle and increase the competitive demand for managerial excellence. As a consequence:

○ Capably managed companies will intensify the pace of competition by identifying more new opportunities for growth and improvement and implementing them faster and more effectively. Poorly managed firms will wither rapidly.

○ The executive will solve more problems, and more kinds of problems, with increasing speed and decreasing margin for error.

○ Top executives will learn to delegate authority more completely to front-line groups to assure a rapid corporate response to changes in the business environment.

These effects will be pervasive. They will profoundly affect top, middle, and front-line management in companies both large and small, whether manufacturers, wholesalers, retailers, or whoever. They will affect everyone concerned —production men, accountants, marketers, line and staff officers, and all their associates.

I believe these changes are coming fast. I shall try to explain why they have been so long delayed, and then sketch more specifically what these changes are likely to mean to the shape of corporate organization over both the short and long term. I think it is possible to reach some conclusions on how the businessman can prepare himself for the new roles he must fill in the future. Naturally, many of my ideas are speculative, and the passage of time is bound to prove some of them wrong. You will have to judge which you are willing to accept. My primary point is that dramatic changes are welling up fast, and we must begin to anticipate them now.

The pump is primed

No further technological breakthroughs are required to start the "revolution"—the computer technology and analytical techniques we possess as of this moment are adequate. Important advances are coming up in these fields—there is no doubt whatever of that—but they will merely kick the ball that is already beginning to roll down the hill. The main job now is to adapt this body of technology and techniques to fit particular circumstances and needs.

As analytical techniques become more adaptable and more accessible via the computer memory bank, management will be free to explore larger sets of alternatives under a wider variety of circumstances—in short, to simulate. These analyses will consider a larger number of factors (although never all factors) under more rigorous procedures. Analyses will be available promptly —in days, if not hours. The cost? A full set of analyses for a modestly complex problem can now be finished for a few hundred dollars, and this cost will shortly fall sharply. Let me describe an actual three-stage computer-programmed system used to evaluate acquisition prospects for a merger-minded organization:

The first stage crudely screens a candidate's history and then projects future growth rates, cash flows, capital requirements, earnings, ROI, and other quantities. The machine cost for one screening is $10; this provides all the printouts the company management needs to identify more likely prospects.

The second stage analyzes the promising candidates intensively. Management feeds in its own judgments about growth prospects, synergistic benefits, coordinating costs, cyclical risks, uncertainties, and other factors, and requests the computer to regenerate its projections. Management can ordinarily test out 15 to 20 different sets of assumptions about a candidate in one day's time, at a machine cost of $150.

The third stage permits management to test a variety of financing formulas to find the one that best meets the needs of the two parties. Factors of importance to both buyer and seller, such as earnings per share, income benefits, growth prospects, ROI, and risk implications, are measured under both normal and cyclic conditions. About 12 runs are necessary to identify the best compromise, and the machine time required is four hours, costing $80.

Several side benefits come from this acquisition-evaluation system. Management can use its time more efficiently by focusing quickly on the promising prospects and thus free itself to concentrate on making qualitative assessments and judgments. Significantly, the quantitative perspective available from two days' machine input multiplies by a hundredfold the information available to management to help it reach purchase decisions. Management is, in short, geared to move *faster* with *better perspective*.

There is no need to multiply examples. This one merely points up the fact that management can now analyze more alternatives more vigorously, much faster, and at lower cost than it could before. Other examples would easily show exponential increases in the speed and sophistication of forecasting, the amount and quality of data available, the cheapening cost of quantitative research, and the demand for quick executive response. Most of the problems that will be analyzable ten years hence can be solved efficiently today. As far as analytical techniques are concerned, only the "software gap" needs to be bridged before management can step into tomorrow's world.

The hardware is here

No spectacular breakthroughs are required in hardware, either. The salient point here is that the development of the remote-access terminal has made the decentralization of computer operations possible. Analysis can now be recoupled with action; an executive can now turn his swivel chair around, ask a complicated question through his personal console, and obtain a quick, comprehensive, current, and well-digested answer.

The costs of owning and operating a remote computer terminal should also fall sharply in the next few years. A teletype terminal can be purchased for much less than $1,000 today—soon it will be more compact, more versatile, and less expensive. It is only a matter of time before most key executives will want a computer terminal on their desk next to their phone, and operating time will soon cost only a few times what phone service does now.

Many specialists are projecting continued technical progress in computer equipment, although at a slower rate than in recent years. Within 10 to 15 years, it appears, this progress will bring costs of solving specific problems down to less than 10% of what they are now, using the most efficient present equipment—this equipment itself being about 1% as costly, decision for decision, as it was 15 years ago. These improvements will assuredly facilitate wider application in the immediate future, but the point remains that present equipment can *already* be applied economically to many decision areas. Shortages of reliable data are more of a handicap at this moment.

We know the limits

We took a great step forward when we began to grasp the theoretical limitations of the creativity of the computer. That limit is low, as this example makes clear:

□ Several men, working independently, have programmed computers to play chess "heuristically"; i.e., the computer is programmed to focus quickly on the more promising plays and retain a memory of its own mistakes—to learn from its own experience, as it were. The machine also observes the play of great chess masters and learns from it as well. It practices tirelessly. What are the results?

In one instance, at least, a computer has learned to play a pretty fair game of chess—it won a local tournament—but it is not good enough to beat its mentor with consistency. I suppose that this is not a bad record for a ten-year-old with an infinite life expectancy. But the computer's rate of learning has slowed ma-

terially. Furthermore, the brainchild is still operating at the subgenius level on a game board that is structured to restrict freedom and creativity. Compared with business, chess is a simple, constrained, unimaginative, albeit highly challenging game.

The point is that routine decisions can be handled by equipment—indeed, they already are—but true management tasks in the future will still be handled by men. Vision, creativity, intuitive heuristic skills, leadership, and so forth, will all be important in the future of management. The computer has realistically been redefined as a data *processor* that can at best assist effectively in the complex, but very human, business of making business decisions.

Why the delay?

Since the technology and hardware are comparatively well in hand, and since we now have a more accurate concept of the computer as a device of assistance, why, many ask, has the "revolution" not yet materialized? The reasons are simple, even obvious:

□ Manpower has been short. At the moment there are probably only 19,000 qualified men with a deep interest in management science who also have the professional competence to apply sophisticated operations research tools to business decisions of more than modest complexity. Of this number, perhaps only 20% are actually working in business; the balance are academically oriented or serve computer manufacturers.

Change is in the making, however. Shortly we shall be graduating 10,000 thoroughly trained operations research personnel a year, most of whom will go into business. The present shortage of technical specialists will turn into a surplus in the 1970's.

□ Executives have not yet been educated in the possibilities of computer applications. They must understand what a particular model can and cannot accomplish in a particular analytic situation. Equally important, management must appreciate what factors remain to be considered after an analytic perspective has been drawn together into a quantitative conclusion. Management has not prepared itself to use sophisticated analyses and therefore has not been able to form a solid estimate of their worth. Currently MBA students at leading schools are receiving thorough training in these applications; when they reach the business world, they will know how to use these tools effectively, and will want to employ them. Pressures for expanded use of the computer will grow from the bottom up, if not from the top down.

Most operations researchers have been trained to avoid suboptimization. They have consequently tended to work primarily on the grand scale, and hence have emphasized long-term, slow-developing projects. These initial efforts, naturally enough, often proved disappointing and ineffective in the end because scope was allowed to submerge value. Increasingly, however, management has learned to channel the operations-research technician's efforts toward short-term payoffs. Results have improved remarkably; and grander schemes have begun to evolve of themselves, easily and organically.

☐ Ready-made programs that a company can use directly in its decision making have been extremely scarce and insufficient, and the enormous cost of program development has inhibited in-house experimentation. Today, however, most larger computer manufacturers and service organizations are rapidly building libraries of such programs, as are leading companies in industry. While at first the programs in these libraries tend to be general-purpose, later they tend to be designed for solving specific problems. The cost of adapting available programs in existing libraries to the specific needs of corporations will be much lower in the future, and inventories of programs tailored to solve specific problems will be built more rapidly. Indeed, we expect that the programming task will be past its peak in leading companies by 1975.

☐ Upper level executives have shied away from personal involvement with the computer, largely because they have feared getting bogged down in the details of quantitative analysis and the computer sciences. As many are now learning, these are not real barriers at all.

An executive can be taught how to write programs and how to use a computer terminal effectively in less than three days. After this brief course, he can write programs, so far as his mathematical background allows him; more importantly, when his background begins to peter out, he knows how to call out more sophisticated programs created by others, including his own staff.

Hence, there are good reasons why companies have been adopting advanced techniques of quantitative analysis and employing computer programs for decision making at a slower pace than was once expected. There are also excellent reasons now to expect this pace to accelerate sharply. What will be the result?

Basic areas of change

In thinking about the future, it is important to distinguish between short-term and long-term developments. These differ markedly in character and scale, just as weather and climate differ. Management must prepare itself to deal with both kinds of trends, especially because short-term changes, if thoughtlessly made, can easily block the development of those postures that will be advantageous in the long run.

The quantitative revolution, like other revolutions, will involve two stages: a short-term setting-up period and a long-term operating period. During the setting-up phase, overhead costs rise sharply and technical specialists carry major responsibilities. Once into the operating phase, however, the pendulum will swing the other way: overhead costs will fall, and line personnel will bear the brunt of the work load. Because the work involved in the transition has been enormous and protracted, some executives are making the mistake of considering the present, long-continuing setting-up period to be the permanent condition. To the extent that they do this, they are undermining what competitive lead they may now possess.

The short-term changes will be the foundations for even more dramatic management upheavals that will commence before the decade of the 1970's has run its course. I can distinguish seven basic areas of change, both short-range and long-range, that will profoundly affect the manager.

Pace of decision making

The pace of decision making is now slowing down; it will shortly begin accelerating to a speed that will seem breathtaking by today's standards.

As management has come to understand more completely the factors at play in important decisions, they have taken more time to analyze and test the consequences of alternatives before acting. The pace of decision making consequently has slowed down. Introducing a new product, for example, takes much longer and requires more costly analysis today than it did a few years ago because sharpened competition has left less room for error.

Hand-drawn analyses, however, are already inefficient in the time they take and the quantity of reliable information they produce. The companies that begin to study the critical decision-making processes as a production process like any other, to increase efficiency and effectiveness by taking advantage of newly available technology, will gain a major competitive advantage. Thus not only will the quality of analysis increase, and costs fall, but decision making will take place faster. It has always been important to be first into the market with a new idea. Tomorrow, to be first will require sharply increased efficiency as well as effectiveness in decision making, and time scales may well be the most critical element.

Skill versus art

Analytical skill will continue to increase in importance; but the *art* of management will eventually reestablish its ascendancy.

At present, seat-of-the-pants, reactive managerial styles are already on the wane, and increased emphasis is being placed on "scientific" analysis and planning. Experience is still invaluable (if it is up to date), but it must be used with greater discipline. Analysis is now more rigorous, and computer techniques permit more alternatives to be analyzed in greater depth. But, most important, formal planning is being used as a basis for *action*, not merely for *pro forma* exercises. Ten years ago this sort of planning was a rarity.

A new plant investment provides an excellent example of formalized planning. Size, location, technological facts, risk, product mix, market promise, and other quantities are now analyzed rigorously and extensively in leading companies. Their methods of analysis, thanks to the computer, employ increasingly sophisticated techniques for measuring income potential, risk potential, and the like. Thus much more perspective on choices is available for decision making than was true a decade ago.

The pendulum is still swinging toward increased depth of analysis via computers; but in the second stage *art*, rather than scientific method, will reemerge as the most critical *management* skill. Strength in computer-related management techniques affords a competitive advantage to some companies now, but this advantage will be submerged as other companies adapt

their analytical systems to close the technical gap. Also, it will be easier and cheaper for these corporations to build their own systems and analytic procedures rapidly than it has been for the front runners.

Eventually, then, depth of experience will count for more, and the quality of experience will have been jacked up well above existing standards. Quick response to shades of difference emerging in the environment will pay big dividends, and the manager will have to be alert for the nuance in the data outputs available to him. Science will thus have laid the cornerstone for deeper, broader applications of managerial craftsmanship. With similarity of information and processes established, the value of sound judgment will be critical and determinative in tomorrow's sharper competition.

The availability of preprogrammed analyses in a wide variety of business areas will also afford executives more time to concentrate on qualitative subtleties of a situation and to develop effective implementation programs. Skill and judgment differentials in these areas—not the analytical formats—should increasingly distinguish successful from unsuccessful management teams.

Even at lower levels, data will still need to be interpreted in a situational context; and this will be the job of the man on the firing line. He will need more freedom to respond quickly to the emerging situation. The policies that guide and limit him must be more fluid, more in tune with the times. Middle management will have to carry a larger share of the burden of overseeing, of spotting the need for very swift strategic changes in product-program emphasis, of making these changes, and of keeping the trench ranks full and well motivated. Spans of control, in turn, will shrink as complexity rises.

Company size

Large corporate size will be helpful at first; then, in the second stage, economies of scale will diminish, and businesses that couple great size with a bureaucratic tendency will stand at a disadvantage.

Initially, that is, the costs of building effective program libraries and gathering and organizing useful analytic data will be enormous. Large companies are of course in a better position to swallow costs of this magnitude. Also, the cost of building an analytic model that can solve similar problems in a variety of circumstances is not substantially higher than that for programming for a single specific application. The large company will be in a position to surge ahead of its smaller competitors as the result of its depth and breadth of analytic competence.

Subsequently, in the second stage, the easy availability of low-cost, computer-based analyses will multiply the power of small, mobile, line-oriented managements disproportionately, therewith neutralizing some of the advantages of "staff depth" enjoyed by today's industrial powerhouses.

It is also significant that continuing market segmentation and localization will splinter the mass-marketing and production capabilities of many of the larger companies and make economies of scale more difficult to achieve. Efforts at market segmentation are already growing as companies seek to appeal to the increasingly discriminating tastes of smaller consumer groups. These efforts are constrained by the limitations of currently existing distribution systems, but these familiar constraints may not apply in tomorrow's world.

Consider shelf space, for example: tomorrow the consumer may be making more of his routine purchasing decisions on a computer console in his home; he may even be using such a console for comparison shopping. Traditional retail display and inventory facilities may lose a good deal of their importance under such conditions.

If the consumer continues to become more discriminating, if he seeks out more information on product characteristics, prices, and so forth, and has convenient and suitable tools at hand for doing so, many economies of scale that exist in marketing today may be undermined. Many small companies today carve out market niches that are too small or too mundane to appeal to the big boys. There will be even more niches of this kind in tomorrow's world.

Again, no matter how consumer shopping patterns are changed by the home computer console, information on sales is likely to be available before deliveries are made. Data will be available not only by product and territory, but also by class of consumer. Trends will be apparent sooner, and quicker actions will be required to capitalize on them or to arrest declines. The company geared to move quickly at the local product-market level should have a great advantage.

At the same time, planning costs will fall markedly. Companies with limited product lines and sales volumes may be able to afford information and forecasting systems that are just as good as their larger rivals'. As smaller managements focus on analyzing fewer products and markets, they will be able to respond faster than their larger rivals (at least where technological barriers are low).

In the large corporation, the key to future competitive success will be to shift responsibility downward without losing control. Key local decision makers—encumbered by long lines of communication, procedural burdens, and inflexible policy—will lumber with the grace of the tortoise in the age of the cheetah. Highly maneuverable companies will be poised to compete effectively for niches; a large company must therefore rejoin tactical know-how with enterprise, and fashion controls that permit freedom and entrepreneurial motivation to flourish at the lower organizational levels.

Strategy & tactics

Marketing mobility will be a crucial strategy in the immediate future; in the longer run, tactical and contingency planning will increase in importance until they match or overshadow it.

Companies that have technological or market muscle are redefining and diversifying their product-market specializations to cover a broader array of products and markets. Entry into promising new market areas has become increasingly competitive and is now dominated by larger companies. Old industrial sectors such as distribution, recreation, retailing, labor-saving equipment, and housing are being revitalized by the entry of strong, new competitors. The more successful of these diversification moves have usually involved centralized strategy carried out by managements strong both in decision-making know-how and in systematic control and planning techniques.

Subsequently, in the second stage, tactical and contingency planning will blossom in importance. Although strategic planning will still remain vital, the companies best geared to implement their programs under a variety of subtly different circumstances will have the edge. Marketing programs will have to be more flexible; corrective response to the consequences of ill-conceived assumptions will have to be quicker, and will afford smaller margins for error; and all planning, in short, will have to be geared for rapid change—change that may differ markedly from one market locale to another.

By that time, also, forecasting will be more sophisticated and comprehensive. In election forecasting, for example, computers employ direct sampling techniques to predict results. By drawing data from early-return and bellwether precincts, they produce reliable predictions fast. In the future, these same forecasting techniques will be widely used in industry to predict such quantities as market demand by product and territory.

However, the reliability of forecasts will be more short-lived. Businessmen will pore over these forecasts to identify new opportunities for enhancing their competitive position and to mobilize for quick pointed thrusts. This reaction should affect the action. The pace of change will increase exponentially, and forecasts will be less prescient over the long run. Skills in reading forecasts perceptively and in anticipating competitive reactions will be more vital. As a consequence, the character of competition should become more intense, more local, and faster moving. Tactical adaptation will prove critical.

Changing roles of staff

Central staff activities will mushroom at first, as will staff size; then central staff positions will decrease in number, but the demands on staff creativity will be higher.

To be successful in the immediate future, a company must build distinctive quantitative competencies in a broadening number of managerial areas. This condition of success, coupled with the greater competitive need for analytical depth in reaching strategic and tactical decisions, will naturally advance the cause of the staff specialist. Management is also in a transition period in terms of its ability to cope with the exponentially increasing amounts of data it is attempting to use to control operations and plan changes. Similarly, increasing scale and diversity of operations of many companies has increased the need for synthesis and summary. Staffs have been expanded, and will continue to be expanded, to deal with these problems.

Ultimately, however, staff support will be smaller in quantity but more creative. Specialist knowledge will be stored in computer banks, as will specific analytical procedures. However, the task of effectively drawing on these stored resources will demand more from the creative energies of the specialist. He will have more problems to handle rigorously and less time to get the job done; he will have to be more sensi-

tive to situational peculiarities, and be more incisive, if not decisive. Organization of effort toward payout, not multiplication of organizational slots, will be the real keystone to effective decision making, and thus the company that is burdened by unwieldy staff will be severely handicapped on the fast-moving treadmill of change.

Experimental research, for example, will become cheaper and richer in insights as time goes by. Data collection costs today make test marketing and other experimental programs expensive. As a result, only limited features of a marketing program can be pretested. Striking an ideal balance between packaging, promotion, pricing, message selection, media selection, and budget size is still an expensive trial-and-error process. The greater availability of low-cost information on a large number of local markets should make experimentation much less expensive and time-consuming in the future.

Two results should come from this. The first is a more accurate understanding of certain economic parameters, such as the impact of advertising on sales volume. However, competitors will learn about these economic characteristics just as readily. Imagination and daring—in short, qualitative skills—in designing marketing programs will again be the critical ingredient of success. Emphasis will shift from analysis to action, where the quality of analysis will be superior.

Second, experimental analysis will be able to penetrate further into the planning, research, production, finance, and distribution areas. But once the effective techniques of exploration are common knowledge and low in cost, differences in achievement will depend more closely on the perception with which these tools are used. Staff will have to be much more than technical specialists; they will have to be experienced *judges* of changing business realities. In this sense, the staff will move closer to the line.

Front-line management

Front-line management ranks will thin at first; then they will grow again and absorb new functions, many of them from staff areas.

Many historic factory and marketing-management jobs involve a considerable amount of routine. These routines have been important and have required the formulation and discriminating application of good rules of thumb. In several areas, such as forecasting, production

scheduling, and inventory management, routines can be and already have been reduced systematically to mathematical programs capable of performing substantially all the analytical steps required for decisions. The main task of front-line managers is accordingly being reduced to dealing with exceptions born of special situations. Line-management economies are the direct result.

In the long run the need for more and better trained front-line managers will grow, however, and their functions will change. There will be more products and more markets, each subtly different, for each product. The data available on these local markets will be voluminous and current, and decisions on how to adapt marketing programs to suit special local, transient conditions will be necessary to success. Local marketing managers—a rarity today—will need more freedom to capitalize on momentary lapses of competitors, to respond to changes in their tactics, and to take full advantage of the immediacy of information. With conceptual thinking embodied in the information flows, situational thinking will be at a premium, and demands for quick response at relatively low levels will increase. Good strategies will fail, in other words, if they are not supplemented by effective tactical decision-making capacities at all organization levels. Organizations of the future must consequently realign themselves for action, not for staff analysis.

The increase in tactical flexibilities and pressures will increase the danger of mistimed or inappropriate action; it will be easier to make a blunder. A thoughtful, insightful awareness of situational particulars will therefore be necessary to minimize the risk of action failure, and hence skill in dealing wisely with contextual perspective will be more critical. Line specialization, in other words, will grow. Organizations of the future will need executives who are both skilled and experienced in the art of line management, and these men will need much of the background we today associate with staff specialization to function with real effectiveness. The problems of readjusting an organization of today to these circumstances are clearly staggering.

Executive mobility

Executive mobility will increase at first, and then decline.

Competent managers are increasingly being

called on to shift from one operation to another one that is dramatically different in character. Young men with high potential, particularly, are skyrocketing up the organizational ladder. Any individual with unusual skills in administrative leadership and unusual savvy in solving problems systematically tends to be mobile today. Immediate experience, in contrast, counts for less, as do company loyalty and job security. In general, the fluidity of management has been accented by shortages in top-grade talent. In the years immediately ahead, executive mobility should continue to increase, provided, of course, our economy remains dynamic and expanding.

Eventually, however, the "man for all seasons" will find it hard to compete with the typical manager of tomorrow, for this manager will be a man who has both breadth of training and depth of experience in a semi-specialized niche. A new job will require a man to master more material and allow him less time to adapt to its special conditions before it exerts pressure on him to take decisive action. Competition will be poised to take devastating advantage of the strong man in his weakest moments.

Even at top-management levels, the problems of coordinating the rapid tactical changes taking place in numerous market areas will require deeper appreciation of the subtleties of the situation. One of top management's major roles will be to manage decision makers lower down—decision makers who, like themselves, must necessarily operate on reduced time scales under highly intense and diverse pressures. This role will involve top management heavily in day-to-day control activities in addition to its present common functions of leading and developing men. Increasingly, it will need to understand all the phases of the work it oversees with enough depth and richness to assure itself that each man on the team is functioning at first-rate efficiency despite the rapidly shifting loci of challenge to which he must respond.

Changing skill requirements

The business world of tomorrow will have all the fluidity of military maneuvers. Strategy will be important, but success will depend chiefly on the ability to initiate tactical decisions in the field. More of the "hows" will have to be delegated to allow unit commanders to deal with the unique and fast-changing characteristics of local positions. As circumstances change in the field, strategies will have to be quickly revised and unit missions will have to be redefined and recoordinated.

This very fluidity will increase uncertainty, nothwithstanding the availability of increasingly comprehensive intelligence. Using the available intelligence promptly and wisely will be absolutely critical. Logistic support will also have to be made more flexible and be more thoroughly planned. What does all this imply about the management skills required in the long-range view? Here are my answers:

☐ Decisiveness will be at a premium.

☐ Decision making will require more courage. The decision maker at every level will stand increasingly on his own; his performance will be measured more extensively; and he will be held more accountable. Yet he will have to perform more tasks within narrower time spans under tougher competitive conditions, and the consequences of error will be much greater and more apparent than ever before.

☐ Decisions will have to be more finely tuned to realities. Skillful decision making will require a deeper appreciation of the intangibles of a situation as these change rapidly. An intensive, intuitive feel for the concrete realities of a situation, for the *context* of the data he is using to make his decisions, will be an immensely valuable asset.

☐ Skill in solving ill-structured problems will grow in importance. While computer analyses will take the routine out of decision making, the burden of recognizing and coping with the non-routine will remain. An executive will have to recognize data shortfalls for what they are; and, when under pressure of time, he will have to know how to call out additional informational perspective from his computer facilities or how to develop them from environmental sources.

☐ Decisions will require more flair and imagination. As the qualitative aspects of decision making loom larger, the value of the stylistic nuance will increase. Given technical competence, the quality of a man's flair will determine his competitive edge.

☐ Skills used in implementing decisions will increase in importance. Reaching a decision is one thing; putting it into effect is quite another. As the proportion of line executives and activities in an organization grows, as it almost certainly will in the long run, more managers must be capable of doing both.

☐ As the diversity of line activities grows, and channels of communication and coordination increase, the demands for effective leadership at the top will be proportionately greater.

Demands on managers

A sophisticated analytical tool does not in itself guarantee a valuable and sophisticated analysis. The manager must clearly know enough to judge confidently whether (a) he is using the tool that is really appropriate to the problem at hand, and (b) it is giving him the right information for making his decisions and for further information processing. Executives do not now commonly have the ability to recognize the right tool or the right data when they see them. Yet they *must* be able to do so if they are to do more than generate elegant nonsense. This is truly a management responsibility; the mere existence of a large operations research department does not ensure that the manager has a proper base on which to take action.

As I have already implied, this does not mean that the manager must become a mathematician. He must, however, learn what the various quantitative tools are designed to do and what the limits of their capabilities are. He must be able to understand what the staff specialist is attempting to achieve by a particular analysis, and to discuss the appropriateness of alternative procedures sensibly. He must fully understand the variables a model will and will not consider, and be able to evaluate whether the relationships among variables are sensible. The executive cannot use an analytical tool wisely unless he fully comprehends what the assumptions are, what the analysis achieves, and how its conclusions are to be adapted to changing circumstances and intangible considerations.

Further, quantitative methods impose a discipline that may at first be troublesome. Problems must be defined exactly and reduced to a conceptual framework. The relevant factors must be clearly identified, and assumptions about how each bears on the ultimate decision must be described independently and with recognition of interacting characteristics. Data must be selected to test out theories. Management has been performing these activities for years, of course, but to articulate them rigorously is a new demand. All this involves a more thorough understanding of *operations*, not of mathematics.

The executive must develop his ability to spot patterns in data outputs that suggest hypotheses worthy of his further exploration. If he attempts to reduce his decision making to a mere routine mechanically based on computer output, he will miss the very patterns that will forewarn him of changes which it is his function to exploit. Indeed, he will be handing competitors an edge.

It is also necessary that management develop skill in communicating with the operations-research specialist. This is an old problem with a new twist. Businessmen and lawyers, for example, tend to think about common problems with different thought processes and from contrasting frames of reference; yet they still manage to discuss matters to mutual advantage. The concepts of operations research can be made just as comprehensible to the businessman as those of the law.

These quantitative demands sound imposing to the uninitiated, but they are not. Some university programs provide men of low mathematical aptitude with the necessary foundation in approximately 50 classroom sessions. It is the nonquantitative, interpretive skills, actually, that are difficult to develop in adequate measure. In this sense, the quantitative revolution, as it affects executives, will raise old, familiar strengths to a higher plane by virtue of the new muscles developed in the process of transition.

Final note

The quantitative revolution is already under way in some leading companies. Its first fruits are beginning to exert broader effects on competition that will force other companies to adopt the new methods rapidly.

The main difference between the increasing pressure from the quantitative areas and other forces for change lies in the magnitude and pervasiveness of its impact. It will affect every facet of business organization. No executive can afford to ignore the new demands it will make on management and still expect to be successful beyond the next five to ten years. These demands, I believe, will prove personally more onerous to many executives than they have any reason to expect from their past experience.

The companies that will survive and prosper will be the ones whose managers have mastered the techniques of generating and using perceptively the information that can be provided by data banks. A craftsman by definition intimately understands the tools he has at his command; this will surely be true for the masters of the art of decision making in tomorrow's fast-paced business world.

MOTIVATION FOR GROWTH

11

PYGMALION IN MANAGEMENT

J. Sterling Livingston

Foreword

Pygmalion was a sculptor in Greek mythology who carved a statue of a beautiful woman that subsequently was brought to life. George Bernard Shaw's play, *Pygmalion* (the basis for the musical hit, "My Fair Lady"), has a somewhat similar theme; the essence is that one person, by his effort and will, can transform another person. And in the world of management, many executives play Pygmalion-like roles in developing able subordinates and in stimulating their performance. What is the secret of their success? How

are they different from managers who fail to develop top-notch subordinates? And what are the implications of all this for the problem of excessive turnover and disillusionment among talented young people in business? Such are the questions discussed here. The title of the article was inspired by *Pygmalion in the Classroom*, a book by Professor Robert Rosenthal and Lenore Jacobson that describes the effect of expectations on the intellectual development of children.

I n George Bernard Shaw's *Pygmalion*, Eliza Doolittle explains:

"You see, really and truly, apart from the things anyone can pick up (the dressing and the proper way of speaking, and so on), the difference between a lady and a flower girl is not how she behaves, but how she's treated. I shall always be a flower girl to Professor Higgins, because he always treats me as a flower girl, and always will; but I know I can be a lady to you, because you always treat me as a lady, and always will."

Some managers always treat their subordinates in a way that leads to superior performance. But most managers, like Professor Higgins, unintentionally treat their subordinates in a way that leads to lower performance than they are

capable of achieving. The way managers treat their subordinates is subtly influenced by what they expect of them. If a manager's expectations are high, productivity is likely to be excellent. If his expectations are low, productivity is likely to be poor. It is as though there were a law that caused a subordinate's performance to rise or fall to meet his manager's expectations.

The powerful influence of one person's expectations on another's behavior has long been recognized by physicians and behavioral scientists and, more recently, by teachers. But heretofore the importance of managerial expectations for individual and group performance has not been widely understood. I have documented

Author's note: This article is a condensation of my forthcoming book, *High Expectations in Management*, to be published by the Sterling Institute Press.

this phenomenon in a number of case studies prepared during the past decade for major industrial concerns. These cases and other evidence available from scientific research now reveal:

○ What a manager expects of his subordinates and the way he treats them largely determine their performance and career progress.

○ A unique characteristic of superior managers is their ability to create high performance expectations that subordinates fulfill.

○ Less effective managers fail to develop similar expectations, and, as a consequence, the productivity of their subordinates suffers.

○ Subordinates, more often than not, appear to do what they believe they are expected to do.

Impact on productivity

One of the most comprehensive illustrations of the effect of managerial expectations on productivity is recorded in studies of the organizational experiment undertaken in 1961 by Alfred Oberlander, manager of the Rockaway District Office of the Metropolitan Life Insurance Company.[1] He had observed that outstanding insurance agencies grew faster than average or poor agencies and that new insurance agents performed better in outstanding agencies than in average or poor agencies, regardless of their sales aptitude. He decided, therefore, to group his superior men in one unit to stimulate their performance and to provide a challenging environment in which to introduce new salesmen.

Accordingly, Oberlander assigned his six best agents to work with his best assistant manager, an equal number of average producers to work with an average assistant manager, and the remaining low producers to work with the least able manager. He then asked the superior group to produce two thirds of the premium volume achieved by the entire agency the previous year. He described the results as follows:

"Shortly after this selection had been made, the men in the agency began referring to this select group as a 'super-staff' since, due to the fact that we were operating this group as a unit, their esprit de corps was very high. Their production efforts over the first 12 weeks far surpassed our most optimistic expectations . . . proving that groups of men of sound ability can be motivated beyond their apparently normal productive capacities when the problems created by the poor producer are eliminated from the operation.

"Thanks to this fine result, over-all agency performance improved 40 percent and stayed at this figure.

"In the beginning of 1962 when, through expansion, we appointed another assistant manager and assigned him a staff, we again utilized this same concept, arranging the men once more according to their productive capacity.

"The assistant managers were assigned . . . according to their ability, with the most capable assistant manager receiving the best group, thus playing strength to strength. Our agency over-all production again improved by about 25-30 percent, and so this staff arrangement was continued until the end of the year.

"Now in this year of 1963, we found upon analysis that there were so many men . . . with a potential of half a million dollars or more that only one staff remained of those men in the agency who were not considered to have any chance of reaching the half-million-dollar mark."[2]

Although the productivity of the "super-staff" improved dramatically, it should be pointed out that the productivity of men in the lowest unit, "who were not considered to have any chance of reaching the half-million-dollar mark," actually declined and that attrition among these men increased. The performance of the superior men rose to meet their managers' expectations, while that of the weaker men declined as predicted.

Self-fulfilling prophesies

However, the "average" unit proved to be an anomaly. Although the district manager expected only average performance from this group, its productivity increased significantly. This was because the assistant manager in charge of the group refused to believe that he was less capable than the manager of the "super-staff" or that the agents in the top group had any greater ability than the agents in his group. He insisted in discussions with his agents that every man in the middle group had greater potential than the men in the "super-staff," lacking only their years of experience in selling insurance. He stimulated his agents to accept the challenge of outperforming the "super-staff." As a result, in each year the middle group increased its productivity

1. See "Jamesville Branch Office (A)," MET003A, and "Jamesville Branch Office (B)," MET003B (Boston, Sterling Institute, 1969).

2. "Jamesville Branch Office (B)," p. 2.

by a higher percentage than the "super-staff" did (although it never attained the dollar volume of the top group).

It is of special interest that the self-image of the manager of the "average" unit did not permit him to accept others' treatment of him as an "average" manager, just as Eliza Doolittle's image of herself as a lady did not permit her to accept others' treatment of her as a flower girl. The assistant manager transmitted his own strong feelings of efficacy to his agents, created mutual expectancy of high performance, and greatly stimulated productivity.

Comparable results occurred when a similar experiment was made at another office of the company. Further confirmation comes from a study of the early managerial success of 49 college graduates who were management-level employees of an operating company of the American Telephone and Telegraph Company. David E. Berlew and Douglas T. Hall of the Massachusetts Institute of Technology examined the career progress of these managers over a period of five years and discovered that their relative success, as measured by salary increases and the company's estimate of each man's performance and potential, depended largely on the company's expectations of them.[3]

The influence of one person's expectations on another's behavior is by no means a business discovery. More than half a century ago, Albert Moll concluded from his clinical experience that subjects behaved as they believed they were expected to.[4] The phenomenon he observed, in which "the prophecy causes its own fulfillment," has recently become a subject of considerable scientific interest. For example:

☐ In a series of scientific experiments, Robert Rosenthal of Harvard University has demonstrated that a "teacher's expectation for her pupils' intellectual competence can come to serve as an educational self-fulfilling prophecy."[5]

☐ An experiment in a summer Headstart program for 60 preschoolers compared the performance of pupils under (a) teachers who had been led to expect relatively slow learning by their children, and (b) teachers who had been led to believe their children had excellent intellectual ability and learning capacity. Pupils of the second group of teachers learned much faster.[6]

Moreover, the healing professions have long recognized that a physician's or psychiatrist's expectations can have a formidable influence on a patient's physical or mental health. What takes place in the minds of the patients and the healers, particularly when they have congruent expectations, may determine the outcome. For instance, the havoc of a doctor's pessimistic prognosis has often been observed. Again, it is well known that the efficacy of a new drug or a new treatment can be greatly influenced by the physician's expectations—a result referred to by the medical profession as a "placebo effect."

Pattern of failure

When salesmen are treated by their managers as supersalesmen, as the "super-staff" was at Metropolitan Rockaway District Office, they try to live up to that image and do what they know supersalesmen are expected to do. But when salesmen with poor productivity records are treated by their managers as *not* having "any chance" of success, as the low producers at Rockaway were, this negative expectation also becomes a managerial self-fulfilling prophecy.

Unsuccessful salesmen have great difficulty maintaining their self-image and self-esteem. In response to low managerial expectations, they typically attempt to prevent additional damage to their egos by avoiding situations that might lead to greater failure. They either reduce the number of sales calls they make or avoid trying to "close" sales when that might result in further painful rejection, or both. Low expectations and damaged egos lead them to behave in a manner that increases the probability of failure, thereby fulfilling their managers' expectations. Let me illustrate:

☐ Not long ago I studied the effectiveness of branch bank managers at a West Coast bank with over 500 branches. The managers who had had their lending authority reduced because of high rates of loss became progressively less effective. To prevent further loss of authority, they turned to making only "safe" loans. This action resulted in losses of business to competing banks and a relative decline in both deposits and profits at their branches. Then, to reverse that decline in deposits and earnings, they often "reached" for loans and became almost irrational in their acceptance of questionable credit risks. Their actions were not so much a matter

3. "Some Determinants of Early Managerial Success," Alfred P. Sloan School of Management Organization Research Program #81-64 (Cambridge, Massachusetts Institute of Technology, 1964), pp. 13-14.

4. Robert Rosenthal and Lenore Jacobson, *Pygmalion in the Classroom* (New York, Holt, Rinehart, and Winston, Inc., 1968), p. 11.

5. Ibid., Preface, p. vii.

6. Ibid., p. 38.

of poor judgment as an expression of their willingness to take desperate risks in the hope of being able to avoid further damage to their egos and to their careers.

Thus, in response to the low expectations of their supervisors, who had reduced their lending authority, they behaved in a manner that led to larger credit losses. They appeared to do what they believed they were expected to do, and their supervisors' expectations became self-fulfilling prophecies.

Power of expectations

Managers cannot avoid the depressing cycle of events that flow from low expectations merely by hiding their feelings from subordinates. If a manager believes a subordinate will perform poorly, it is virtually impossible for him to mask his expectations, because the message usually is communicated unintentionally, without conscious action on his part.

Indeed, a manager often communicates most when he believes he is communicating least. For instance, when he says nothing, when he becomes "cold" and "uncommunicative," it usually is a sign that he is displeased by a subordinate or believes he is "hopeless." The silent treatment communicates negative feelings even more effectively, at times, than a tongue-lashing does. What seems to be critical in the communication of expectations is not what the boss says, so much as the *way he behaves*. Indifferent and noncommittal treatment, more often than not, is the kind of treatment that communicates low expectations and leads to poor performance.

Common illusions

Managers are more effective in communicating low expectations to their subordinates than in communicating high expectations to them, even though most managers believe exactly the opposite. It usually is astonishingly difficult for them to recognize the clarity with which they transmit negative feelings to subordinates. To illustrate again:

☐ The Rockaway district manager vigorously denied that he had communicated low expectations to the men in the poorest group who, he believed, did not have "any chance" of becoming high producers. Yet the message was clearly received by those men. A typical case was that of an agent who resigned from the low unit.

When the district manager told the agent that he was sorry he was leaving, the agent replied, "No, you're not; you're glad." Although the district manager previously had said nothing to the man, he had unintentionally communicated his low expectations to his agents through his indifferent manner. Subsequently, the men who were assigned to the lowest unit interpreted the assignment as equivalent to a request for their resignation.

☐ One of the company's agency managers established superior, average, and low units, even though he was convinced that he had no superior or outstanding subordinates. "All my assistant managers and agents are either average or incompetent," he explained to the Rockaway district manager. Although he tried to duplicate the Rockaway results, his low opinions of his men were communicated—not so subtly—to them. As a result, the experiment failed.

Positive feelings, on the other hand, often do not come through clearly enough. For example:

☐ Another insurance agency manager copied the organizational changes made at the Rockaway District Office, grouping the salesmen he rated highly with the best manager, the average salesmen with an average manager, and so on. However, improvement did not result from the move. The Rockaway district manager therefore investigated the situation. He discovered that the assistant manager in charge of the high-performance unit was unaware that his manager considered him to be the best. In fact, he and the other agents doubted that the agency manager really believed there was any difference in their abilities. This agency manager was a stolid, phlegmatic, unemotional man who treated his men in a rather pedestrian way. Since high expectations had not been communicated to the men, they did not understand the reason for the new organization and could not see any point in it. Clearly, the way a manager *treats* his subordinates, not the way he organizes them, is the key to high expectations and high productivity.

Impossible dreams

Managerial expectations must pass the test of reality before they can be translated into performance. To become self-fulfilling prophecies, expectations must be made of sterner stuff than the power of positive thinking or generalized confidence in one's fellow men—helpful as these concepts may be for some other purposes. Subordinates will not be motivated to reach high levels of productivity unless they consider the boss's high expectations realistic and achievable. If they are encouraged to strive for unattainable goals, they eventually give up trying and settle for results that are lower than they are capable of achieving. The experience of a large electrical manufacturing company demonstrates this; the company discovered that production actually declined if production quotas were set too high, because the workers simply stopped trying to meet them. In other words, the practice of "dangling the carrot just beyond the donkey's reach," endorsed by many managers, is not a good motivational device.

Scientific research by David C. McClelland of Harvard University and John W. Atkinson of the University of Michigan[7] has demonstrated that the relationship of motivation to expectancy varies in the form of a bell-shaped curve, like this:

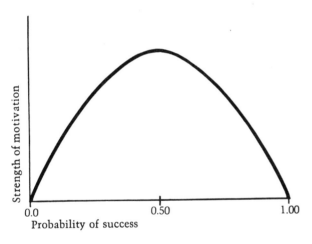

The degree of motivation and effort rises until the expectancy of success reaches 50%, then begins to fall even though the expectancy of success continues to increase. No motivation or response is aroused when the goal is perceived as being either virtually certain or virtually impossible to attain.

Moreover, as Berlew and Hall have pointed out, if a subordinate fails to meet performance expectations that are close to his own level of aspirations, he will "lower his personal performance goals and standards, his . . . performance will tend to drop off, and he will develop nega-

tive attitudes toward the task activity or job."[8] It is therefore not surprising that failure of subordinates to meet the unrealistically high expectations of their managers leads to high rates of attrition; such attrition may be voluntary or involuntary.

Secret of superiority

Something takes place in the minds of superior managers that does not occur in the minds of those who are less effective. While superior managers are consistently able to create high performance expectations that their subordinates fulfill, weaker managers are not successful in obtaining a similar response. What accounts for the difference?

The answer, in part, seems to be that superior managers have greater confidence than other managers in their own ability to develop the talents of their subordinates. Contrary to what might be assumed, the high expectations of superior managers are based primarily on what they think about themselves—about their own ability to select, train, and motivate their subordinates. What the manager believes about himself subtly influences what he believes about his subordinates, what he expects of them, and how he treats them. If he has confidence in his ability to develop and stimulate them to high levels of performance, he will expect much of them and will treat them with confidence that his expectations will be met. But if he has doubts about his ability to stimulate them, he will expect less of them and will treat them with less confidence.

Stated in another way, the superior manager's record of success and his confidence in his ability give his high expectations credibility. As a consequence, his subordinates accept his expectations as realistic and try hard to achieve them.

The importance of what a manager believes about his training and motivational ability is illustrated by "Sweeney's Miracle,"[9] a managerial and educational self-fulfilling prophecy:

☐ James Sweeney taught industrial management and psychiatry at Tulane University, and he also was responsible for the operation of the Biomedical Computer Center there. Sweeney believed that he could teach even a poorly educated man to be a capable computer operator. George Johnson, a black man who was a former hospital porter, became janitor at the computer center; he was chosen by Sweeney to prove his conviction. In the morning, George Johnson

7. See John W. Atkinson, "Motivational Determinants of Risk-Taking Behavior," *Psychological Review*, Vol. 64, No. 6, 1957, p. 365.

8. David E. Berlew and Douglas T. Hall, "The Socialization of Managers: Effects of Expectations on Performance," *Administrative Science Quarterly*, September 1966, p. 208.

9. See Robert Rosenthal and Lenore Jacobson, op. cit., pp. 3-4.

performed his janitorial duties, and in the afternoon Sweeney taught him about computers.

Johnson was learning a great deal about computers when someone at the university concluded that, to be a computer operator, one had to have a certain I.Q. score. Johnson was tested, and his I.Q. indicated that he would not be able to learn to type, much less operate a computer.

But Sweeney was not convinced. He threatened to quit unless Johnson was permitted to learn to program and operate the computer. Sweeney prevailed, and he is still running the computer center. Johnson is now in charge of the main computer room and is responsible for training new employees to program and operate the computer.

Sweeney's expectations were based on what he believed about his own teaching ability, not on Johnson's learning credentials. What a manager believes about his ability to train and motivate subordinates clearly is the foundation on which realistically high managerial expectations are built.

The critical early years

Managerial expectations have their most magical influence on young men. As subordinates mature and gain experience, their self-image gradually hardens, and they begin to see themselves as their career records imply. Their own aspirations, and the expectations of their superiors, become increasingly controlled by the "reality" of their past performance. It becomes more and more difficult for them, and for their managers, to generate mutually high expectations unless they have outstanding records.

Incidentally, the same pattern occurs in school. Rosenthal's experiments with educational self-fulfilling prophecies consistently demonstrate that teachers' expectations are more effective in influencing intellectual growth in younger children than in older children. In the lower grade levels, particularly in the first and second grades, the effects of teachers' expectations are dramatic.[10] In the upper grade levels, teachers' prophecies seem to have little effect on a child's intellectual growth, although they do affect his motivation and attitude toward school. While the declining influence of teachers' expectations cannot be completely explained, it is reasonable to conclude that younger children are more malleable, have fewer fixed notions about their abilities, and have less well-established reputations in the schools. As they grow, particularly if they are assigned to "tracks" on the basis of their records, as is now often done in public schools, their beliefs about their intellectual ability and their teachers' expectations of them begin to harden and become more resistant to influence by others.

Key to future performance

The early years in a business organization, when a young man can be strongly influenced by managerial expectations, are critical in determining his future performance and career progress. This is shown by a study at American Telephone and Telegraph Company:

☐ Berlew and Hall found that what the company initially expected of 49 college graduates who were management-level employees was the most critical factor in their subsequent performance and success. The researchers concluded: "The .72 correlation between how much a company expects of a man in his first year and how much he contributes during the next five years is too compelling to be ignored."[11]

Subsequently, the two men studied the career records of 18 college graduates who were hired as management trainees in another of the American Telephone and Telegraph Company's operating companies. Again they found that both expectations and performance in the first year correlated consistently with later performance and success.[12]

Berlew and Hall summarized their research by stating:

"Something important is happening in the first year.... Meeting high company expectations in the critical first year leads to the internalization of positive job attitudes and high standards; these attitudes and standards, in turn, would first lead to and be reinforced by strong performance and success in later years. It should also follow that a new manager who meets the challenge of one highly demanding job will be given subsequently a more demanding job, and his level of contribution will rise as he responds to the company's growing expectations of him. The key ... is the concept of the first year as a *critical period for learning*, a time when the trainee is uniquely ready to develop

10. Ibid., pp. 74-81.

11. "Some Determinants of Early Managerial Success," pp. 13-14.

12. "The Socialization of Managers: Effects of Expectations on Performance," p. 219.

or change in the direction of the company's expectations." [13]

Most influential boss

A young man's first manager is likely to be the most influential person in his career. If this manager is unable or unwilling to develop the skills the young man needs to perform effectively, the latter will set lower standards for himself than he is capable of achieving, his self-image will be impaired, and he will develop negative attitudes toward his job, his employer, and—in all probability—his career in business. Since his chances of building a successful career with his employer will decline rapidly, he will leave, if he has high aspirations, in hope of finding a better opportunity. If, on the other hand, his manager helps him achieve his maximum potential, he will build the foundation for a successful career. To illustrate:

☐ With few exceptions, the most effective branch managers at a large West Coast bank were mature men in their forties and fifties. The bank's executives explained that it took considerable time for a man to gain the knowledge, experience, and judgment required to handle properly credit risks, customer relations, and employee relations.

However, one branch manager, ranked in the top 10% of the managers in terms of effectiveness (which included branch profit growth, deposit growth, scores on administrative audits, and subjective rankings by superiors), was only 27 years old. This young man had been made a branch manager at 25, and in two years he not only improved the performance of his branch substantially but also developed his younger assistant manager so that he, in turn, was made a branch manager at 25.

The man had had only average grades in college, but, in his first four years at the bank, he had been assigned to work with two branch managers who were remarkably effective teachers. His first boss, who was recognized throughout the bank for his unusual skill in developing young men, did not believe that it took years to gain the knowledge and skill needed to become an effective banker. After two years, the young man was made assistant manager at a branch

headed by another executive, who also was an effective developer of his subordinates. Thus it was that when the young man was promoted to head a branch, he confidently followed the model of his two previous superiors in operating his branch, quickly established a record of outstanding performance, and trained his assistant (as he had been trained) to assume responsibility early.

Contrasting records: For confirming evidence of the crucial role played by a person's first bosses, let us turn to selling, since performance in this area is more easily measured than in most managerial areas. Consider the following investigations:

☐ In a study of the careers of 100 insurance salesmen who began work with either highly competent or less-than-competent agency managers, the Life Insurance Agency Management Association found that men with average sales aptitude test scores were nearly five times as likely to succeed under managers with good performance records as under managers with poor records; and men with superior sales aptitude scores were found to be twice as likely to succeed under high-performing managers as under low-performing managers. [14]

☐ The Metropolitan Life Insurance Company determined in 1960 that differences in the productivity of new insurance agents who had equal sales aptitudes could be accounted for only by differences in the ability of managers in the offices to which they were assigned. Men whose productivity was high in relation to their aptitude test scores invariably were employed in offices that had production records among the top third in the company. Conversely, men whose productivity was low in relation to their test scores typically were in the least successful offices. After analyzing all the factors that might have accounted for these variations, the company concluded that differences in the performance of new men were due primarily to differences in the "proficiency in sales training and direction" of the local managers. [15]

☐ A study I conducted of the performance of automobile salesmen in Ford dealerships in New England revealed that superior salesmen were concentrated in a few outstanding dealerships. For instance, 10 of the top 15 salesmen in New England were in 3 (out of approximately 200) of the dealerships in this region; and 5 of the top 15 men were in one highly successful dealership; yet 4 of these men previously had worked

13. Ibid., pp. 221-222.

14. Robert T. Davis, "Sales Management in the Field," HBR January-February 1958, p. 91.

15. Alfred A. Oberlander, "The Collective Conscience in Recruiting," address to Life Insurance Agency Management Association Annual Meeting, Chicago, Illinois, 1963, p. 5.

for other dealers without achieving outstanding sales records. There seemed to be little doubt that the training and motivational skills of managers in the outstanding dealerships were the critical factor.

Astute selection

While success in business sometimes appears to depend on the "luck of the draw," more than luck is involved when a young man is selected by a superior manager. Successful managers do not pick their subordinates at random or by the toss of a coin. They are careful to select only those who they "know" will succeed. As Metropolitan's Rockaway district manager, Alfred Oberlander, insisted: "Every man who starts with us is going to be a top-notch life insurance man, or he would not have received an invitation to join the team." [16]

When pressed to explain how they "know" whether a man will be successful, superior managers usually end up by saying something like, "The qualities are intangible, but I know them when I see them." They have difficulty being explicit because their selection process is intuitive and is based on interpersonal intelligence that is difficult to describe. The key seems to be that they are able to identify subordinates with whom they can probably work effectively—men with whom they are compatible and whose body chemistry agrees with their own. They make mistakes, of course. But they "give up" on a subordinate slowly because that means "giving up" on themselves—on their judgment and ability in selecting, training, and motivating men. Less effective managers select subordinates more quickly and give up on them more easily, believing that the inadequacy is that of the subordinate, not of themselves.

Developing young men

Observing that his company's research indicates that "initial corporate expectations for performance (with real responsibility) mold subsequent expectations and behavior," R.W. Walters, Jr., director of college employment at the American Telephone and Telegraph Company, contends that: "Initial bosses of new college hires must be the best in the organization." [17] Unfortunately, however, most companies practice exactly the opposite.

Rarely do new graduates work closely with experienced middle managers or upper-level executives. Normally, they are bossed by first-line managers who tend to be the least experienced and least effective in the organization. While there are exceptions, first-line managers generally are either "old pros" who have been judged as lacking competence for higher levels of responsibility, or they are younger men who are making the transition from "doing" to "managing." Often, these managers lack the knowledge and skill required to develop the productive capabilities of their subordinates. As a consequence, many college graduates begin their careers in business under the worst possible circumstances. Since they know their abilities are not being developed or used, they quite naturally soon become negative toward their jobs, employers, and business careers.

Although most top executives have not yet diagnosed the problem, industry's greatest challenge by far is the underdevelopment, underutilization, and ineffective management and use of its most valuable resource—its young managerial and professional talent.

Disillusion & turnover

The problem posed to corporate management is underscored by the sharply rising rates of attrition among young managerial and professional personnel. Turnover among managers one to five years out of college is almost twice as high now as it was a decade ago, and five times as high as two decades ago. Three out of five companies surveyed by *Fortune* magazine in the fall of 1968 reported that turnover rates among young managers and professionals were higher than five years ago. [18] While the high level of economic activity and the shortage of skilled personnel have made job-hopping easier, the underlying causes of high attrition, I am convinced, are underdevelopment and underutilization of a work force that has high career aspirations.

The problem can be seen in its extreme form in the excessive attrition rates of college and university graduates who begin their careers in sales positions. Whereas the average company loses about 50% of its new college and university graduates within three to five years, attrition rates as high as 40% in the *first* year are common

16. Ibid., p. 9.

17. "How to Keep the Go-getters," *Nation's Business*, June 1966, p. 74.

18. Robert C. Albrook, "Why It's Harder to Keep Good Executives," *Fortune*, November 1968, p. 137.

among college graduates who accept sales positions in the average company. This attrition stems primarily, in my opinion, from the failure of first-line managers to teach new college recruits what they need to know to be effective sales representatives.

As we have seen, young men who begin their careers working for less-than-competent sales managers are likely to have records of low productivity. When rebuffed by their customers and considered by their managers to have little potential for success, the young men naturally have great difficulty in maintaining their self-esteem. Soon they find little personal satisfaction in their jobs and, to avoid further loss of self-respect, leave their employers for jobs that look more promising. Moreover, as reports about the high turnover and disillusionment of those who embarked on sales careers filter back to college campuses, new graduates become increasingly reluctant to take jobs in sales.

Thus, ineffective first-line sales management sets off a sequence of events that ends with college and university graduates avoiding careers in selling. To a lesser extent, the same pattern is duplicated in other functions of business, as evidenced by the growing trend of college graduates to pursue careers in "more meaningful" occupations, such as teaching and government service.

A serious "generation gap" between bosses and subordinates is another significant cause of breakdown. Many managers resent the abstract, academic language and narrow rationalization typically used by recent graduates. As one manager expressed it to me: "For God's sake, you need a lexicon even to talk with these kids." Noncollege managers often are particularly resentful, perhaps because they feel threatened by the bright young men with book-learned knowledge that they do not understand.

For whatever reason, the "generation gap" in many companies is eroding managerial expecta-

tions of new college graduates. For instance, I know of a survey of management attitudes in one of the nation's largest companies which revealed that 54% of its first-line and second-line managers believed that new college recruits were "not as good as they were five years ago." Since what a manager expects of a subordinate influences the way he treats him, it is understandable that new graduates often develop negative attitudes toward their jobs and their employers. Clearly, low managerial expectations and hostile attitudes are not the basis for effective management of new men entering business.

Conclusion

Industry has not developed effective first-line managers fast enough to meet its needs. As a consequence, many companies are underdeveloping their most valuable resource—talented young men and women. They are incurring heavy attrition costs and contributing to the negative attitudes young people often have about careers in business.

For top executives in industry who are concerned with the productivity of their organizations and the careers of young employees, the challenge is clear: it is to speed the development of managers who will treat their subordinates in ways that lead to high performance and career satisfaction. The manager not only shapes the expectations and productivity of his subordinates, but also influences their attitudes toward their jobs and themselves. If he is unskilled, he leaves scars on the careers of the young men, cuts deeply into their self-esteem, and distorts their image of themselves as human beings. But if he is skillful and has high expectations of his subordinates, their self-confidence will grow, their capabilities will develop, and their productivity will be high. More often than he realizes, the manager is Pygmalion.

12

WHO IS TO BLAME

FOR MALADAPTIVE MANAGERS?

Harry Levinson

By the time a man enters management, many businessmen believe it is too late to change his "character." To a great extent this belief is true; the experiences of childhood and adolescence are indeed crucial. Many of the troublesome attitudes and actions of managers which are typically blamed on "character," however, can be traced to management itself. In other words, although "character" is relatively enduring, many of management's "people problems" are partly products of its own making. Again and again, in my observation of industry, I find that the undesirable behavior of subordinates is precipitated or aggravated by the unintentional actions of their superiors. Such a statement is not news to subordinates — to them it is by now a cliché — but it is often disdained by their bosses as sheer rationalization.

In one sense, this observation is a discouraging commentary on the practice of management today. In another sense, it is a reason to be encouraged. For, to the extent that "people problems" *are* created by management, it has the

AUTHOR'S NOTE: I am indebted to Drs. William C. Menninger, Roy W. Menninger, Herbert C. Modlin, and Richard O. Sword, and to Mr. Arthur Mandelbaum, all of The Menninger Foundation, for their many comments and suggestions which I have incorporated into this article.

immediate power to solve them by changing its approach. It does not have to defer the solution until long-range training programs and education have had a chance to work.

In this article I shall discuss six common management actions which lead to troublesome or problematic behavior among subordinates, and suggest supplemental or alternative actions which might be taken to avoid the difficulty. This analysis is based on an examination of 287 cases presented by participants in 15 executive seminars held at The Menninger Foundation during the past nine years (for more details, see the color spread on pages 128 and 129.)

Problem-Creating Actions

The actions that I shall describe frequently seem to make sense at the time they are taken. But while they may be defensible in the short run, in the long run they turn into liabilities. From the standpoint of sound organizational growth, they must be judged as errors.

Error #1: Encouragement of Power Seeking

No single kind of subordinate pleases his superiors more than the man who is able to assume responsibility for a crisis task, jump to his task with zest, and accomplish it successfully with dispatch. Such men become the "jets" of industry, the "comers," the "shining lights." They are usually bright, energetic managers who have considerable ability and even more promise. Sometimes, as revealed in our cases, they rescue some part of the organization from failure or produce outstanding results in resolving difficult problems almost single-handedly.

Naturally, higher management rewards such men for their capacity to organize, drive, and get results. Management therefore encourages them in their wide-ranging pursuit of personal power. Then what happens? Management abruptly changes the signals. At a certain point, further advancement hinges not on what the men themselves can do alone but on their ability to lead, not drive, others.

Of our 287 cases, 12 revolve around just such men. Although this number is small, the group nevertheless is a highly important one because of the talents the men have. The men are described as problems because they reportedly over-dominate their staffs; they are unable to coach and develop subordinates; they concentrate decision making in their own hands while driving their subordinates unnecessarily hard. In short, they are *authoritarian*. Their individual achievements have led to promotion, and the aura of their record has obscured for a considerable time the fact that they are now destroying or failing to build some part of the organization.

These are the very sort of men of whom it is frequently said that they could be outstandingly successful if only they could "work with people." Since they cannot, they will either have to leave their companies or be doomed to the continued frustration of their ambitions. Whether they cannot work well with others because of the kind of people they are, or because of organizational pressures to produce, is not always clear from the cases. It is clear, however, that *both* factors usually are involved.

Possible Alternatives

Top management has several alternatives with such men in those cases where it is not already too late. If management is primarily concerned with building an organization and with making it possible for men to grow into larger organizational responsibilities, then, contrary to popular conceptions, it must provide for close supervision of them. Such supervision must be pointed to helping support subordinates and to rewarding team, rather than individual, productivity. True,

some of the "jets" may not be able to work in harness no matter what is done, and may therefore have to leave; but they will do so without having developed expectations that they can succeed in the organization by hard driving alone and before management builds up unrealistic expectations about their future development.

If a situation is such that it calls for heroic rescue or rebuilding efforts by a single person, both he and his superiors should recognize together the unique value of his talents in a particular situation and the likelihood that he may have to find a similar task elsewhere when this one is completed. My own observations suggest that a heroic organizing or rebuilding task takes from three to five years. After that, individual efforts, which by then have resulted in an organizational structure, must give way to group effort. Rarely is it possible for people who have ranged far and wide in an organization to accept increasing circumscription of their behavior. Usually, at the end of the initial building period a whole new group of managers must be introduced whose talents lie less in their own vigorous attack and more in coordinating and supporting the problem-solving abilities of groups. This phenomenon is an old story in many different contexts, ranging from offensive and defensive platoons in football, to guerrilla units in the military and reform movements in politics. It is not yet widely recognized in business.

Error #2: Failure to Exercise Controls

Senior executives, according to some of our cases, often seem to condone behavior which is beyond the bounds of common courtesy. The result is devastating to those who are subject to such behavior and detrimental to the organization. The cost of tolerating this behavior is reflected particularly in that group of 15 cases which I call *the angry ones*. These are executives who reportedly spew their anger about them — at colleagues, subordinates, and superiors. These are the people who are described as being unnecessarily critical, as arguing too long and too much, as being crude and rude to others, and as seeming to flail at their working environment.

Again, it is sometimes difficult to determine how much of this behavior results from what is going on in the organization and how much from the personalities of the men themselves. But what is clear is the fact that they have got away with their outbursts, that the undesirable behavior seems to increase in intensity, that others are hurt by it, and that the angry ones themselves often feel guilty and contrite after their outbursts.

In another group of 20 cases, self-centeredness seems to be the most conspicuous aspect of the problem. The major form this self-centeredness takes is the exploitation of and attack on others as part of the subject's efforts to maintain or increase his own status. He differs from those who are authoritarian and directive in that he is more manipulative. The self-centered man is more clearly out for his own self-aggrandizement and often seems not to care what he does to others in the process; the authoritarian executive more frequently is sympathetic to others in a paternalistic way.

The striking aspect of both the angry and the self-centered executives is the manner in which they are able to intimidate others and get away with it. *Some of them have been permitted to go on in this way for years*, often for the reason that the man in question has some particular skill or talent which the organization needs. Even when the responsible executive knows that such behavior is destructive to the organization, to other subordinates, and to the man himself, he often permits it to go on. He excuses it with such words as "temperamental," or "the problem you have with creative people."

Such behavior may be a way of demonstrat-ing power or a way of getting attention. For some people, any attention, whether criticism from superiors or loving kindness from oneself, is better than none. Anger or self-centeredness may also be an expression of increased insecurity and anxiety, particularly if job burdens are felt to be too heavy and failure threatens. Whatever the reason, as long as higher management condones the behavior or tolerates it, the problem is swept beneath the managerial rug.

What seems to happen in such cases is that the superior is taken aback by the aggressive outbursts or the chronic hostility of the subordinate. The superior may feel afraid of the subordinate's anger, being cowed by it just as lower-level employees are, and may then back away from confrontation or control for fear of precipitating even more anger. Or the hostility of the subordinate may arouse the superior's anger to the point where the superior feels guilty because of his angry thoughts toward the subordinate. If the superior feels inordinately guilty about his own angry feelings and doubts his ability to control them once they are unleashed, he may be paralyzed into inactivity as a way of coping with his own feelings.[1]

In either case, the subordinate is left free to vent his spleen on others. Those who are victims resent both him and the superiors who permit him to behave in this way. Working relation-

Cases Analyzed

There were 287 cases available for analysis for this article. Each of these cases was submitted in written form, in advance of a week-long seminar, by an executive participating in the seminar, for purposes of discussion in a small seven-man group. The participant was instructed that his case should be about a problem between people, preferably one in which he was one of the parties, and one which had been particularly troublesome. He was asked to describe in the case the circumstances of the problem and the nature of the discussions between himself and the other person. He was free to write the case in any way he chose, disguising it sufficiently so that it was not identifiable. In the small group discussions he did not have to identify his case unless he wished to do so, although in such a small group it was often apparent which case belonged to which participant. I reviewed each of these cases and, on the basis of the most prominent aspect of behavior described, assigned it to one of five categories:

1. *Nonmanagement Problems* — Of the total submitted, 27 cases did not constitute individual problems; 25 more were not problems of executives (middle management and above, but not first-level foremen). These cases have not been used in this article.

2. *Mental Illness* — This category includes 15 cases in which psychiatric illness had already been diagnosed or in which the symptoms as described by the presenter were so severe that they were clearly indicative of illness. In 4 of these cases the subjects were manipulative to the point of dishonesty, exploiting customers as well as subordinates, colleagues, and superiors, and clinically would be called pathological character disorders. These cases, too, are excluded.

3. *Hostility* — This is the most conspicuous symptom or underlying feeling in 125 of the remaining 220 cases. Of these cases, 15 cover a wide range of hostile behavior; the other 110 cases fall into four subgroups: (a) the authoritarian ones, (b) the angry ones, (c) the self-centered ones, and (d) the wounded ones.

ships with colleagues are impaired. The superior feels angry with himself for not stopping the aggressive behavior; and the angry subordinate, whose behavior is really a cry for help, continues to thrash about, to his own detriment and that of the organization. Thus when the responsible executive does not exercise adequate control, he contributes to the malfunctioning of those subordinates who are unable to maintain their own controls.

Asserting Control

The first step in the control process is to define the problem. As long as others put up with an angry one's behavior, he has no reason to stop it; there is no problem. He can easily feel that he must be right in his anger or manipulation if everyone else puts up with it, particularly if his own superiors tolerate it despite the complaints and turnover of lower level personnel.

Once the superior has defined which aspects of the subordinate's behavior are unacceptable and has confronted the subordinate with a statement of the problem as he sees it, then the two need to look at their own relationship. There may be features of the superior's behavior which provoke and sustain the anger of the subordinate. There may be role conflicts among superiors which tear the subordinate apart psycholog-ically. Work stresses may take their toll. It may well be that the subordinate unconsciously is asking for more support from his superior. Whatever the case, the two of them need to examine the situation together for possible causal influences. The superior needs to be alert to possible fears and anxieties which the subordinate cannot express, such as the fear of failure or a sense of inadequacy in the supervision of others.

Regardless of whether there are mitigating circumstances, the superior must draw the line for what is permissible. He simply cannot permit destructive behavior to go on. If environmental circumstances which precipitate anger cannot be altered, if indeed there seem to be no problems of such proportion as to induce such anger, then it is a reasonably safe assumption that the problem is primarily within the individual and therefore he himself must do something about it. The chances are that he will have to seek professional help. If this is the case, bear in mind that the organization does not have to put up with the man's behavior until he solves his problem. If he still cannot control his outbursts after the line is drawn, then he should be removed from his job.

[1] See my book, *Emotional Health: In the World of Work* (New York, Harper & Row, Publishers, 1964), Chapter 18, for further elaboration of this point.

4. *Limited Personalities* — This group includes 48 men classified into four subgroups: (a) the anxious ones, (b) the rigid ones, (c) the dependent ones, and (d) the impulsive ones.

5. *Misplacement* — In this group are 47 men who had either been placed in the wrong job (the hapless ones) or who had been outgrown by the job (the helpless ones).

The categories were derived from an inspection of the cases; they had not been previously established. They reflect my interpretation of the behavior of the person described in the case. The categories, therefore, are based on the problem as the presenter saw it — on the data as he perceived and reported them, though not necessarily as he interpreted his own data. They are not diagnostic categories in the clinical sense. Nor are they mutually exclusive, for they have been evolved from that aspect of the individual's behavior which I understood from the case description to be the most salient.

These cases, then, are reports by senior executives of problems they have had with subordinate executives. The acute or painful aspect of the problem as presented is the behavior of the subordinate executive. But as the discussion elaborates, it turns out that the senior executive also has a part in each of these problems. His part results from lack of self-scrutiny, indifference, inadequate understanding, or some other nonfunctional behavior. This is not to say that the senior executive or the organization "caused" the problem. There are always multiple causes for all behavior. Yet in each one of these groups of cases, senior executives have made certain repetitive managerial errors that relate specifically to the kind of behavior which the subordinate displays. This correlation between managerial error and subordinate behavior enables us to focus on the former as a means of pointing toward more proficient managerial practice.

The executive must not assume that undesirable behavior can be stamped out by forbidding it. Discussion of problems means just that — self-critical examination by both parties of their working relationship. It does not mean that the superior tells the subordinate he must stop behaving as he does and that the conversation ends there. Follow-up is needed. For instance, the superior strengthens the structure of the organization by seeing to it that the subordinate makes use of those organizational avenues, policies, and procedures which presumably are the agreed-on ways by which problems are to be dealt with in the company.

When a superior finds himself condoning hostile behavior or procrastinating in doing something about it because the subordinate is "too valuable to lose," the chances are that he is taking an expensive, short-run view of the problem. More often than not, when pinned down, the senior executive admits that the subordinate is more trouble than he is worth and that his failure to act arises from his own feelings of anger and guilt.

Error #3: Stimulation of Rivalry

The central problem in a group of 36 cases is rivalry. Sometimes the executive presenting the problem recognizes this, but more often he does not. He may, for example, concentrate his attention on the hostility between two subordinates without recognizing why they became hostile, although the rivalry aspects of the problem often seem clear from his own description. For example:

◖ A man is promoted to a position in which he becomes a rival of a senior person. He is instructed to "light a fire" under the senior person or is promised the senior man's job, as, for example, when the chairman of the board chooses an executive vice president to prod the president. But the subordinate "freezes" in his job, failing to show the previously successful behavior which brought him his promotion. His seniors cannot understand why.

Frequently the rivalry is between department heads or different functions — for instance, between sales and production; and here again the underlying psychological reasons for the rivalry may not be recognized. Thus:

◖ A production-minded president sees the need for a strong sales effort and employs a competent sales executive, only to resent his success. He then rejects or sabotages the sales executive without being aware of what he is doing or knowing why.

The destructive effects of rivalry thus stimulated are rarely recognized by the presenting executives, in my experience. Executives are not aware of the deep-seated psychological roots of rivalry and the guilt feelings which immediate personal competition can arouse in many people. Often they have consciously encouraged rivalry on the assumption that all competition is good. They cannot understand why a hard competitor will suddenly stop competing, let alone see the psychological trap in which the subordinate has been placed.

Although executives usually recognize why two colleagues can no longer be friends after one is promoted, or that older subordinates will rebel against a younger boss, generally they do little to prevent or ameliorate such frictions. Some young executives promoted rapidly over the heads of older men have guilt feelings about taking the opportunities of the older men. Such feelings are not recognized by superiors either. *In none of the cases with rivalry problems described in our seminars was the issue of rivalry discussed, either by the rivals themselves or by their superiors, as preparation for dealing with their new jobs.*

Rivalry, by definition, is the essence of competitive enterprise. But in such an enterprise, where the desirable end product is the result produced by the organization, all effort should be focused on the collective attainment of that result. When a superior plays subordinates off against each other, overstimulates rivalry in other ways, or acts competitively with his subordinates, he forces them to divert energies from competition with other organizations into interpersonal rivalry. Less attention is focused on problems which the organization has to solve. In addition, the subordinates become defensive, or destroy cooperative possibilities by attacking each other, or maneuver for the favor of the boss. The more intensely intraorganizational rivalry is stimulated, the more acute the problem of company politics becomes.[2]

Constructive Discussion

Open discussion of and joint solution of mutual problems make it possible for managers

[2] See Edgar H. Schein, *Organizational Psychology* (Englewood Cliffs, New Jersey, Prentice-Hall, Inc., 1965), pp. 80–87.

to use much more profitably the energy which might otherwise be dissipated in destructive rivalry. In dealing with this problem the superior needs to take a critical look at his own motivation with possibilities like these in mind:

√ *He may consciously or unconsciously encourage rivalry because he likes to see a good fight, rationalizing his pleasure by believing that the better ideas or the better men will survive.*

Men in executive positions have strong feelings of rivalry that are sufficiently aroused by real problems, if the executives are given enough freedom to attack them; the range of ideas in a problem situation is generally wide enough to produce ample differences and critical examination. Playing men off against each other is merely psychological goading. Those who are not moved by the problems themselves will not be moved by goading either. Instead, they will be even more rigidly paralyzed. One can only wonder about the motivation of an executive who has to goad his subordinates into fighting each other, just as one would wonder about a parent who does the same with his children.

√ *He may be angry at one of the rivals and use the other as a weapon to displace his own hostility.*

This is a subtle phenomenon which happens frequently. The senior executive can ask himself to what extent he avoids one subordinate, speaks harshly of him behind his back, and disdains his communications. If he finds himself doing these things without clearly being aware of it, his behavior is one clue to what may be influencing the conflict between the two subordinates. He would do better to talk directly to the man with whom he is angry than to get at him by using another man as a weapon.

√ *He may fear the rivalry of subordinates for his own position, and either keep them off balance or permit them to destroy themselves by encouraging their rivalry of each other.*

Few men can grow older without envying and fearing the younger men who will take their places, no matter how much they like and respect the younger men. Such fears, though natural, are hard for a man to accept in himself. According to the folklore of our culture, he is not supposed to have them. Why should he not retire in due time without regret or recrimination? He has it made; what more does he want? But our feelings are simply not that logical. Moving up through executive ranks is much like playing the children's game, "King of the Mountain." A man often feels as if he is always pushing the man ahead of him off the top — even if it is only a small hill. Inevitably, it is difficult for him to relinquish his position without feeling he is being pushed, too. If he feels that way and is unaware of it, he will perforce defend his position in many subtle ways. If he can accept such feelings as legitimate, he is then in a better position to control their expression.

√ *The two rivals may well represent his own inner conflicts about his identification with different parts of the business.*

Often executives rise through the ranks on the basis of their identification with a particular capacity, skill, or experience. Then, on reaching a high level, they find that new business requirements make their old skill relatively obsolete or compel them to evolve multiple skills. For example, many a production man has risen to chief executive only to discover that we are now in a marketing economy and that he must either shift his own focus from production to marketing or at least become more knowledgeable about marketing.

To change one's focus or to broaden one's perception can also mean that a man has to change his image of himself. A production man who looks on marketing as manipulation, for example, may have considerable conflict within his own conscience about becoming a manipulator. Even though he may well recognize the need for marketing, he may still not want to be a salesman. The conflict within himself between the wish to continue being what he always was and the wish to have the organization compete successfully by competitive marketing may then reflect itself in his inability to make decisions.

It will also reflect itself in conflict between the men who have to carry on the two responsibilities about which he is in conflict. In hardly discernible ways he will support one, then the other, or make an ally of one and then the other. The two subordinates soon find themselves on opposite sides of a fence whose origin is then attributed to "poor communications" or the supposition that "salesmen are always like that." Perhaps only after the third successive sales vice president has been fired might it dawn on the president that something more than a "personality clash" is afoot. The clash within himself clangs loudly in the behavior of those who report to him.

In the promotion or transfer of any executive, careful attention should be given to the rivalry aspects of the situation. These should be *talked about frankly* as problems to be dealt with in the new job. And for those who must accept a new superior or colleague, it can be helpful to reassure them honestly of their own value, to recognize openly with them the inevitable presence of rivalry feelings, and to indicate that, though such feelings exist, the task is still to be done and the new boss has the superior's full support in managing that group toward the required goals of the organization.

Error #4: Failure to Anticipate the Inevitable

Many experiences in life are painful to people. Some, like aging and its accompanying physical infirmities and incapacities, are the lot of everyone. Others are specific to a man's work life, e.g., failure to obtain an expected promotion or the prospect of retirement. We can speak of such painful experiences as *psychological injuries.*

Such injuries are inevitable. Yet there is little in our 287 cases to indicate that companies recognize their inevitability and have established methods for anticipating or relieving them. The result is that those who are hurt in this manner have considerable hostility which is repressed or suppressed. Sometimes the thought of retirement is what hurts. Those men to whom prospective retirement is a psychological injury often refuse to train subordinates and become obstructionists, displacing their repressed or suppressed hostility on both subordinates and organization. Physical changes such as hearing loss and heart attack also leave residues of resentment as men attempt to deny their incapacity. Other sources of psychological injury are:

• Not being promoted to a job one has expected.

• Having one's judgment rejected.

• Having some of one's responsibilities given to someone else.

• Lonesomeness — wishing to be gregarious but being unable to act that way, and therefore feeling rejected by others, with a resulting hypersensitivity to further psychological wounds.

Helpful Steps

Judging from our executive seminars during the past nine years, superiors are more aware of psychological injury than any other form of impairment, and they try to do more about it. Yet they typically have great difficulty dealing with such problems, especially because the older men who are more subject to them are managers of long service. In the many cases where superiors have done a good job of providing support for the "problem people" and have saved their jobs, they have done it by hard work and heroic rescue attempts.

However, such extraordinary measures — and the pain and frustration which usually attend them — can often be made unnecessary by advance preparation in anticipation of possible injury. People not only have a right to know what is likely to happen to them as far ahead as such events can be anticipated, but also *they* can then prepare themselves for the eventuality or choose alternative courses of action. If they are not informed and then experience a sudden blow from higher management, they have every reason to feel manipulated and exploited.

The organization contributes to executive malfunction when it does not —

. . . systematically prepare people throughout their work careers for the realities which inevitably will come their way;

. . . provide shock absorbers, in the form of counseling services, to help people cope with psychological injury.

Every important change should be discussed with each man involved before it occurs. A major part of such discussion should be the opportunity for him to express his feelings, without embarrassment or fear, about the change. When a man can say to his superior how he feels about the latter's decision or an organizational decision, the acceptance of his feelings conveys to him that he is accepted and respected as an individual. This in turn supports his feelings of self-esteem and makes it possible for him to deal with the change and his feelings more reasonably. No amount of sugarcoated praise will substitute for being heard.

When a person has help in absorbing the shock of injury and support in recovering from it, he is in a much better position to mobilize his resources to cope with what has happened to him. More often than not, a senior executive who would quickly offer a supporting hand to a man with a sprained ankle, and indeed get him medical attention, has difficulty seeing psychological injuries in the same light.

Error #5: Pressuring Men of Limited Ability

The characteristic and futile way of trying to deal with men of limited ability is by frontal assault. Repeatedly the senior executives attempt to persuade a rigid person to stop being rigid, exhort a dependent person to become independent, or cajole an impulsive person to gain better self-control. Although the executives may know in their minds that the subordinate is inflexible or unable to accept responsibility or assume initiative, they tend to *act* as if they could compel or stimulate him to change. Thus:

❡ It is difficult for most successful executives to understand that grown men can be frightened and dependent. Sometimes, in a misguided effort to stimulate the subordinate, they open up the possibilities of greater responsibility and more active participation in decision making.

Such gestures are even more threatening to men who are already immobilized than exhortation is. Sometimes seniors actually promote the problem man in the vain hope that he will change when he has more responsibility or when he is sent off to a management development course. It is not understood that such pressure on a person who is already devoting so much effort to controlling or protecting himself (which is what the aberrant behavior means) will only increase the intensity of the undesirable behavior. If a man is characteristically rigid, dependent, or impulsive, he is likely to become more so under increasing stress, which is what the pressure exerted by the boss becomes.

❡ Impulsive men present another problem for their superiors. Because so often they are intellectually competent, even gifted, their superiors are reluctant to face the problems of their behavior squarely and thus can only continue to chafe at their episodic failure. Our seminar cases included eight instances of men who do their jobs well "when they want to." However, they are frequently absent, often embroiled in multiple family difficulties, and sometimes irresponsible with respect to getting their work done or doing it thoroughly. Here also are the men who, though not alcoholic, will drink too much in the presence of their superiors, and others whose worst behavior will occur when they are with highest-level superiors. The self-defeating aspects of such behavior are obvious.

Poor impulse control and low frustration tolerance usually reflect considerable anxiety and insecurity. More often than not, such behavior reflects the need for professional counsel. Repeated admonitions usually serve little purpose.

❡ Inflexibility is the most prominent reported behavior of 14 men in our cases. For nearly half of these men, the problem is characterized as an inability to plan for or accept change. Several others seem to resist change not because they are personally inflexible, but because the organization has prepared them poorly and they are angry. In one case, the *organization* was so rigid that the best man available for a given post was not going to be promoted because he did not believe in God!

Rigid people find their self-protection in well-ordered lives. Often they have high standards for themselves. Those who become more rigid under stress are in effect building a protective shell for themselves.

Management Action

How should management try to deal with problems of the sort just described?

First, it should so delimit the person's duties that he can confine himself to standardized, detailed work, with clear policy guidance. It should be made clear to him what his responsibilities do *not* include.

Secondly, higher management should consider what demands have made the person more anxious and defensive. As earlier pointed out, change always requires support from superiors if it is to take place with a minimum amount of stress. Much of the time senior management takes it for granted that people can and will change; few can do so without stress. The most effective kind of support lies in joint problem solving — in making changes together step-by-step so that the person can feel he is still master of himself and his fate instead of being arbitrarily buffeted about by anonymous forces over which he has no control.

Thirdly, management should take a hard look at the "climate" of the executive organization. In our seminar cases a frequent corollary of inability to perform as expected is the report by the presenting executives that the problem men were previously suppressed in an excessively authoritarian structure for years. Some are able to function reasonably well as long as they have the close support of their superiors. Some cannot make decisions themselves.

Undoing dependent behavior is no easy task, particularly when the organization continues to demand conforming behavior. Where conformity is the first rule of survival, no amount of exhortation will produce initiative. Where mistakes are vigorously hunted out and held against a person thereafter, few men will take a chance on making a mistake. Therefore, close, minute supervision of a man as he assumes greater responsibility is not an unmixed blessing. There are rewards for such supervision — and costs. This situation often creates great conflict among senior executives — the wish that subordinates demonstrate initiative versus the wish to be in complete control.

Error #6: Misplacement

Despite the plethora of psychological consultants, assessment and rating scales, and a wide-ranging literature on promotion, there is little indication in our cases that careful assessments are regularly made to indicate a man's limitations or predict his inability to carry greater responsibility. In cases where men have been outgrown by their jobs, there seems to have been almost no anticipation that such an eventuality would come about. As a result, there has been no continuing discussion of the problem, which might help the man become aware of what he will have to do to keep up with his job. Nor is there support for him in facing his feelings about becoming less competent to do the job or having to give it up. Instead, whatever the reason a man has not grown, often he is left to flounder in his job because superiors recognize it is not his fault that he is failing, but theirs for having placed him in that position. Thus the failure is compounded.

In 47 cases of misplacement, by my interpretation, half of the men placed in the wrong job are unable to function adequately in the face of larger responsibilities. Often these are men who did well in jobs of lesser responsibility and who seemed to have promise of being able to carry on a more responsible job. Some men, however, have been placed in managerial positions despite the fact that their limitations are known, particularly their inability to supervise others. Some have moved up through the ranks because of their technical knowledge at a time when it was thought that technical knowledge was the most important qualification which a leader could have. The remaining men in this group could not consistently meet the demands of their present jobs. Often they could do some aspects of their jobs well, but not others.

About one third of the cases involve men who reportedly cannot keep up with the continuing growth of the organization and the particular jobs they hold. In most of these instances the executive simply does not have the knowledge or the skill for the expanding job. His growing job has gone beyond his training and experiences and beyond his capacity for organizing and making judgments. This problem is even more painful when the incumbent has had long service in the position or when he has made highly significant contributions to organizing and developing an activity, sometimes even the company itself. In these situations the superior bears considerable pain because he feels compelled to take action against a man who has contributed so much to the organization. His anger toward the man who "forces" him into such a situation arouses his guilt feelings, and his conscience punishes him severely.

How much of the failure to keep up with the growth of the company was passive aggression — failure to do what a man was capable of doing

as a way of defeating the company — I have no way of knowing. Often rigidity and plateaus in performance are products of passive aggression. One way of being aggressive covertly is by not changing, not doing what is expected of one, letting the boss down in one way or another. Passive aggression is an extremely widespread phenomenon.

Recommended Approach

The single most helpful practice for dealing with misplacement is to have a *continuing and consistent relationship* with a psychological consultant. Psychological testing and evaluation are no better than the person who does them. His judgments and predictions can be no better than his knowledge of the man, the position, and the company. If he is to serve all three, then he must develop a feel for the company, knowledge of specific jobs and the men who supervise them, and, finally, some understanding of the candidate. Standardized batteries given by psychologists who see neither the company nor the probable position of the candidate among others in the company have limited value. Mail-order testing has even less value (apart from the ethical question involved). Occasional referral to a local psychologist is hardly enough to keep the latter in touch with the climate of the organization.

Growth is the essence of living. All of us like to feel that we are becoming wiser as we grow older. Most men seek opportunities for continued growth. Some, however, cannot or do not. This problem is likely to occur with increasing frequency as executive roles become more complex. To avoid failures, companies will have to evolve methods for anticipating and coping with misplacements before they become a painful and destructive fact. In a continuing professional relationship the psychologist can be in contact with executives from day to day, know when they are under particular stress, and provide support and counsel as necessary. In growing companies one of his continuing tasks should be to keep an eye out for those who are not keeping pace.

Conclusion

The contemporary management scene is characterized by frequent complaints about the inadequacies of subordinates and potential executive successors. The validity of such complaints would seem to be verified by the widespread use of management consultants for every conceivable purpose and by the repetitive reorganizations of businesses. These phenomena reflect the chronic pain of management, enormous dissipation of human energy, and the palliative nature of the attempted cures. Dr. Karl Menninger coined the term "polysurgical addiction" to describe people who repeatedly demanded operations to cure their multiple, repetitive complaints.[3] It would not stretch the analogy too far to speak of "polyconsultative addiction" to describe this all too frequent mode of solving managerial problems.

This phrase is not meant to reflect on consultants any more than Menninger's phrase was a criticism of surgeons. Both practitioners serve highly important purposes. Rather, it refers to a characteristic managerial way of looking at problems as caused by someone or something foreign to oneself, and as being resolvable by excision or reconstruction, also by someone else. The tragedy of such a tendency is that the executive, like the patient who wants someone else to cut out the presumably offensive part, often has within himself the power to cope with managerial problems. This is especially true

with respect to those problems which are of his own (if inadvertent) making.

In this article I have outlined, from cases reported by executives, six common managerial errors in the supervision of subordinates, and I have suggested ways which may help avoid or correct each error. Most management problems seem to call for increased investment, more experts, and long periods of planning and execution before results can be expected. The problems described in this article do not. Though few managerial difficulties are more troublesome than those which have to do with people, the solutions to them are often relatively simple, given a modicum of attention and sensitivity. The manager needs only to examine more carefully his own actions. Of course, some problems, like those which arouse feelings of guilt, will remain difficult no matter how simple the solutions seem. Even these, however, will be somewhat easier to cope with if the underlying issue is more visible. Perhaps, then, the greatest self-healing managerial talent, as the psalmist would put it, is to "make wise the simple."

[3] Karl Menninger, *Man Against Himself* (New York, Harcourt, Brace & Co., 1938).

13

CONDITIONS FOR

MANAGER MOTIVATION

M. Scott Myers

• Motivation of the manager is strongest when he is realizing his potential — becoming what he has the capacity and desire to become.

• Motivation is strongly related to the supervisory style of the immediate boss: "developmental" supervisors stimulate motivation; "reductive" supervisors inhibit motivation.

• Motivation is highest among top management.

• Style of supervision is uniformly distributed through all levels of management; however, high level managers tend to know the "right" answers about supervisory practice better than lower level managers.

• All managers prefer a developmental supervisor regardless of their own values or the style of supervision they practice themselves.

• Reductive supervisors are generally insensitive to their propensity for quashing motivation, and in fact rate themselves on a par with developmental supervisors.

These and other interesting conclusions are supported by a recent survey of motivation at Texas Instruments (see box on page 138). Based on a study of attitudes of 1,344 managers at all levels and the application of the findings within the company, this article isolates and describes three conditions under which managers and their subordinates are motivated. The motivation of managers is dependent on:

1. Interpersonal competence.
2. The opportunity to work toward meaningful goals.
3. The existence of appropriate management systems.

In the balance of this article, I propose to discuss each of these conditions under which managers can motivate and be, in turn, motivated. *Interpersonal competence*, for example, describes a developmental style of supervision which meets one of the requirements for higher motivation, self-realization, and positively expressed creativity. *Meaningful goals* illustrates ways of giving direction to these positive motivations by providing company goals which offer opportunity for achieving personal goals, and keeping the goals clearly in view at all times by slashing away the underbrush of red tape, protocol, and irrelevant objectives. And *management systems* describes the vehicles for speeding positively motivated people on to the achievement of their organization goals, thereby reinforcing and perpetuating this motivation.

Interpersonal Competence

A motivation index was computed for each manager on the basis of his responses to the motivation items on the questionnaire. Managers were then sorted into three groups according to level of motivation. The top 30% group of 403 managers was labeled "high motivation"; the middle 40% group of 538, "partial motivation"; and the bottom 30% group of 403, "low motivation." EXHIBIT I shows the relationship between level of motivation and level of management.

AUTHOR'S NOTE: I am indebted to Warren J. Bowles, Charles L. Hughes, and Earl D. Weed for their help in interpreting survey data, and to Patrick E. Haggerty and Carl J. Thomsen for concepts of Texas Instruments' goals and systems which provide the framework for the application of research results.

EXHIBIT I. RELATIONSHIP OF MOTIVATION TO LEVEL OF MANAGEMENT

LEVEL OF MOTIVATION

LEVEL OF MANAGEMENT	NUMBER	HIGH	PARTIAL	LOW	TOTAL
UPPER	91	57%	31%	12%	100%
MIDDLE	683	32%	39%	29%	100%
LOWER	570	23%	43%	34%	100%
TOTAL	1,344	30%	40%	30%	100%

Upper managers — those in key decision-making roles and more closely identified with the overall performance of the organization — understandably derive a higher degree of proprietary enthusiasm from their jobs. From their vantage point, and through the process of getting there, they experience rich satisfaction of their growth, achievement, responsibility, and recognition needs.

Though the incidence of high motivation is much higher at the upper level (57%) than at the lower level (23%), it should be noted that the 91 upper level managers comprise only 7% of the survey group (91 ÷ 1,344), which means that there are only 52 highly motivated upper managers (.57 × 91); whereas the figures for highly motivated lower and middle managers come to 350, thus outnumbering the highly motivated upper managers almost seven to one (350 vs. 52). Stated otherwise, 87% of the company's highly motivated managers are below the upper management level, thereby reflecting the relatively minor role which organizational level per se plays as a motivator.

Style of Supervision

As noted earlier, managers were asked to select items which described the supervisory style of their immediate supervisors. These items describe the boss's style in terms of his ability to stimulate enthusiasm, the level and consistency of his expectations, his recognition of performance, his accessibility and willingness to listen to new ideas, his practices related to dispensing company information, his attitude toward risk taking and mistakes, his manner in dealing with mistakes, and his sensitivity to the feelings of others.

Supervisors described favorably in these terms were labeled "developmental" because of their demonstrated effectiveness in developing subordinates. Supervisors described unfavorably in these terms were labeled "reductive" to denote their propensity for reducing or inhibiting positive expressions of initiative and creativity, and for inducing withdrawal into protective patterns of conformity. Developmental supervision is synonymous with Theory Y supervision, and reductive with Theory X.[1]

Following the same procedure used for grouping managers by levels of motivation, the 1,344 managers were again separated into three groups — this time according to their descriptions of their supervisors' styles. The top 30% was comprised of the 403 managers having the most developmental bosses, and the bottom 30%, the 403 managers having the most reductive bosses. The middle 40% consisted of the 538 managers whose supervisors fit a pattern description between the developmental and reductive styles, labeled here as "traditional," since it probably more nearly characterizes the majority of supervisors who through intuition, experience, and maturation have learned to avoid many of the practices of reductive supervision, yet whose supervisory skills and understanding of human motivation are below requirements for the developmental label.

EXHIBIT II shows the relationship between levels of motivation and these three supervisory styles. Of the highly motivated managers, one half have developmental bosses and only 8% have reductive bosses. By contrast, almost two thirds of poorly motivated managers have reduc-

[1] For a brief explanation of Theory X and Theory Y, see HBR November–December 1963, p. 165; for more details, see Douglas McGregor, *The Human Side of Enterprise* (New York, McGraw-Hill Book Company, 1960).

Texas Instruments' Survey

This study is based on data obtained from 1,344 managers in the Dallas divisions of Texas Instruments. The breakdown was as follows:

• Upper managers participating in the study totaled 91 and included company officers, department heads, and key staff personnel.

• Middle managers numbered 683 and were usually at the branch and section head levels.

• There were 570 lower managers, primarily first- and second-level supervisors.

The information was gathered through 99 multiple-choice questions, designed to measure attitudes toward the company and its administrative climate, feelings about status symbols, opportunities for self-actualization, and assumptions about human be-

havior and supervisory styles of managers.

The 1,344 completed returns were factor analyzed by computer.* This analysis identified the eight factors shown in the diagram below. These are the primary factors influencing the managers' responses to the questionnaire.

The relative strength of these factors corresponds approximately to the areas of the circles. Note, for example, that *motivation on the job* had about five times as much influence on responses to questions as did *job pressure*.

Overlap among circles indicates that more than one factor influenced responses to certain questions. However, the amount of overlap is relatively small, which signifies a high degree of objectivity by the respondents and absence of item ambiguity.

Factors Influencing Management Questionnaire Responses

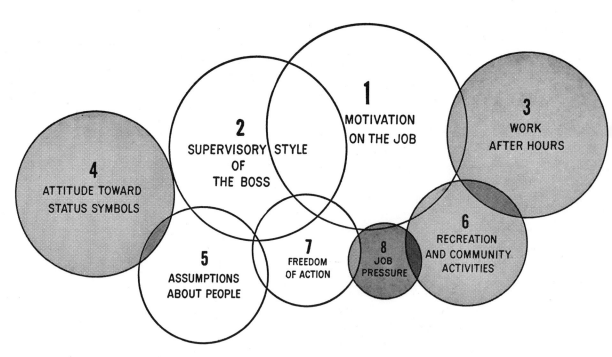

* The 96-item correlation matrix was analyzed by the principal components method with varimax rotation. Technical data and detailed factor definitions may be requested from the author at Texas Instruments Incorporated, Post Office Box 5474, Dallas, Texas 75222.

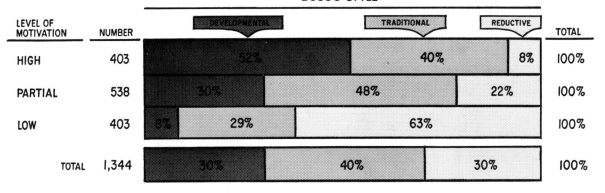

EXHIBIT II. RELATIONSHIP OF MOTIVATION TO BOSS'S STYLE

LEVEL OF MOTIVATION	NUMBER	BOSS'S STYLE			TOTAL
		DEVELOPMENTAL	TRADITIONAL	REDUCTIVE	
HIGH	403	52%	40%	8%	100%
PARTIAL	538	30%	48%	22%	100%
LOW	403	8%	29%	63%	100%
TOTAL	1,344	30%	40%	30%	100%

tive bosses, and only 8% developmental bosses.

It might seem logical to hypothesize that upper level managers are more developmental, and therefore the relationship of motivation to level of management as shown in EXHIBIT I is just an expression of the impact of supervisory style. However, EXHIBIT III disqualifies that explanation, for it shows that style of supervision is rather uniformly distributed throughout all levels of management.

The study indicated that higher level managers have a good intellectual understanding of developmental assumptions about people. It is not surprising to see greater sophistication at the higher levels where sheer age and experience have provided more opportunity to learn the theoretical answers to questions about human relations. But, from the viewpoint of the subordinate, this intellectual advantage has not been translated into supervisory practice. This phenomenon merely underscores the fact that developmental behavior does not occur automatically as a result of intellectual understanding. Rather, intellectual understanding is but a foundation (and a necessary one) on which hab-

its of interpersonal competence are developed and emotional maturity is acquired.

Managers are generally more objective in describing their boss's style and his effectiveness in motivating subordinates than they are in appraising their own effectiveness. Contrary to expectations, reductive as well as developmental managers are more highly motivated under developmental supervision. Furthermore, though many reductive managers accurately describe their own style of supervision, they often fail to recognize its negative impact on subordinates. EXHIBIT IV illustrates the relationship between self-ratings and subordinates' ratings of their ability to stimulate people to be enthusiastic about their work.

For all managers, the major difference is at the lower end where only 3% of the managers admitted failure, while 19% were rated as failures by their subordinates. The pattern is reversed for developmental managers whose subordinates rated them slightly higher than they rated themselves. But the most spectacular case of introspective myopia is illustrated by reductive managers who rate themselves almost on a

EXHIBIT III. DISTRIBUTION OF STYLE OF SUPERVSION

LEVEL OF MANAGEMENT	NUMBER	BOSS'S STYLE			TOTAL
		DEVELOPMENTAL	TRADITIONAL	REDUCTIVE	
UPPER	91	32%	42%	26%	100%
MIDDLE	683	26%	43%	31%	100%
LOWER	570	34%	37%	29%	100%
TOTAL	1,344	30%	40%	30%	100%

EXHIBIT IV. ABILITY TO MOTIVATE — SELF-RATINGS VS. SUBORDINATES' RATINGS

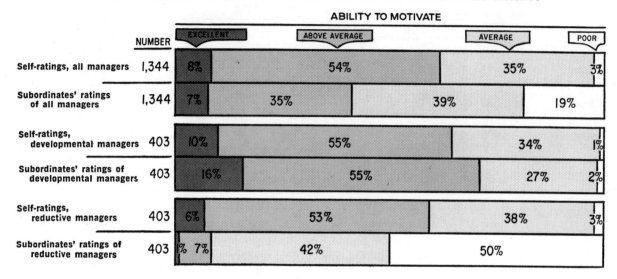

par with developmental supervisors. Their subordinates see them differently, however, and rate fully half of them as unsuccessful, and only 8% of them as above average or better.

EXHIBIT V presents the collective description of supervisory style by the 403 highly motivated managers (top 30%) as compared to the description of supervisory style by the 403 poorly motivated managers (bottom 30%).

Highly motivated managers rather consistently characterize their supervisors as persons who are approachable and open-minded, maintain high expectations, provide ready access to company information, encourage initiative and risk taking, help them learn from mistakes, and give credit for top performance. This description of supervisors clearly qualifies them for the Theory Y or developmental label.

Poorly motivated managers, though less consistent in describing their supervisors, more often describe them in terms that match Theory X, or reductive supervision. Their supervisors are typically authority-oriented, not usually receptive to conflicting ideas from subordinates, tend to oversupervise and discourage initiative and risk taking, are intolerant of mistakes (particularly those that might embarrass them), are prone to look for someone to blame for mistakes, tend to overlook successes and stress failures.

It is traditional for researchers at this point to conclude that better human relations is the key to organizational effectiveness. Members of the growing cult of sensitivity training [2] offer valid testimonials for its role in improving human relations in work groups, but they provide

only spotty evidence of its success in achieving organization goals. It is my belief that sensitivity training can contribute to organization goals, but only if interpersonal competence can find expression through *meaningful goals* and *facilitative systems*. Ideal human relationships in the absence of the other two conditions can, at best, permit cathartic expression for frustrated achievement needs and lead to the trade-off of motivation for satisfaction and complacency.

Meaningful Goals

The manager's job is to achieve organization goals. He does this through management systems and the proper utilization of human resources.

The foregoing material has dealt primarily with the human factor, and has shown the consequences of developmental and reductive styles of supervision on interpersonal competence. The following discussion attempts to show the synergistic relationship between *interpersonal competence, goals,* and *systems*.

Successful goal setting is a function of:

- Being able to relate personal goals to organization goals.

- Having helpful systems for setting and achieving goals.

- Being ready to respond favorably to organization goals.

[2] For a discussion of sensitivity training, see Chris Argyris, "T-Groups for Organizational Effectiveness," HBR March–April 1964, p. 60.

EXHIBIT V. HOW THE MANAGER SEES HIS BOSS

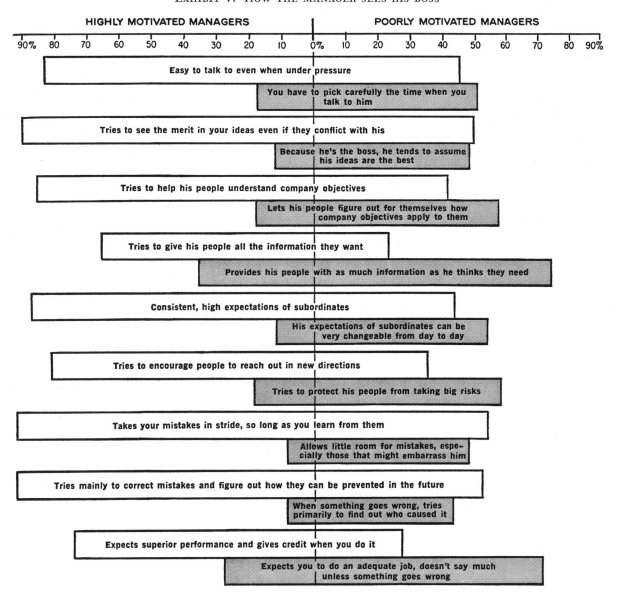

Effective management systems are those systems which —

. . . enable individuals to achieve personal goals by achieving organization goals;

. . . are managed by the individual (rather than manage the individual) in the achievement of goals;

. . . reflect a developmental philosophy of supervision.

Motivation for the manager (as well as for the nonmanager) is usually a consequence and symptom of effective job performance, which in turn influences and is influenced by any of the stages in the developmental cycle. EXHIBIT VI

reflects the cyclical relationship of supervisory style, goal setting, and management systems.

The developmental cycle is initiated by conditions of interpersonal competence, opportunity to work toward meaningful goals, and the existence of helpful management systems. These conditions maximize the manager's opportunity to achieve goals and earn approval and reward. The resultant motivation or self-actualization colors his perception of life, his work, and the company, encouraging him to reach out for greater achievements. His positive outlook reinforces the conditions of interpersonal competence, supporting and perpetuating his developmental cycle for as long as these conditions prevail. Job success is both a consequence and cause of the various stages in the developmental cycle.

The reductive cycle, in its extreme, is characterized by interpersonal conflict, unattractive goals, and hopeless red tape. These conditions typically lead to failure, to disapproval and punishment, and to feelings of guilt, frustration, despair, and apathy. The manager's defenses take the form of cynicism, hostility, and efforts to seek gratification from sources unre-

lated to the goal. This behavior further aggravates interpersonal relationships, reinforcing and perpetuating his cyclical plight.

In actual circumstances individuals seldom find themselves stabilized clearly in one cycle or another. Most persons follow a wavering path in the middle ground of the traditional cycle, from time to time crossing the developmental and reductive borders into the characteristic highs and lows of industrial life. The following case example of goal-setting opportunities,

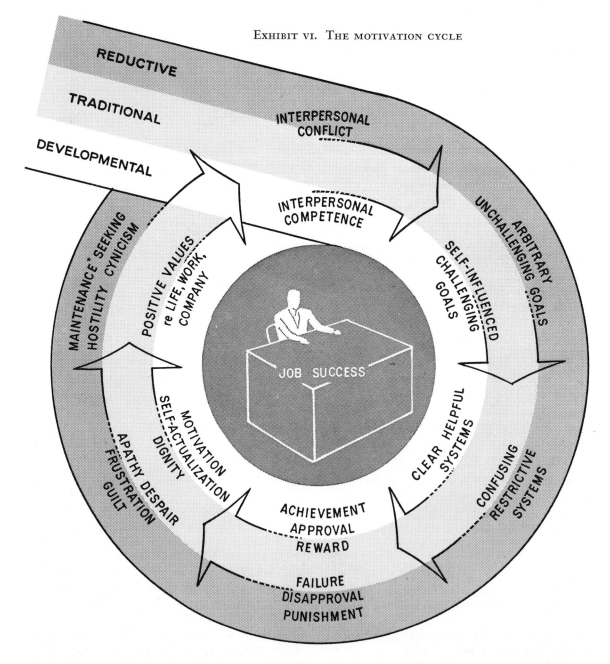

EXHIBIT VI. THE MOTIVATION CYCLE

* Maintenance needs are described in my earlier article, "Who Are Your Motivated Workers?" HBR January–February 1964; see particularly page 86, where maintenance is contrasted with motivation.

though not immune to reductive mismanagement, is presented as a model for implementing developmental management.

Goal-Setting Model

Having reached the brink of bigness in 1949, with 800 employees and annual sales of $6 million, Texas Instruments managers recognized continuing organizational growth as a requisite for company survival, and also for the personal and professional growth of its members. Had growth leveled off at that point, the more competent and highly motivated individuals would have most likely departed for greener pastures, leaving the company to stagnate in the hands of the less competent. Consequently, deliberate growth was planned through strategies related to the following factors:

- Investment in product R & D.
- Product diversification.
- Aggressive and innovative marketing.
- Investment in capital improvements.
- Mergers and acquisitions.
- Expansion to international operations.

These six factors individually, and in a mutually reinforcing manner, resulted in the rapid growth of TI to its 1965 level of 34,000 employees and sales nearing the half-way mark to the 1973 goal of $1 billion as shown in Exhibit VII. This organization goal has obvious implications for the achievement of individual goals — in a circular fashion stimulating the enthusiasm necessary for their mutual attainment.

Delegation Process. TI's corporate growth and geographical deployment led to the choice of the decentralized product-customer center as the basic organizational unit for pushing goal setting and decision making down to the action areas of engineering, manufacturing, and mar-

EXHIBIT VII. TEXAS INSTRUMENTS GROWTH CURVES AND GOAL

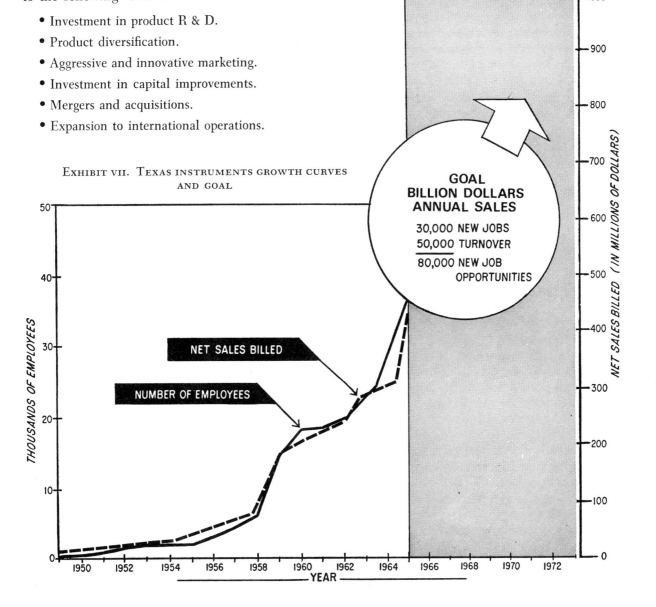

keting. Organized around a product or family of products (or services) the product-customer center is a miniature of the parent organization in terms of its organizational role.

Charged with a broad responsibility which, within the bounds of sound management practice, includes the development, manufacture, and marketing of a product or service, and judged in terms of balance sheet criteria, there is little opportunity or incentive for the manager of the product-customer center to dally with irrelevant objectives. Instead of limiting opportunity for autonomy to a few major division heads, the formation of product-customer centers thrust into the eager hands of over 40 young "presidents" of these "small companies" an opportunity for each to build an empire.

This delegation process requires managers of product-customer centers (and their staff counterparts in the supporting and performance-maximizing centers such as industrial engineering, accounting, and personnel) to establish goals and keep score on themselves in the process of achieving them. Motivation abounds under such circumstances, requiring little stimulation from higher company management. Indeed, management influence under these conditions often must include safeguards against overcommitment or overmotivation, and admonishments to be mindful of home and community responsibilities and the developmental needs of the members of their organizational teams.

Administrative Climate. Goal orientation, as opposed to authority orientation, is encouraged at TI. The distinction between these approaches is subtle on the surface, but significant in determining the administrative climate of the organization. The authority-oriented person is typically an "outer-directed" person performing in blind obedience to orders from superiors. His boss calls the shots, giving him little incentive or opportunity to become a thinking person who relates his job to the big picture. Automaton conformity, or obedient "jumping through hoops," is little better than a pattern for "serving time" on the job, even for high-level managers who are generally assumed to be exempt from such domination. The reductive style of supervision described earlier fosters authority orientation.

The goal-oriented person is more likely to see job goals as a meaningful part of the broader organizational objective, and as steppingstones to his long-range personal goals. Unlike the authority-oriented person who becomes overdependent on his boss for direction and affirmation, the more "inner-directed," goal-oriented person receives meaningful feedback and satisfaction directly from work itself and the achievement of goals. His grasp of the job enables him to initiate self-correction and to grow with his accomplishments.

Status, Not Symbols. Deliberate attempts are made at TI to minimize the status symbols which traditionally reinforce authority orientation and undermine goal orientation. Dining and coffee-bar facilities are shared by all employees, identification badges are color-coded on a job-tenure basis, parking privileges and office space are assigned on the basis of factors other than level of responsibility, a hierarchy of office furnishings is nonexistent, and mode of attire is not standardized (and often consists of informal sports apparel at any level). Employees commonly address each other on a first-name basis (vertically as well as horizontally) and communicate with each other (and conduct business) through the informal and fluid grapevine which exists (though is not always recognized) in every organization. The net effect of such a system is to orient employees on a competence basis rather than to sensitize them to, and sandwich them into, an authority hierarchy.

Contrast this, for example, with the class distinctions sometimes created through dining and parking privileges, office size and furnishings, identification badges, mode of attire, and similar status privileges. Symbols associated with these authority-oriented privileges increase social distances and inhibit communication. They create and exaggerate an hourly salaried cleavage of the work force into the "privileged management" group, whose tactics often become manipulative and defensive; and the "exploited worker" group, whose wrath is exploited, and alternately appeased and aggravated, by labor unions.

Not all status symbols are harmful. For example, attractive grounds and buildings and tenure-coded identification badges are not authority oriented, and probably enhance the cohesiveness of the work force. Thus the selective reinforcement and reduction of status symbols serves a key role in improving interpersonal competence and goal setting.

It should be noted that the points enumerated

above apply to status *symbols* and not status itself. Status itself differs in terms of amount of accountability, salary, and freedom of action. Increased status is a major incentive for personal and professional growth, and for those who have the talent and desire to achieve it. Earned status is its own reward, and the flaunting of symbols or other reminders of inequality is symptomatic of immaturity which serves only to undermine feelings of dignity and worth of those of lesser status on whom higher status individuals depend for their continued success.

Management Systems

The foregoing discussion has illustrated the interdependence of interpersonal competence and goal setting. Though the means and philosophy for achieving goals — such as the product-customer center and minimized status symbols — are in a broad sense management systems, they do not define or adequately illustrate the role of formalized systems for catalyzing interpersonal competence and achieving company and employee goals.

A management system is broadly defined at TI as the organization of a manager's effort to accomplish his purpose. Management systems are perceived and serve as extensions of the managers who direct them and, as such, have the same (or greater) motivating, dissatisfying, supporting, or threatening impact that the managers would have without the systems. That is, a system reflects the supervisory style or takes on the "personality characteristics" of the person running it or thought to be running it.

Conversely, the characteristics of a management system impute to its manager a supervisory style. For example, a supervisor's implementation of a company policy to check all expense accounts might tend to brand him as reductive, whereas the existence of company policy encouraging self-audit practices tends to give supervisors a more developmental image. Hence, the design and staffing of a system must take into account the fact that, with few exceptions, people are the media through which systems function. Moreover, the ideal system is both intrinsically well designed and managed in such a manner that people are able to understand and support it.

Five widely used TI management systems are discussed briefly in the following pages to demonstrate their role in satisfying customer-company and employee needs. Before turning our attention to each of these systems, it may be useful to know the reasoning behind their inclusion in this article. Consider:

• The *planning process* is presented as an illustration of a general management system with far-reaching impact on both customer-company and employee needs.

• Both the *performance review* and the *attitude survey* are examples of personnel management systems which, in addition to their unique roles, also serve the common function of measuring managerial effectiveness.

• *Work simplification* is a system for providing expression for employee creativity in the management of the company.

• *Inventory control* is presented as a typical materials management system which attracts little attention unless it fails.

Planning Operation

At TI the planning process includes the ten-year plan, the annual plan, quarterly reviews, sales and billings meetings, technical seminars, and various other regular and ad hoc group meetings. Annual and long-range planning are discussed here to illustrate the many-faceted role of planning in serving customer-company and employee needs.

Managers from worldwide TI operations convene in Dallas each December to participate with company officers in reviewing and finalizing annual goals. Meeting in a large working session of selectively varied memberships, each manager in a 15- to 30-minute period reviews his past year's targets and accomplishments, and outlines his plans for the year ahead. This presentation serves four basic purposes. It is designed to —

. . . communicate goals and achievements to all managers;

. . . appraise managerial effectiveness in planning and achieving organization goals;

. . . establish understandable, acceptable, challenging charters;

. . . develop managers through their involvement in the planning process.

The annual planning presentations spring from a more profound Objective-Strategy-Tactics (OST) system for managing innovation. Objectives are formal statements of ten-year goals for business areas such as materials, exploration, and electronic components, or for intracompany staff functions such as personnel, facilities, and marketing. Objectives are pursued through one or more supporting "strategies" which, in turn, are implemented through detailed 12- to 18-month. "Tactical Action Programs," or TAPs. Strategies and TAPs are the basis for managing innovation in the various create-make-market and staff support groups. Each product-customer center defines its long-range mission through formal strategies, and reports its current effort toward the strategy on the standard TAP form for top management approval and review. Let us look at two typical illustrations:

Specific ten-year goals have been established for the broad field of functional electronics, and these goals are pursued through several strategies such as one currently implementing the planned evolution of integrated circuits. This strategy is supported by TAPs in the areas of R & D, manufacturing, and marketing.

Similarly, as an example of a staff implementation of the OST system, personnel supports a strategy for locating and developing the company's managerial talent. TAPs supporting this strategy include development of a personnel information retrieval system, identification of criteria and predictors of managerial effectiveness and obsolescence, refinement of a performance measurement and merit compensation procedure, and definition of processes for developing managers.

Reviews of selected strategies and TAP's are presented monthly to the office of the president by strategy and TAP managers who are, in most cases, several organizational levels below the president. This presentation directly to company officers serves several vital purposes not usually satisfied in the large organization. First, it circumvents the traditional multilayer, upward screening process and presents the president and other senior officers with firsthand progress reports on important projects. Second, it also keeps the officers posted on developing technologies. Third, this direct reporting gives the project head immediate feedback, undistorted by the traditional multilayer, downward filtering process, and enables him to align his efforts more directly to the needs of the corporation. Needless to say, the recognition afforded by this process increases the incentive and opportunity for maximum effectiveness.

In short, planning at TI is a dynamic process for involving employees in goal setting, communicating company goals, maximizing profes-

sional growth, and earning recognition. More importantly, it is a system for bypassing the traditional impediments to communication, decision making, and involvement which quash innovation and undermine the corporation's capability for competing successfully with smaller and more agile competitors.

Performance Review

This is a dual-purpose management system for setting goals and reviewing accomplishments, and for determining and communicating pay status to employees twice per year. The system, which is implemented through the relationship of the individual to his supervisor, maximizes opportunities for self-direction and self-review. The salaried review form consists of a single sheet on which the ratee fills in three kinds of information — his accomplishments during the past year, his short-term (six months or less) goals, and his long-range (a year or more) goals.

The next step is a discussion with his supervisor which focuses on these accomplishments and goals, their priorities, and the means of achieving them. After talking things over with his supervisor, the subordinate recaps on the reverse side of the form the consensus of their discussion regarding priorities, action plans, and schedules agreed on. Hence, for the salaried person, the systematic review is a performance-planning process in which the subordinate rather than the supervisor is the initiator of corrective action. In this respect, TI's performance review process is similar to General Electric's work performance and review program.[3]

The supervisor of the hourly person typically uses a traditional report card approach based on job-related factors such as quality, quantity, and reliability, but has the option of using a goal-setting approach. If goal setting has little meaning for hourly employees, it is not so much an indictment of the capabilities of the hourly person as it is a consequence of a historical tradition of failing to delegate meaningful chunks of work to him which would provide opportunities and incentives for him to develop initiative, creativity, and company identification.

Attitude Surveys

These are administered annually at TI as a system for helping managers monitor their own

[3] See Herbert H. Meyer, Emanuel Kay, and John R. P. French, Jr., "Split Roles in Performance Appraisal," HBR January–February 1965, p. 123.

effectiveness, and to provide a basis for diagnosing problems and planning remedial actions. Supervisors compare attitude survey results for their department against a current company profile and their own profile for the previous year. Managers appoint and work through committees to review survey results, and formulate recommendations for improvement. These working committees, particularly when they involve non-supervisory salaried and hourly persons who traditionally have little influence on policy and practice, enable employees to understand organizational problems and to make meaningful contributions to their solution.

Attitude surveys often encounter the traditional circular problem: good supervisors have better survey results and freely provide opportunities for employees to participate in the improvement process; inept supervisors receive unfavorable survey results (which they often attempt to rationalize or ignore) and are reluctant to let employees become involved in the improvement process.

Work Simplification

This is perhaps the most potent management system for encouraging creativity at organizational levels where it is traditionally suppressed.[4] It replaces traditional motion-and-time study on the dual assumption that (1) most job incumbents have creative potential for improving their own jobs, and (2) self-initiated change is positively motivational while change imposed by an authority figure (standing behind them with a clipboard and stopwatch) is more likely to evoke fear and hostility.

Skills in work simplification are acquired through a standardized company training program — usually totaling about 24 hours — to learn principles of motion and time economy, process flow charting, cost analysis, and human relations. Endowed with this new ability, an assembler, for example, ceases to be just a pair of hands performing in a routine unthinking capacity. Instead, the individual has a new outlet for personal creativity — involving work planning with supervisor and associates, earning recognition, growing professionally, and in general strengthening self-identification with the company.

Though the major purpose of work simplification is the harnessing of employee creativity,

improvements effected through the training program result in considerable savings. Ultimately, these savings are returned to employees through profit sharing, which undoubtedly does much to change the image of profit sharing from that of a handout to an earned reward. Work simplification sensitizes individuals to job processes and develops a proprietary consciousness of proper use of company resources.

Manufacturing processes have, in some instances, narrowed the machine operator's job to the point that opportunities for individual task improvements have been reduced. To adapt to these circumstances, a "work simplification task force" process has been developed to involve all members of a work group in the review and improvement of their total operation.

Guided by a staff conference leader who establishes ground rules against personal accusation, this process usually begins with a meeting of top managers to identify and classify operation bottlenecks. An initial meeting might typically result in the identification of 25 to 50 specific problems which are then classified into perhaps 2 to 5 operation areas. The next step takes a deeper dig into the organization through committees to deal with each of these bottlenecks, and may ultimately involve all employees in the department.

Invariably, improvements in operations and attitudes, both of which translate into cost reductions, are the result. Individual and group work improvement processes, if properly goal-oriented, provide opportunities for the growth and recognition of individuals and for the improved achievement of customer-company goals.

Inventory Control

The purpose of an inventory control system is to maintain a proper balance between too lean and too fat an inventory. Too great an inventory increases costs of warehousing, insurance, obsolescence, interest, and price declines; too lean an inventory increases costs of buying, handling, record keeping, and production downtime.

Inventory control is rarely the focus of attention unless something goes wrong. Depletion of a key item can become a serious dissatisfier on the production line. The foreman, for example, faced with the threat of 30 idle assemblers on his hands, scrambles out on a scrounging foray to find the needed part, finding time in the rush to admonish the manufactur-

[4] Auren Uris, "Mogy's Work Simplification Is Working New Miracles," *Factory*, September 1965, pp. 112–115.

ing engineer and inventory control people. If he fails to find the part, he tries to avoid idle-time costs by hurriedly farming the assemblers out to other operations. If he succeeds in placing them, he still faces the possibility of tardy delivery, and the cost and personal inconvenience of overtime.

The assemblers' feelings are mixed, depending on factors such as their attitudes toward the work they are doing, frequency of stoppages, nature of the stopgap assignment, pressure to make up schedules, their feelings about overtime, and their attitudes toward their supervisor and the company.

The inventory control manager has problems even when all is well on the production line. He must be ever alert for the surprise opening or closing of a shift or assembly line. He is continuously preoccupied with shortages, obsolescence, and the cost of inventory on hand, particularly when preparing the monthly inventory cost report. If he has done his job well, maintaining a lean and balanced inventory and avoiding work stoppages, his accomplishments may only cause his boss to urge even tighter controls.

Nonetheless, most jobs in inventory control have potential for satisfying motivation needs; and inventory control clerks, when adequately trained and not overloaded, usually enjoy their work. Their responsibility for monitoring the system, organizing their work, and initiating large purchase orders offers opportunities for the satisfaction of achievement needs.

Inventory problems, from shrinkage to imbalance, usually have their origin in the attitudes of those who administer and are influenced by the system. Attitudes, in turn, are traceable in a circular fashion to one or more of the three conditions set forth in this article — interpersonal competence, opportunity to work toward meaningful goals, and the existence of good management systems. Inventory control, as a specimen materials management system, illustrates the potential of such a system for reflecting the positive and negative aspects of the other two conditions.

Conclusion

Just as the nonmanager is dependent on his boss for motivational opportunities, so is the manager dependent on his boss for conditions of motivation which have meaning at his level. Since the motivation of an employee at any lev-el is strongly related to the supervisory style of his immediate boss, sound motivation patterns must begin at the top. Being closer to the policy-making level, the manager has more opportunity to understand and relate his work to company goals. However, high position alone does not guarantee motivation or self-actualization.

Motivation for the manager, as well as the nonmanager, is usually both a consequence and a symptom of effective job performance. Job success is dependent on cyclical conditions created by interpersonal competence, meaningful goals, and helpful systems. After sustained conditioning in the developmental cycle, an individual has amazing capacity and incentive to remain in it. Moreover, if forced into the reductive cycle, unless he has pathological needs to remain there, organizational conditions must be remarkably and consistently bad to suppress his return to the developmental cycle.

Sustained confinement of a large percentage of the work force in the reductive cycle is symptomatic of organizational illness. It is usually a culmination of a chain of events beginning with top management, and is reversible only by changes at the top. Consequences of reductive conditions such as militant unionism and other forms of reactive behavior usually provoke management into defensive and manipulative behavior which only reinforces the reductive cycle. The vicarious pleasure sought by the rank and file through seeing the management giant felled by their union is a poor substitute for the self-actualization of being a whole person doing a meaningful job, but, in the absence of motivational opportunities, it is an understandable compromise.

The seeds of concerted reactive behavior are often brought to the job from broadly shared frustrations arising from social injustice, economic deprivation, and moral decadence either to sprout in a reductive climate or become infertile in a developmental climate. Hence, the unionization of a work group is usually precipitated by management failure to provide opportunities for employees to achieve personal goals through the achievement of organization goals. Organizations survive these failures only because most other companies are equally handicapped by the same failures.

Management failures in supervision do not, of course, stem from intentional malice. They may result, in part, from a lingering tradition of "scientific management" which fractionated tasks and "protected" employees from the need to think, and perpetrated management systems based on automaton conformity. But more often such failures stem from the manager's insensitivity to the needs and perceptions of others, particularly from his inability to see himself as others see him.

Insensitivity or the inability to empathize is manifested not only as interpersonal incompetence, but also as the failure to provide meaningful goals, the misuse of management systems, or a combination of both. Style of supervision, then, is largely an expression of the personality characteristics and mental health of the manager, and his potential for inducing developmental or reductive cyclical reactions.

14

BETTER MANAGEMENT
OF MANAGERS' CAREERS

Lawrence L. Ferguson

• Why do about one-half of the carefully screened, highly promising new college graduates hired by large corporations leave during the first three to six years?

• What causes an increasing number of mature men of demonstrated high capacity to leave or seek to leave a company?

• Why do so many really high-potential individuals end up in dead-end situations?

• What job situations cause incumbents consistently to be overrated by their peers and supervisors?

• What are the characteristics of "graveyard" jobs — jobs in which no individual ever looks good and which can damage the career of a highly promising man?

• What characteristics (other than previous performance in lower-level jobs) are critical for success in top jobs of broad responsibility?

• Why do so many successful managers say, at the midpoints in their careers, that they do not know the real promotion criteria in their company?

• How many managerial manpower planning programs now have a rational long-range base, and how many of them consider each problem of selection and training for a job opening a task by itself?

• How many times has the solution to one pro-

motion-and-placement problem unknowingly generated many more problems because practical means for examining all the subsequent effects were not available?

If these seem like nagging questions that top executives and personnel managers have been asking for years, then how about these:

◖ Can a comprehensive simulation model of the entire career-growth process for managers be developed that will give coherence and relevance to all the fragmented pieces of the selection, training, motivating, planning, and promotion processes?

◖ Can the variables actually exerting major influences on business career progress be identified, stated, and understood?

◖ Can these variables then be used to develop a comprehensive, continuous-flow process of manpower development that will enhance growth opportunities and contributions for the benefit of the individual and the corporation?

The answer to these latter questions is *yes!* Why? Because the time *has* now come when American industry can — and will — move into an exciting new world of scientific personnel management that was completely impractical just a few years ago. Two coinciding advances make this possible:

(1) The development of highly effective, flexible, time-shared, real-time computer systems, with matching advances in analytical techniques for processing data.

(2) The increasingly significant progress that social scientists are making in providing insights into the manager development and management processes.

It is now possible and practical for us to examine critically the validity of many of our beliefs about managerial growth. Moreover, as this article will indicate, *it is now possible to replace intuition with scientific analysis in the personnel area*, just as intuition has successively given way to analysis in engineering, finance, production, and marketing.

Time for Action

What will be said in this article is neither utopian nor futuristic. Some U.S. companies are already well beyond the Model T stage so far as managerial career planning goes. Today there is little doubt that social scientists clearly demonstrate significant abilities to separate personnel with high probabilities of success in specific management jobs from those who have low probabilities. And we are certainly at the stage where this predictive information can be — and is being — put on computers. But there is still a long way to go before today's pre- and post-Model T forms of manpower management develop into Thunderbirds — or even Mustangs. Here is why.

Next Big Step

Despite the fact that we are using computers for storing and analyzing information on personnel, the common process today is for a manager to call a personnel man, tell him about a coming vacancy, and say he wants a replacement with certain kinds of characteristics to fill the job. In-depth requirements of the job in terms of task demands and specific personal attributes, however, are more often than not left in very general or vague terms.

The personnel man then goes back and asks the computer — or other, less advanced forms of data storage — for information. He gets a packet of personnel files containing comparatively limited data, and brings them to the manager for review. From these reports the manager chooses a few men he wants to interview; after interviewing, he finally selects a replacement. All the while, however, he may be wondering somewhat apprehensively if his solution to his problem is not producing complications and other problems elsewhere in the company, now or for the future.

Unless there is available a comprehensive analytic and storage facility such as a computer system can provide, there is no way that an individual manager, making a sound decision in relation to his immediate problem, can have any idea of the impact of his decision on the many more distant aspects that are necessarily involved. As a consequence, solutions to a problem that are arrived at without an awareness of the total scene may, *and more often than not do*, create a host of additional problems of which most individuals are completely unaware.

How would things be different if the manager possessed a better understanding of the behavioral criteria and other data that are important for various kinds of positions? He could turn, say, to a small console beside his desk and ask the computer center directly about the availability of individuals who meet the qualifications he believes to be most important. The information would then be fed directly to him in a matter of seconds, together with indications of the effects of the considered move on the individual's career and the corporation's manpower needs and plans. To be more specific:

Suppose our manager of the future is looking for new men for a position where the major future problems seem to be in two areas: (a) improvement in design and performance, and (b) lower manufacturing costs. The goal is to make the product substantially more competitive in order to gain a larger share of the market.

Instead of looking merely for individuals with an engineering background and some success in the area of cost reduction and manufacturing (as would have been the common practice in the past), our manager will seek, in addition, many other talents which previous social science research has identified. These might be the individual's capacity to:

√ Accept risk.
√ Make decisions with varied amounts of information.
√ Correlate data.
√ Gather specific kinds of information.
√ Analyze data.
√ Exercise leadership.

√ Integrate the skills of specialists (such as application engineers, material specialists, quality control people, plant layout specialists, and purchasing agents).

The manager may also ask the computer to search for individuals who have revealed on previous tests special aptitudes, such as high analytical ability with quantitative problems or mechanical talents. The computer could also be asked to identify, among those so far qualified, particular men who have had prior success in jobs with demands similar to those for the job in question, and to identify the relative importance of various personal attributes that have correlated with previous successful performance.

Continuous-Flow Process

Such a process is infinitely superior to the intuitive methods now used by the majority of companies. It represents, roughly, the kind of advance that the efficient continuous-process chemical plants and refineries have made over the crude-batch and individual-still operations of a few decades ago. Accurate knowledge of processes; understanding of the effects of temperature, pressure, catalysts, and reagents on raw materials; and data on kinds of output in greatest demand — such resources make today's complex plants highly effective, low-cost producers that benefit everyone.

Manpower planning to date has been pretty much a short-term "batch" process, managed for the most part by the good judgment and intuitive skills of successful persons who apply the distillation of their experience to individual problems. But the opportunities are at hand to move toward a broader understanding of all the forces involved. With better predictive information, with better knowledge of what a manager's work actually consists of, and with comprehensive information storage (i.e., with analytical and retrieval systems *coupled* to research systems and corporate planning), it has become practical to develop techniques for continuous-flow processes for manpower planning, development, and utilization that can benefit everyone involved.

In short, *the scientific revolution has at last reached the field of personnel management.*

Expensive Intuition

In no area of management is failure to substitute science for guessing more costly than in personnel. There is little doubt that inadequate managerial skills in critical positions can well be the most serious limitation to the growth and profitability of a corporation. When largely intuitive methods continue to be relied on by management, both individuals and organizations suffer. Let us examine several reasons for this.

1. *Intuitive methods of selection and promotion are impossible to quantify, and difficult to communicate even to the more perceptive young managers.*

Consequently, because of our current reliance on these largely intuitive methods, the process by which an ambitious employee moves from early training assignments to a top managerial position is cloaked in mystery, uncertainty, and often ridiculous historical precedents. Early in his career, therefore, he can only guess at the actions on his part that will be most effective in moving him along the course he wants to follow.

This uncertainty often causes the individual to devote so much time, energy, and thought to conforming to assumed criteria for promotion that the company suffers a triple loss: (a) from energies diverted from real work objectives; (b) from failure to encourage fresh, innovative behavior; and (c) from active efforts to find more attractive opportunities elsewhere. In addition, under these conditions the individual loses the feeling of effective personal influence over his destiny that is so important to highly motivated individuals and essential for real involvement in an employer's problems.

Why is there not greater clarity and specific information about the promotion processes in a particular company? Mainly because most employers themselves do not possess the necessary information about the critical factors that significantly affect career progress. Consequently, they have not been able to develop integrated progression programs for a business lifetime that can be explained and consistently followed.

2. *Attempts to predict a man's success cannot be made scientific with mechanical devices.*

Progression tables, runner-up charts, and lists of promising young men are all staple items in the manpower planning repertoire of most companies. But just how meaningful are such devices? There are few, if any, precise measurements. However, repeated, after-the-fact examinations at General Electric and other companies indicate quite consistently that, for all but a few exceptional companies, *less than 30% of the individuals identified as being the leading candidates for a position ever actually achieve it.* Similar kinds of results are found when we examine the histories of individuals who do achieve top-level managerial positions. More often than not, less than one-half of such individuals have appeared on the most-promising-young-men lists early in their careers, or have been paid in the top quartile of their age group.

This fact is often obscured by the presence of readily visible "comers" for whom outstanding success is predicted and who do fulfill all expectations. It is true that the odds on advancement to the top are better for some groups than for others. For example, one examination of the histories of top leaders in General Electric Company indicated that:

For men up to age 35, the odds for an individual in the top compensation decile *for his age group* eventually achieving a position in the top 1% of the company are five times greater than those for a randomly chosen individual in the lower deciles for the same age group.

At age 40, the odds for his achieving it are up to about 15 to 1.

At age 45, the odds are as high as 45 to 1!

Although a comprehensive examination of salary history data always produces a range of possibly significant interpretations, these data at least suggest that a man in the top decile from age 30 on does have a much better chance of becoming a company leader than do those who are not in this stratum. However, we must remember that there are nine times as many individuals in the lower nine deciles, and *from these lower nine deciles it is common to find that about* twice *as many company leaders are finally drawn as from the top decile alone!*

It is also true that because the opportunities outside a company are high for the most able individuals, the odds that individuals in the top decile will leave are higher than for individuals in lower strata. As a consequence, in most companies there is a constant attenuation of top-level talent and a progressive dilution of the concentration of top abilities (see EXHIBIT I). This often goes unnoticed — or blandly ignored — because of the always available supply of individuals moving up from below who are, it is hoped, very nearly as good as the individuals they replace. Thus it is only over an appreciable

time interval that the effects of higher losses from the top are evident, if at all.

3. Guesswork in selection and development leads to high turnover — especially at the beginning levels.

Better ways of handling manager progression — the selecting, rewarding, training, and planning process for careers — must be developed so that both the individual's needs and the corporation's are better realized. A recent *Wall Street Journal* study reported:

"Firms complain increasingly that they are laying out as much as $10,000 a man to recruit and train talented college graduates for management posts in the $7,500 to $10,000 a year range — and then losing about half of them within three to five years. . . .

"Many of the youthful managers call on executive recruiting firms to find them new jobs. 'We get from 30 to 50 unsolicited queries from these restless young comers each work day, compared with only 10 to 15 daily in 1958,' says a partner in one management recruiting concern." [1]

Some of this turnover points up the increasing magnitude of "people problems" plaguing American industry. Paul B. Wishart, Chairman of the Board of Honeywell Inc., emphasized this recently, stating that the need for 200,000 more top managers is a "practical, not a theoretical, problem." [2]

Looking ahead, we do not find the need diminishing. Industry usually recruits its executive talent primarily from the 34–54 age group. In the next ten years, this population will remain constant at about 46 million persons. Yet the total population in the United States is expected to grow from the present 195 million to about 225 million over the same decade. This means that industry will have to dip into the expanding 20–34 age group for managerial talent to a greater extent than ever before, and must make promotion commitments with less on-the-job experience data to draw on than has been the case in the past.

These facts accentuate American industry's need for outgrowing its current intuitive methods and developing much more reliable instruments. The crucial need is to help get the "right" men in the "right" jobs faster, more consistently, and with fewer mistakes of the kind

[1] January 21, 1965.
[2] *Management Review*, March 1965, p. 4.

EXHIBIT I. TYPICAL PATTERN OF MANAGER MOBILITY

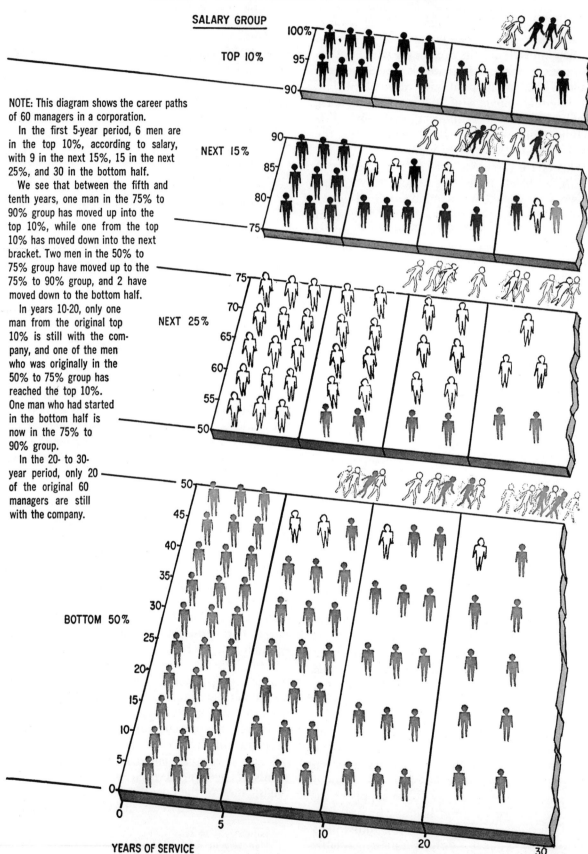

NOTE: This diagram shows the career paths of 60 managers in a corporation.

In the first 5-year period, 6 men are in the top 10%, according to salary, with 9 in the next 15%, 15 in the next 25%, and 30 in the bottom half.

We see that between the fifth and tenth years, one man in the 75% to 90% group has moved up into the top 10%, while one from the top 10% has moved down into the next bracket. Two men in the 50% to 75% group have moved up to the 75% to 90% group, and 2 have moved down to the bottom half.

In years 10-20, only one man from the original top 10% is still with the company, and one of the men who was originally in the 50% to 75% group has reached the top 10%. One man who had started in the bottom half is now in the 75% to 90% group.

In the 20- to 30-year period, only 20 of the original 60 managers are still with the company.

SALARY GROUP

TOP 10%

NEXT 15%

NEXT 25%

BOTTOM 50%

YEARS OF SERVICE

that are so costly to correct in terms of time, money, and personal relations.

Why Fear Science?

Impeding the progress toward achieving this goal is the fear some managers have of the encroachment of science into the personnel area. Moral issues such as invasion of privacy and the like are quickly raised as objections. Yet moral reasons also cry out for making the management selection, development, and promotion process *more* scientific, objective, and openly communicated. Why, if it is at all possible to have it otherwise, should a man's career progress be left to chance or to the potential whim of one or more lower-level supervisors making the recommendations?

In an era when continuous retraining is necessary for managers on the rise, selection for advanced training programs is crucial. Yet being selected for such programs is often dependent on the ability of the individual to perform *early* technical or routine assignments — even though these may not reveal the broader, more general abilities required of top-level managers. The selection process, if it is not made more objective, may merely reflect the biases of a man's particular manager at a particular time — a manager, moreover, who does not have the knowledge, skill, or long-term responsibilities for the man's development.

Actually, if we think about it, we see clearly that *it is managers at the lower levels who determine just which person it is whom higher-level managers will have the opportunity to consider for promotion.* Although boards of directors normally elect officers to the one or two top executive positions, first-line supervisors *every day* are determining which individuals the directors will *never* have an opportunity to consider. Lack of understanding of changing job requirements at higher levels often results in lower-level supervisors eliminating those persons who, though not well matched to their jobs at present, might be especially well qualified to perform higher-level tasks at some later time.

Above-Board Treatment

Aspiring managers have every right to expect equitable treatment in career planning just as they have in other areas of contact with their company. Objections to scientific approaches to psychological testing and research on moral grounds miss the real moral imperative — that of frankness and openness with the individual about how his capacities match up against company position requirements.

This is not the place to discuss the strengths and shortcomings of personnel testing, but the true moral implications of in-depth personnel research are brought out clearly in the following excerpts from a letter by a scientist closely involved in an in-company research program of unquestioned merit:

"If our research tells us (as it does) that lack of emotional stability contributes strongly to executive failure, do we have the right to subject a man to the ravages of a job that he does not have the emotional strength to cope with? . . .

"If we can predict promotability to a first-line supervisory position with approximately 70% accuracy (as we can), would we be right if we allowed a man to get into that position if the chances of succeeding are overwhelmingly against him? . . .

"If we test a couple of thousand employees and then file their tests away for five years (as we did), and then check on their respective job progress and find that psychological tests are better predictors of what will eventually happen to employees than are supervisory ratings (as our research has demonstrated), would we then be justified in withholding the use of psychological tests as a supplement to supervisory judgment? . . .

"If we can say with great assurance (as our research allows us to do) that the psychological characteristics of the executive leader stand in close relationship to the quality of morale he produces, and that the leader's psychological characteristics are, to a very large extent, determinants of employee morale (as they are), would we be right if we did not influence the working atmosphere of hundreds and thousands of people through the medium of initial selection of executive leaders?"

How moral is it for companies — inadvertently or otherwise — to keep aspiring managers in the dark about their chances for advancement in the organization? The extent of the confusion now rampant about what it takes to advance in companies is indicated by a number of surveys at General Electric and elsewhere. About one-half of those managers in the 30–40 age group who are viewed as outstanding candidates for substantial future advancement commonly say that:

1. They do not know what the present promotion process is.

2. Whatever it is, it is different from what they have been told.

3. The process is not uniformly administered.

4. They know that just doing an outstanding job will not assure them of consideration for promotion, but they are uncertain about what else they "should" do.

5. They cannot aim for a particular job because of lack of knowledge beforehand about probable or actual opportunities.

6. They are unable to discern any consistent historical patterns in the promotions made.

7. As a consequence, they do not know how best to prepare themselves for the next possible advancement and are often less effective and purposeful in their present jobs than they would be if there were a consistent, rational, well-understood basis for review and selection of individuals for promotion to key jobs.

Consequently, the moral question should not arise when companies use all scientific methods at their disposal for matching the right men to the right jobs. It should arise when companies do *not* put more objectivity into the selection process. Issues should also be raised when companies fail to be frank (but confidential) with individuals about what the odds are that their particular attributes and prior achievements will lead to success in the career of their choice.

Potential for Progress

A few companies, such as General Motors, IBM, Du Pont, Sears Roebuck, Standard Oil of New Jersey, American Telephone & Telegraph, and General Electric, have made a good start toward bringing scientific knowledge and methodology into their selection, development, and promotion programs. Their programs are based on serious, systematic attempts to collect, analyze, apply, and test new kinds of information and procedures which may help them do a better job of predicting the future growth of managers.

These pioneering programs have disclosed much — especially about the mutual benefits that the individual and the company can obtain from working together. For example, it is increasingly evident that most individuals are realistic in evaluating their capacity, the probable maximum achievement level for which they can qualify, the necessary rate of progress they must maintain to reach specified goals, and the probable actual maximum achievement level they will attain.

It also appears that individual prediction is greatly improved, adjustment to reality facilitated, and individual motivation increased by the open dissemination of reliable information about job requirements and rewards, the promotion process really being followed, the current and probable future state of promotion opportunities, and the criteria actually used for selection.

Steps Toward Improvement

Just pointing up the costs of intuition and the advantages of a more scientific selection, development, and promotion program, as I have done, is not enough. What steps should companies take in order to gain these advantages?

Underlying these steps is one absolute necessity: *Any company interested must first secure the support of its top officers for a long-range personnel research program.* For only from such research, conducted *within* the individual company and with top management support, can a truly integrated long-range manpower development program result. Then, once this support is obtained, the following data and capabilities must be developed:

1. *Predictive information* — Management has need of the kinds of information that reliably predict further growth of an individual. ("Growth" here is defined in terms of his being able to handle specific responsibilities of greater scope and accountability.)

2. *Understanding of what a manager's work actually is and will be* — Required is an understanding, in behavioral terms, of what the critical managerial performance demands will be in the future, in the light of specific corporate business and organization plans.

3. *Information storage, analysis, and utilization* — There must be a system for storing and processing comprehensive data on personal attributes and nature of tasks.

4. *Monitoring, research, and corporate manpower planning* — Management needs a feedback-and-research system for analysis, evaluation, and alteration of the managerial growth process.

Each of these requirements will be examined in order. Please remember, however, that I am *not* suggesting a mechanistic substitute for managerial decisions and manpower planning. Rather, I am suggesting a means of augmenting a manager's capacity to consider a wide array of complex data and reduce the information, at his command, to forms he can consider thoughtfully, evaluate, and use as an improved basis for manpower decisions.

Predictive Information

Developing reliable early predictors of a manager's future progress is difficult. Individual careers do not follow smooth composite percentile curves. Yet in our personnel planning we often *act* as if they did.

Actually, every person has a period (or periods) in his career when, as a result of some synthesis, his potential effectiveness increases enormously. Certainly, there are no instruments now available to help us predict when or how often this "blossoming" is most apt to occur in individual cases. But psychologists who are studying learning processes and many business managers do know that when the blossoming happens under favorable conditions, the individual makes contributions that are literally phenomenal. The application of existing knowledge about work characteristics and socialization processes can unquestionably make such rapid growth stages occur more often.

Of course the blossoming of an individual should be reflected in his compensation — and we do have some limited data about this. In one study of a group of top leaders in General Electric, for example, it was found that the individuals who achieved salary increases of 30% or more at least once in a single year had a much better than average probability of going on to substantially higher maximum achievement levels later in their careers. Such findings suggest the value of collecting long-term career data and progress patterns to (a) assess the predictive value of compensation and other personnel data and (b) increase the likelihood of timing the matching of men and situations so that more nearly optimal results are obtained.

Some insight into reasons for managerial success or failure can be obtained from trying to reconstruct the careers of successful men. Usually, however, retrospective efforts of this type are not very rewarding. What is needed is more analytical, less historical (or repertorial) information. Companies need to collect data on both successful mature managers and highly promising young men which show in depth:

— What they actually *do* in their various jobs.

— What methods they use.

— What the situational factors are which surround their successes and failures.

— How they make decisions and implement them.

— What opportunities they have to make mistakes.

— What results (good or bad) they achieve.

— What other factors impinge on individual managerial effectiveness.

Needed is information as to the proportion, degree, relationship, and consequences of "good" and "bad" decisions, and as to the relative importance of sound thinking, vigorous action, intellectual skills, personal style, interpersonal skills, and other characteristics that are required for success. Needed also is information on the factors that produce slowdown or relative ineffectiveness in individuals formerly enjoying a rapid growth rate, as well as a host of other important pieces of knowledge.

Advances in managing careers will come as understanding increases and as sound theories are developed and tested. New and insightful information, coupled with thoughtful analyses, can go far in illuminating the critical considerations that affect an individual's career and govern his potential for future accomplishments.

Getting the Facts

How are companies to go about obtaining such information? Much uncorrelated data are already available. Other information is becoming available from special studies validated in actual working conditions by social scientists. But it is most likely that any individual company will make the best progress by developing the information it needs from within its own operations. This will surely involve utilizing the skills of social scientists experienced in the management development process to determine the critical interrelationships that are peculiar to each business enterprise.

But social scientists cannot be solely relied on to gather necessary data. This has to be a joint activity of managers and social scientists. Social scientists, for the most part, almost never have a sound and complete understanding of what a manager's job really is. They do not understand the kinds or degrees of stresses and strains under which the manager operates. They do not understand the rationale for the way the manager spends his time, and they are critical of the "foolish" decisions he sometimes makes. They often wonder why things appear to be done so illogically and unreasonably in business operations. Mainly they feel this way because they do not have an understanding of the kinds of forces that operate on a manager at work.

But even though they may not understand the entire process of business operations, social scientists are in a position to help determine the characteristics of individuals who can operate best under certain prescribed conditions. The task calls for cooperation. Managers must provide information about task needs and goals, about operating limitations, situational variables, procedures, plans, present personnel, and other work-related factors. In turn, social scientists must be able to ascertain the psychological attributes needed by the holder of a particular job. What skills in terms of conflict resolution, deductive reasoning, information processing, analysis, decision making, persuasion, risk acceptance, ambiguity tolerance, and a dozen other things are desirable for maximum performance? And by matching such job requirements with an individual's psychological and educational makeup, the social scientist can determine if he has a high probability of being successful in the new position.

Team Approach Needed

Managers are very often unaware of all the skills required and used in their jobs. For example, rarely is a manager today consciously aware even of the existence of processes such as conflict resolution. Nevertheless, from a social scientist's standpoint, the possession of such psychological skills is an important factor in the performance of a successful manager. This makes it desirable for managers and social scientists to team up in doing the research.

Such a team can obtain much information by employing existing standard psychological tests, business games (such as the one devised by Charles H. Kepner and Benjamin B. Tregoe [3]), and simulation exercises tailored to job characteristics and environmental conditions representative of a company's operations.

The American Telephone & Telegraph Company's "Assessment Center" technique, soundly conceived and supported by continuing research, is an outstanding example of this last approach.[4]

Here actual managerial situations are simulated, and *operating managers have a major role in the scoring and judging of individual performance.* For AT&T, this research effort has already paid off handsomely in practical applications. Specifically:

(1) Managers appointed as a result of Assessment Center evaluation have done a "better than satisfactory" job — in the opinion of their supervisors — with about double the frequency (62% versus 35%) of those appointed without Assessment Center evaluation.

(2) Essentially the same relationship prevailed in the percentage judged by their supervisors as having the potential for further promotion: 67% of the assessed group compared with 35% of the control group.

This approach should be even more rewarding in the future, as further research done under AT&T's long-range "Management Progress Study" provides additional insights into the influences within the company that affect individual career patterns and how these influences correlate with individual attributes and responses.

Role of Self-Perception

Psychological tests, business games, and on-the-job observations are all important sources of information on which to base conclusions about an individual's suitability for increased responsibility. But there is one other aspect that we should never lose sight of: the individual's perception of himself in relation to promotion opportunities.

Dr. Harry Levinson of The Menninger Foundation made this point very clearly when he questioned recently: "Will a promotion be an opportunity — or a big step toward failure?" His answer: "A promotion can be as threatening to one man as it is reassuring to another, because it raises questions that concern his emotional and psychological makeup. . . . How he *feels* about himself is often more critical to his success or failure than what he *is* objectively." [5]

Promotion decisions that rely too heavily on the marvelous capacity of unusually able persons to adapt well to a wide range of demands represent today one of the high cost elements in the promotion process. Often the limits of a person to adapt are exceeded or stressed to the

[3] See "Developing Decision Makers," HBR September–October 1960, p. 115.

[4] See *The Personnel Job in a Changing World*, edited by Jerome W. Blood (New York, American Management Association, Inc., 1964), p. 234.

[5] *Think*, January–February 1965, p. 7.

point where he performs considerably below optimal levels or actively seeks a change.

On-the-Job Behavior

Why is it so important to develop knowledge of managerial work in *behavioral* terms? The reason is that there is almost no comprehensive information available today with respect to *what* a manager actually does and *how* he utilizes his time. Sune Carlson's *Executive Behavior* [6] was the first definitive effort in this direction. Subsequent studies by William H. Whyte, Jr., Robert Dubin, T. A. Mahoney, Tom Burns, and others have, for the most part, served mainly to make more evident the need for specific information about managerial work. Here are some of the findings:

❧ The European managing directors in Sune Carlson's study put in about a 50-hour work week on the average. By contrast, Professor William H. Whyte, Jr. of Cornell reports that American executives put in much longer hours. He states: "Putting all the commitments together, we get a work week something like this: 45 to 48 hours of daytime work, one night working late at the office, two nights working at home, one night entertaining — all in all, some 57 to 60 hours. And this evidently is a minimum; come convention time, a trip, a company emergency, and the work can easily go to 70 or 80 hours." [7]

❧ Tom Burns (of the University of Edinburgh) reported last year that in his survey of 94 British managers (from chairman to middle management) in 10 companies: "The average total commitment of time to work was 43½ hours, a figure which includes all reading, homework, business lunches and traveling for the firm. Moreover, the distribution is rather skewed, and the mode is in fact rather below 42 hours a week." [8]

Widely different results such as these reveal the danger of extrapolating the findings from one study to different cultural or situational backgrounds. Definitive studies must be carried out in the environment where the findings are expected to be applied.

The question still remains: *How* do the managers studied spend their time? Some illumination is again provided by Tom Burns, who reports that "they talk" — for as much as 80% of the time, with the lowest proportion being

about 42%. But *what* do they talk about? In Tom Burns's study, they talk about:

Current production	22%
General management policy	20%
Programming, materials, and production control	20%
Recruitment and personnel	11%
Costs, accounts, and wages	9%
External interests	7%
Research and development	6%
Personal and private	5%

The studies reveal a considerable discrepancy between common *beliefs* about managerial behavior and values and the *actual facts*. Tom Burns reports:

"Among heads of companies, there was a widespread tendency to overestimate attention to production, to underestimate the claims of outside interests on time, but even more discrepancies are encountered among their subordinates. One technical manager and his deputy thought that his colleagues must be spending 70% of their time on current production problems as against an actual 12%. A production manager thought of sales and attention to customers' needs as claiming 5% of the whole group's time as against 23% (actual)." [9]

Specific Data Needs

All this suggests the urgent need to find out the really basic behavioral features that are most important to achieving success as a manager. How *are* managerial decisions transmitted? How *do* individuals allocate their time to various tasks? And, most important, *what* do they do in the execution of what they perceive as needed action?

We need specific information as to what managers actually do in conferences, group meetings, telephone conversations, discussions with subordinates, time alone, meetings with peers, and so on throughout representative business days. For example, how much of a manager's time is spent in resolving conflicts? In influencing the action of other individuals? In persuading? In communicating? In reducing misunderstandings? In information gathering? In information processing? In exercising judgment? In decision making?

And, of course, we need to know also how these activities differ among managers of different functions and with different managerial styles — and what the results are. We need to

[6] Stockholm, Sweden, Stromberg, 1951.
[7] "How Hard Do Executives Work?" *Fortune*, January 1954, p. 108.
[8] "What Managers Do," *New Society*, December 17, 1964, p. 8.
[9] Tom Burns, op. cit., p. 9.

know the nature of the different demands placed on executives in marketing, research and development, production, finance, and so on. We need to know how these demands differ at different levels of the organization hierarchy.

Until valid answers to these and many similar questions are available to serve as a pattern against which to match the skills and capacities of individuals for the various jobs in an organization, our manpower placement and development practices are going to continue to fall far short of any reasonable level of efficiency and effectiveness.

Storing & Using Data

Let us take for granted that it is now possible and important for companies to obtain accurate and more complete information about how — and on what — a manager spends his time. Once we possess this mountain of data, what then? Fortunately, facilities are available for the necessary coding, storage, retrieval, analysis, and study of these and the many other related kinds of data whose significance for manpower planning is as yet little understood or appreciated.

Broadly speaking, there are two kinds of data with which we are concerned:

1. *Quantitative information* — This most companies have on hand, though more complete and comprehensive details may be needed. It is primarily statistical information (i.e., information that can be reduced to numbers, such as salary history, scholastic standing, level of education, training programs, job assignments, test scores, and performance ranking). These data can be put on storage media for direct input to the information system. COBOL, FORTRAN, SIMSCRIPT, BASIC, or Integrated Data Store can be utilized to develop computer programs that are appropriate for the particular company's organizational and statistical processes.

2. *Qualitative information* — This second kind of data presents the major difficulty today. It includes the qualitative information about an individual's experience and his attributes — e.g., his personality traits, interpersonal skills, originality, judgment, tenacity, poise, self-confidence, aspirations, commitment, response to risk, cost consciousness, and the many other related facets of personality and abilities.

There also are a host of other factors which are commonly *presumed* to be important, but for which we have little direct evidence as to their relationship to success or failure on jobs. We real-

ly do not know, and cannot compare, the extent to which training, experience, technical skills, intellectual skills, social skills, personal style, timing of particular work experiences, and personal characteristics actually influence career progress. Such determination would be a major research facet of the comprehensive program outlined in this article.

Improving Decisions

It is important to appreciate that what has been designed here is an on-going process. It is a process in which management goes on much as usual, but always a bit more sophisticatedly, and always a bit more consciously. Although the social scientist may help to clarify a decision, it is still the manager who *makes* it. It is still the manager who must choose just one of several fully qualified candidates for promotion. How is he to select the person best able to cope with future work situations — situations which will themselves certainly change in somewhat unpredictable ways in the future? How can he be sure that today's decision will not unwittingly be causing another problem next month or next year?

It is precisely here that the proposed system (schematically portrayed in EXHIBIT II), with its vast data processing capacity and its informed inputs from the insights and techniques of social scientists, should be of the greatest help to a manager. It will help him make promotion decisions which are compatible with the optimal long-term benefits both to an individual and the corporation.

Analyzing the Record

As the model is now envisioned, the manager would make his selections in a perfectly normal and independent fashion. Any properly qualified manager would have access to the appropriate bank of personnel information in the central data storage and processing system. From his desk, he could ask for and receive — in seconds — complete information about all individuals in the storage bank who meet the specifications he designates. The manager could change the specifications, ask for special analyses, and in general get, to the extent that prior inputs have been adequate, answers to any question he wants to ask the computer.

All he need do is be able to talk in terms of the attributes, characteristics, and limitations he wants to impose. He could, at his command, get

EXHIBIT II. SIMPLIFIED MANAGERIAL MANPOWER SELECTION AND CAREER PLANNING MODEL

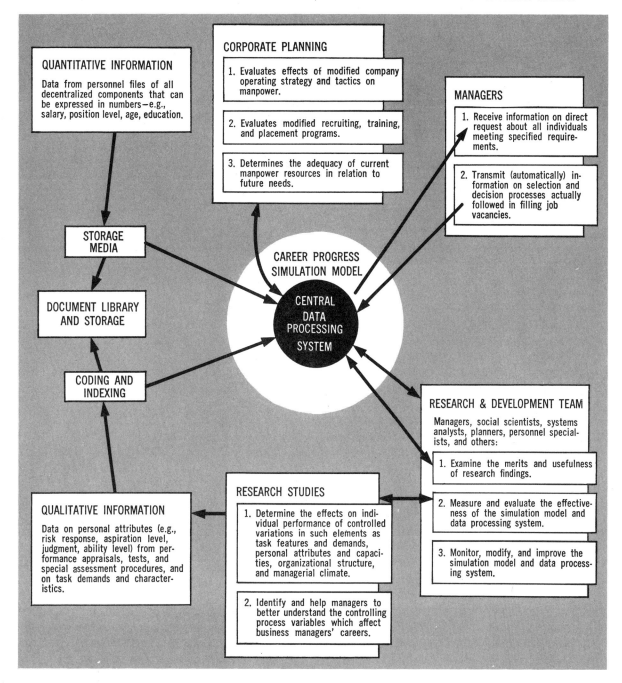

tabular lists, frequency distributions, correlation coefficients, predictive data, and almost anything else he is ingenious enough to think of that might help him reach a decision. From an array of qualified candidates, he would finally make a choice, and a promotion would be accomplished.

But more than this, after such a sequence of actions is completed, there would be available for analysis a complete history of the *process* of selection the manager *actually went through.*

When enough of these selection histories have been recorded, there will then be available for examination and study the evidence of the real selection process managers use in filling subordinate positions.

Thus, this system will allow the individual seeking promotion to receive a confidential "handicapping" of his chances for success along different possible career routes. A person's career history will reveal a series of objectives whose successive attainment — or lack of attainment — provides a basis for more refined estimates as to the likelihood of his achieving more demanding goals. Obviously, then, with such a program in action, it should increasingly become practical to inquire as to the odds that John Jones will become vice president, general manager, or treasurer (or some other position) at some particular age.

And, if the individual finds the odds unfavorable, he can ask the computer to assess — in the light of his present work experience, educational history, special training, personal attributes, age, performance record, and the like — what he must do to have at least a 50–50 chance of reaching his goal within a specific time.

Furthermore, there is no reason why information about current conditions on various career paths could not be periodically summarized. This information could be made available to aspiring candidates in much the same way that status reports on complex technical or production programs are provided today. Individuals could then make effective use of such intelligence to alter their own personal planning so as to match their qualifications and experience to various opportunities in a much more realistic, self-determining, and democratic fashion than is possible under current conditions of limited and inexact information.

Manpower Planning

Research studies can also be conducted on the corporate level to determine the effectiveness of the company's compensation structure in attracting, retaining, and motivating individuals. Such research can also help determine the extent to which various elements in the reward structure — stock options, incentive pay, fringe benefits, and other features — are valued by individuals. Factors affecting the optimal timing of job changes could be studied, as could the extent and nature of changes induced by special training programs. Studies could be made of how an individual's career is influenced by such factors as work climate, aspiration level, managerial style, supervisor values, information flow, perceived opportunity, external job markets, and many other considerations.

These kinds of data, plus an understanding of the magnitude and nature of their influence, will provide inputs which will steadily improve the overall value of the system. Means for more

nearly optimizing the utilization of resources at hand and for predicting the specific nature, costs, and advantages of possible changes will become apparent and can be subjected to objective testing and evaluation.

The complete simulation model proposed here would also provide insight into, and give an understanding of, *how* the important or controlling variables in the personnel system affect the movements of individuals or categories of personnel. With such a system it would be possible for managers and planners to determine in advance the probable effects on business operations of proposed changes in organization structure, recruiting practices, development programs, retirement age, transfer policies, and a host of other factors. This could help develop the combinations that would produce the best overall corporate results.

From a long-range corporate standpoint, the complete system can provide essential manpower data in a central source that reflects the inputs from and status of personnel in hundreds of decentralized components. This makes it possible to examine for an entire corporation the composite effects of individual personnel decisions of hundreds or thousands of managers at any point in time. Consequently, it can simulate the effects of different strategies, tactics, and criteria for decision making.

In addition, corporate planners can examine changes in policies and practices that will optimize the use of available resources and maintain process control for proper distribution of talents. Planners can determine new objectives, monitor their effectiveness, and be prepared to introduce corrective measures quickly if they are needed. Suitable reserves or balanced inventories of talents can be maintained to enable the company to cope with foreseen demands as well as with changing economic, competitive, and international conditions that can be forecast only a few years in advance. It goes without saying that competitive advantages in availability and use of the needed individual talents will be directly translatable into leadership in design, new products, costs, volume, and profits.

Conclusion

There is clear evidence of a critical need to move away from today's all too common personnel practices. Most companies now accept the best man available to fill a job vacancy as long as he is above some minimum level or threshold limit. There is now sound evidence of the near-term practicality of a comprehensive simulation model of business careers that can give coherence and relevance to the various pieces of the selection, training, motivating, and promotion processes. Such a model or system will also provide a rubric or matrix for examining the merits of different research and operating possibilities, and a perspective for planning and testing the means to improve important elements in the costly and relatively primitive process of manager development that is common today.

Eventually, reliable predictive patterns of career progress *will* begin to emerge. Eventually, also, a calculus for the management of human resources will be developed that will provide for differentially weighting personal skills and attributes in relation to corresponding job demands and development opportunities. Intelligently used computers can handle these data processing and analysis problems, still leaving to the personal judgment of those involved the fineline choice between individuals with different characteristics.

Most important, the career planning process will become a more truly participative one. Managers will be in a much more secure position as far as making sound individual decisions is concerned. Subordinates will be in a position to do more intelligent self-planning, based on full and valid information about procedures, values, opportunities, and requirements. At this time, career planning will become a truly two-way process, with all parties more fully aware of the critical considerations that affect them.

15

STRATEGIES FOR SELF-EDUCATION

William R. Dill, Wallace B. S. Crowston, and Edwin J. Elton

The capacity to learn is getting new emphasis as a requirement for managerial success. Alert executives have always recognized the need for continued personal growth. But now, as the pace of change in the business environment and the development of new managerial methods and knowledge accelerate, even an alert and informed executive must wonder occasionally whether he will be nimble enough to survive. Beyond the changes in the world of business which affect his role as a manager, changes in society may outdate his competences and attitudes as a citizen.[1]

The threat of personal obsolescence is a challenge at all levels. The senior manager with 10 to 15 years to serve can no longer count on exploiting his present knowledge and skills comfortably until he retires. The younger man just beginning his career may have confidence in his ability to learn, but must prepare for peak responsibilities two or three decades hence in a world whose characteristics he and his mentors can only dimly foresee. Both the older and the younger man may be diverted from preparing for tomorrow by the pressures of today's job; they may put their trust in the company to define and provide the training they need.

But executives today cannot afford to be diverted or wait for others to provide a vaccine against obsolescence. Knowledge, skills, attitudes, and understanding are possessions which men acquire for themselves, not gifts which a company or a university can bestow. The process of acquisition is a slow one, measured usually in months and years rather than in hours and days. As one noted psychologist has observed, "the nurturing of growth requires the long patience of the husbandman rather than the hasty intervention of the mechanic."[2]

The hand of the mechanic shows all too clearly in many of the solutions proposed for developing and refreshing managers. We look for ways of providing executives with more information that is relevant to their changing world — though they complain that they are choking with too much information already.

[1] For projections of these changes, see *Management and Corporations, 1985*, edited by Melvin Anshen and G. L. Bach (New York, McGraw-Hill Book Company, Inc., 1960); Kenneth E. Boulding, *The Meaning of the Twentieth Century* (New York, Harper & Row, Publishers, 1964); John W. Gardner, *Self-Renewal* (New York, Harper & Row, Publishers, 1963); Gilbert Burck, *The Computer Age* (New York, Harper & Row, Publishers, 1965); Harold J. Leavitt and Thomas L. Whisler, "Management in the 1980's," HBR July–August 1962, p. 41; Margaret Mead, "Why Is Education Obsolete?" (Thinking Ahead), HBR November–December 1958, p. 23.

[2] Robert W. White, *Lives in Progress* (New York, The Dryden Press, 1952), p. 364.

We prescribe more frequent company training programs or returns to the college campus — though the most difficult thing to demonstrate about such programs is that they improve a participant's subsequent performance. We advocate more varied experience through job rotation or similar programs — though when it comes time to evaluate a man's experience, we still more often count the years he has been on the job than measure what he has really learned.

However much the training programs, information services, or variety of job assignments for executives are expanded, they remain a means to an end. The ultimate goal must be, as John Gardner suggests, "to shift to the individual the burden of pursuing his own education."[3] We have largely neglected exploring the process of self-education in management and experimenting with ways of encouraging and facilitating it.

Basic Ingredients

To stimulate such exploration and experimentation, this article reports on interviews with about 70 young managers who are facing the challenge of self-education in order both to qualify for advancement and to stay ahead of still younger men who have the advantage of more recent training. (The men ranged in age from their mid-twenties to their mid-forties. All were alumni of a graduate program in administration, and they were employed in a wide range of jobs and companies. The interviews were recorded, but the format of questioning did not permit meaningful quantitative tabulations of the results.) We asked about:

• *Their agendas for learning*: What are they preparing for? What do they want to learn, and how do they want to change? What parts of their program for self-education have highest priority?

• *Their strategies for learning*: What do they try to learn by reading and conversation or classes with experts? What do they try to learn by experience? What do they try to learn by deliberate probing, testing, and experimenting with the world about them?

• *Their chances for success in learning*: How do they find or make time for learning? What motivates and what discourages their efforts? What kinds of resources and incentives are provided?

Organizational Barriers

Their answers show that self-education is hard for even well-motivated executives to pur-

sue. Managers need help in developing longer range views of the kinds of learning that must be done. They need guidance in devising more effective strategies for learning — particularly in capitalizing on their experience, in cumulating it in meaningful ways, and in supplementing reading and observing with tests and experiments. But, perhaps most of all, managers must get the feeling that their organizations recognize learning as a mainstream activity, not as a residual obligation for evenings and weekends.

To make self-education a mainstream activity, top management can accomplish more by example than by exhortation. More can be done in formal training programs to build bridges for continuing learning on the job. And, as resources and incentives are provided for learning, efforts can be made to clear away the disincentives that impede learning. A basic issue with our current standards for designing and administering organizations is that they yield systems which are much better suited to efficient operations in a stable environment than to perceptive and flexible adjustment to changing conditions. Because of the barriers in many organizations, asking an executive to invest in self-education is like asking a salmon to climb Grand Coulee Dam.

Learning Agendas

Men who know that the world is changing rapidly might be expected to be able to provide:

• Statements of *aims* — changes that they would like to make in their knowledge, skills, attitudes, values, or relationships with other men and organizations.

• Definitions of *areas for study, search, reflection, or testing* — lists of activities, experiences, or questions that can help them accomplish their aims.

• Ideas about *priorities* — feelings of preference or urgency about what should be learned first.

A learning agenda has the same purpose as an action agenda. Both ensure that the time invested will be used efficiently and efforts will be concentrated in a few key areas which promise results. A tempting, but feckless, response to the burgeoning needs for education is to decide to learn a little of everything.

Goal-Setting Barriers

Yet executives apparently cannot easily describe explicit agendas that guide their efforts

[3] John W. Gardner, op. cit., p. 12.

at self-education. Well-stated learning agendas proved to be rare among our interviewees. A few interviewees felt that educators believe too easily in the prospects for change. Typical of their feeling was this response:

"I am not sure obsolescence is anything we have to be concerned about with any college graduate. I am not sure that top management is willing to accept the things that would force out experienced people. I know I am not worried about it myself."

But, for most, the villain was not lack of interest. It was lack of time:

". . . to be perfectly honest, I haven't thought much about what I need to learn. Unfortunately, I have been so busy solving — or trying to solve — a million kinds of problems that I haven't had time to wonder whether I'll be put out of business down the road."

These words came from an officer of a fast-growing company. He knew well that, as the company grew, new markets would have to be developed and new organizational patterns would be required. He wanted to be able to use computers to produce better management reports and to routinize some decisions. He recognized that he ought to delegate more to his subordinates. But he had not progressed beyond the general definition of aims to consideration of means and priorities — to the construction of a program to guide his efforts. For this man, and for many of the others whom we interviewed, the pressures were to survive today, not to prepare for tomorrow.

Of the interviewees who had time and interest to make an agenda, a few lacked the required sense of personal identity. Even successful executives sometimes report doubts about themselves and their goals. Such doubts can lead men to reflect, search, and question in constructive ways. They can stimulate, rather than impede, learning. But such doubts can also overwhelm managers, even men who may be two or three decades into their careers. Conflict-ridden, indecisive, and dependent on others for support and guidance, some men lack the confidence to chart and manage a program of self-education. Men with a weak sense of personal identity have no purposes against which to measure opportunities and no rationale by which to commit their energies. So opportunities for learning slip by.

Another barrier to formulating learning agendas is simply lack of practice. For some men, our request was new — one that parents, teachers, and supervisors had seldom made. Mothers and fathers are more likely to set goals, activities, and priorities for their children than to encourage them to develop their own. Even when parents do not give explicit directions, they give indirect cues that shape behavior. In educational programs from kindergarten through graduate school, the learning agenda is defined by course requirements, assignment schedules, textbooks, teachers' instructions, and experience with examinations. In business a major current issue in theories of leadership and performance appraisal is whether or not supervisors should move from telling employees what to do and what not to do toward helping them decide for themselves.[4]

Although self-sufficiency is a skill which society values and high-level assignments in management require, it is too often a talent that we acquire by stealth, against great odds. Not all of our interviewees had adjusted to making their own decisions.

Opportunities & Problems

Some points of concern appeared on many of the learning agendas. Perhaps to a greater extent than is the case for older executives, the agendas of our young interviewees were job-oriented; they were as often directed toward getting established and getting ahead as they were toward meeting the demands of a changing environment.

A great deal of what today's young managers want to learn is the same as what their predecessors wanted as they moved up the executive ladder. First, they want to become oriented to the company and their co-workers; then, after a few years, to develop skills as a supervisor, become expert in some phase of the business, and learn how to make decisions and persuade others to accept them. Still later, they must gain a broad perspective: the ability to see problems and opportunities for the company as a whole, a concern for long-term goals and plans as well as for today's operations, and a skill for negotiating with many kinds of groups inside the organization and out.

[4] See Douglas McGregor, "An Uneasy Look at Performance Appraisal," HBR May–June 1957, p. 89.

Even in a stable world, the executive's career is evolutionary rather than static. As he grows older, he advances in position. The demands on his competence, wisdom, and capacity to handle stress grow in a way that other professionals — e.g., physicians, teachers, scientists, engineers — seldom experience. Perhaps only lawyers and ministers face the same evolutionary challenge during their careers.

If the concern to qualify for increased responsibilities in the company represents traditional learning needs which are unique to managers, other parts of the learning agendas that were described to us reflect the plight of all professionals in a changing world. Change means new opportunities to exploit and new problems to solve. It also means new knowledge, tools, and resources for managers to apply.

Consider first the new opportunities and problems:

❧ Ten years ago, the young manager who expected to be involved with international operations was exceptional. In our current survey most men reported a desire for greater mastery of such things as international trade, foreign languages, and the art of adjusting American managerial theory and practice to overseas conditions. Most interviewees were at least occasionally involved with overseas questions.

❧ Similarly, ten years ago only a few young managers saw an advantage to learning about computers. In our survey even the men not working directly with computers felt a need to know more about them and their potential for the future.

Many interviewees wanted a better understanding of business-government relations: likely changes in tax and antitrust policy, strategies for survival in the defense business, the consequences of public investment in urban housing and transportation, the prospects for expanded political and trade relations with Communist countries, and guidelines for joint action on providing better employment opportunities for Negroes or contributing to the economic and political evolution of emerging nations, and so on. The federal government, overseas affiliates, and computers loomed largest in the minds of interviewees as spurs to further education.

Other trends, such as changes in patterns of union-management relations and growth of research as a corporate activity, were also mentioned by the men interviewed.

Knowledge & Skills

As the environment changes, so does the need for knowledge and skills that managers can use to cope with it. The obvious developments which the men in our study mentioned as important here are contributions from the management sciences to their ways of making decisions about production schedules, inventory policies, budget allocations, distribution systems, and a variety of other questions. Also prominent are the changes in information, decision, and control practices that a computer-based system permits and the behavioral studies that question traditional approaches to supervision, marketing, training, and organizational design. Although interviewees often questioned some of the new ideas and techniques, they put a high priority on knowing the ones that have proved effective.

This applies even to older men in the sample. Although beyond the level where they themselves might expect to use the new approaches, they have to recruit and supervise expert subordinates who can. Such experts, they found, tend with today's job market to be aggressive in their demands for influence and confident about the methods they have mastered. Since many young recruits lack perspective on the managerial standards against which their work is measured, there is some peril in freeing them from managerial control. But because they are neither docile nor easy to understand as they ply their skills, effective control is difficult for an older supervisor to maintain. Like young scientists in a research and development laboratory, young management trainees today come equipped with language, theories, and tools that an uninitiated supervisor finds hard to understand or evaluate.[5]

The minimum motivation, then, in learning new approaches to managerial decision making is to become a better supervisor, to learn what kind of men to recruit and how to lead them effectively. An additional motivation, particularly among managers between 30 and 45 years of age, is to insure against replacement by more

[5] For a perceptive discussion of the impact of new degrees of expertise on organizations, see Victor A. Thompson, *Modern Organization* (New York, Alfred A. Knopf, Inc., 1961).

recent recruits. Today's recruits from the universities and business schools know more about mathematics, economics, behavorial science, and computers than their counterparts did 5 to 15 years ago. They have been taught more about how these subjects relate to marketing, production, finance, accounting, and personnel decisions. Interviewees generally felt that as a qualification for advancement in management today, good training is worth more than experience *per se*, though the latter is still valuable.

Biases & Omissions

In reviewing the elements which figure in learning agendas, we see that there are three main pressures for self-education: (1) to qualify for advancement in responsibility and power; (2) to recognize new opportunities for making decisions and solving new problems; and (3) to use new information and skills in approaching decisions. The response of many interviewees to these different pressures seemed well in balance, but for some it wasn't. As checks on the soundness and comprehensiveness of learning agendas, we propose four questions.

1. Is the man thinking far enough beyond his present assignment?

Current pressures to learn cannot be ignored, but if they limit a man's response to a changing world, they may also block his growth. The advantages of a long-run orientation are seen in the careers of men who became interested in computers early. Although little in their university training or industrial experience in the early 1950's suggested that the computer would become a significant factor in management, a number of men gambled that it would. Those who grasped the opportunity moved rapidly into positions of major responsibility, first with data processing systems, but later in many cases into general management positions.

The danger is that the significance of new management activities will not be recognized, either by the young men who are trying to plan a career or by the older managers who base their advice on yesterday's experience.

2. Is the man underestimating the rate of environmental change and the power of new methods to enhance the "art" of management?

Executives often oppose new methods because they are complex or quantitative, because they do not produce perfect decisions, or because "no one else is using them." The new methods are rejected on false grounds before their potential has been questioned or tested. The issue is not whether new approaches yield perfect decisions, but whether they yield better ones; not whether they will substitute for managerial intuition and judgment, but whether they can usefully supplement them.

Aspiring managers sometimes share the illusion of many aspiring painters — namely, that creative performance is uninhibited and undisciplined. They ignore the evidence which suggests that great painters, scientists, bridge designers, and businessmen have not built their reputations on imagination alone. Great creators have almost without exception been voracious consumers and exploiters of fact and technique.

The discipline of applying rate of return measures to investment alternatives doesn't preclude making the final decision on pure "hunch," but it may make the hunch a better one. The use of appropriate scheduling and inventory rules in routine situations frees time for exercising intuition on the problems where intuition really helps, or where there is no better alternative. The mere study of research findings concerning the relationship of leadership style to morale and productivity will not produce the perfect supervisor; but by suggesting new alternatives it can enhance the supervisor's native flexibility and judgment.

3. Is the man concentrating too much on the acquisition of knowledge and technique, and too little on the combination of these into effective managerial skills?

The manager's life is dominated by pressure for results. He is evaluated more for what he achieves than for the elegance of the methods he uses. If dice will work as well as linear programming, it is generally cheaper and faster to roll the dice. If ethical considerations cannot be quantified as elements in a decision model, this does not mean they should not be considered.

Younger managers in particular may overemphasize acquisition of knowledge and technique in their learning agendas. At the same time, they may underrate the development of important but ill-defined qualities such as willingness to accept risk and uncertainty, sensitivity to other people without being submissive, foresight in recognizing how people or economic opportunities will develop, and competence in handling issues of personal and social ethics.

4. Is the proposed learning agenda consistent with the probable course of development of the man's career?

Under the best of circumstances this is hard to answer because executives are commonly kept in the dark about what lies ahead. Ambiguity about career prospects, in fact, is probably unavoidable because of the keen competition for top-management jobs. Decisions about what to learn can be as crucial as decisions about what to do, and any choice is a gamble. At least one observer has suggested that, with the uncertainties of executive life, the philosophy of existentialism fits managers better than it does most bohemian intellectuals.[6]

Learning Approaches

Choosing a learning agenda only starts the process of self-education. Executives with well-stated plans for learning may still face difficulty in implementing them. To understand better the problems that arise in implementation, we should first review the three basic learning processes: men acquire or absorb, they experience, and they explore.

Making Them Effective

Many of the managers we interviewed interpreted questions about what they were learning as questions about what they had read or what conferences and seminars they had attended. They saw learning primarily as an *acquisitional* process: knowledge, opinions, or cues to understanding and skill development are absorbed by reading or listening. Although this concept of learning is reinforced by years of experience in school systems and in company training programs, it alone is not enough.

Acquisitional strategies break down if there are no experts to consult or if what the experts offer is difficult to understand and use. The men who wait until computers can be explained in two-syllable words will never lead in exploiting them. And by the time an expert publishes his advice in a secretive field — such as marketing, for example — it is a safe bet that he already knows something else he thinks is better.

Where acquisitional strategies do not suffice, *experiential* strategies may. Managers learn by

[6] See David Braybrooke, "The Mystery of Executive Success Re-Examined," *Administrative Science Quarterly,* March 1964, p. 542.

living, acting, watching and listening for results, and reflecting on the relation between what they see happen and what they expect to happen. An experiential approach is often the only way for a manager to master a new job, improve the complex skills he needs to lead men effectively, or make profitable investments of capital resources.

Experience is limited as a means for self-education because it is easier to "have" than to exploit. It provides diffuse, ambiguous signals which are hard to interpret and which take more effort to understand than executives commonly will invest. Lessons from experience, like advice from an expert, are also likely to be rooted in the past. Since the manager's job is changing so rapidly, what worked yesterday may be a treacherous guide to what should be tried tomorrow.

The third kind of approach — *exploratory* learning — is appropriate when the problems are unfamiliar, or when the costs of finding experts or accumulating experience are high. Exploration is a deliberate, organized search for information and experience. It involves posing questions, testing hypotheses, and running experiments. The end objective may be to find "answers," or it may be only to learn how to pose sharper questions or more believable hypotheses.

A manager using an exploratory approach resembles a trial lawyer building a case through cross-examination, or an engineer evaluating designs in a wind tunnel. Two new tools — computer simulation techniques and experimental methods from the social sciences — promise to increase significantly the executive's capacity for exploratory learning.

An example of the uses of the three approaches may help put them in perspective. A manager interested in capital budgeting can learn a great deal by the acquisitory approach. He can read or listen to accounts of the basic techniques: how they work, where they have been used, and how successful they have been.

From books and articles about leadership and organizational change, he may see how to win acceptance for the new approach in his department. But in evaluating the methods of capital budgeting that he can use, and in deciding how to introduce them, he will be in a stronger position if he has learned from experience something about his own abilities and motivations and something about the capabilities and interests of his organization. He relies on experience to translate the advice of outside experts into realistic action guides for his situation.

Reading and listening to discussions about capital budgeting are also likely to be inadequate if he is contemplating entirely new kinds of applications for the techniques — for example, an application to salary determination for engineers and scientists, or an extension of the techniques to situations where costs and benefits are unusually hard to estimate. Here the task is exploratory, since it is a challenge to formulate questions and to design tests and experiments so that, as new ideas are generated, their value can be estimated.

The methods followed by the men we interviewed did not vary with the nature of the learning task as much as one might expect. Choices of approach tended to rest on a man's ability, his personal preferences, and his experience with different methods in the past. A man who found it hard to read and did not like to read was likely to neglect things that were best learned from books and journals, just as the manager who was timid in interpersonal contacts lost many opportunities to advance his knowledge and skills through conversations and discussions.

Focus & Feedback

Special problems in making each of the methods effective were encountered by the men in our sample. An acquisitory approach, for example, presumes that someone has written about or will talk about a particular problem the executive is interested in. Very often, though, the outsider talks at the wrong level or sets his ideas into the wrong context. Managers in the interviews seemed to grow more critical, as they became older, about sources of information and advice that were not tailor-fitted to their interests, competence level, and job situation.

Sometimes, when appropriate materials were available, a manager was unable to locate them. For a man working in a branch office, remote from staff advisers, company libraries, and other resources, the problem was often to find any material to work with. For others, the problem was to sort out from a flood of material or personal contacts the ones that were worth pursuing. Effective acquisitory learners spent much time building and revising selective lists of topics, journals, writers, or personal contacts that particularly deserved attention.

Successful learning by acquisitory processes also rested on other factors: a willingness to read, converse, or consult on a sustained, rather than a scattershot, basis, and an effort to build in feedback on what was being accomplished. If a man wanted to read something about statistics, he chose a book which showed what statistical methods could do and how they had evolved rather than one which simply described a few applications. He worked sample problems and tried to apply some of the ideas on the job.

If he wanted to improve his leadership skills, he not only listened to lectures, but also asked questions about what he heard. He built agendas for further reading or conversation with people, and tried to modify his own behavior to see whether or not he had learned anything worthwhile, or whether or not he knew how to use it. Many interviewees liked the idea of making reports to associates about new things they were working on because it provided them with a forum for organizing and testing the results of their educational efforts.

If effective acquisitory learning requires selective shifting of information sources and arrangements for self-testing of progress, the key problem in experiential learning is to define what kinds of things should be observed. One man who had just made two major job changes in close succession said:

"I used to rush in to try to learn everything at once, but I found that I was only cluttering my mind. It's better to be wrong for a little while in some things, to absorb things in an organized style by tackling things in sequence."

The people who talked actively about experiential learning tended to have one or two things to which they were devoting most of their attention. It might be observing the differences in behavior between men regarded as good and poor supervisors in the company, or it might be trying to unravel the reasons why dismissal of a subordinate unexpectedly brought criticism from those who agreed the man was incompetent.

The yield from experience can be improved if it is analyzed intensively a little at a time, rather than surveyed superficially all at once. It is also increased if, prior to the experience, a manager has established expectations about what he thinks will occur. To generate expectations or predictions, he must think about the causal links between what he does and what results he gets. These thoughts constitute a rudimentary "model" of the situation and provide something to which later analysis of actions and outcomes can be anchored.

Expectations & Questions

The role of expectations in the analysis of experience is much like the role of questions in an exploratory strategy of learning. The quality of the expectations and questions greatly influences what can be learned. If they are narrow, unimaginative, or imprecise, they are not likely to be of much help.

Recognizing that every person has limits in the way he views the world, several interviewees made a special effort to identify the kinds of bias and inflexibility in perception that most frequently get them in trouble. Some interviewees were effective in probing their world for evidence of cause-effect relationships and for cues to developing simple models about how things work. The most valuable lesson that they had learned, several managers said, was the importance of asking *why* again and again, even about phenomena they assumed they understood.

Another component of an effective strategy for exploration is a sense of the meaning of data. The skilled questioner wanted to know:

- Are the answers I am getting relevant to the questions that I asked?

- Are they reliable or representative of the whole range of answers I might receive?

- Are they free from bias and distortion?

The main contribution of the concept of subjective probability and the neat abstractions of statistical decision theory to management practice is to make the executive more conscious of what he believes, why he believes it, how much he is willing to gamble on his beliefs, and what new kinds of information will change them.

A third component of exploratory strategies is a realization of the difference between observation and experiment. We *observe* that the rates of both cigarette smoking and lung cancer have increased during the last several decades, but this does not establish a relationship. The increase in lung cancer, after all, was also paralleled by increases in the number of television sets per household and by increases in barge traffic on the Mississippi River. We must impose experimental controls in one or both of two ways to test our theory that smoking "causes" cancer. One way is to take advantage of experiments that nature has performed for us —

namely, comparisons of health records of two groups of men, alike in all important respects except that one group smokes and the other does not. The other is to set up controlled conditions of our own to see if laboratory animals injected with cigarette tars develop cancer while a matched group of animals, uninjected, do not.

There may be more understanding among businessmen of the principle of experimentation than willingness to use it. Sometimes the problem is an unthinking insistence on uniformity in company policy. Sales managers have discovered that it is often less expensive to test a new marketing strategy in a limited, controlled way than it is to implement it nationwide with the risk that it may not work. The same kind of approach can help personnel managers and supervisors appraise incentive systems, accountants appraise the value of new reporting procedures, and production men appraise new models for scheduling inventory.

At other times, experiments are performed, but the results are ignored. How much more effective would tobacco industry advertising be if the companies applied the same high standards of experimentation in evaluating plans for brand introduction and promotion that they want medical researchers to use in exploring the links between smoking and cancer? A danger in exploratory learning, as in any other kind of learning, is that we may accept and remember only what we are already conditioned to believe, and ignore information that runs against our beliefs and biases.

A final component of exploratory strategies for learning is a sense of how to cumulate questions, tests, or experiments so that they build on one another in sequence. The good lawyer does not build a cross-examination on one or two questions. He plans his attack through a sequence of questions and usually with a sequence of witnesses. Some of the most important parts of his strategy are the guides he develops for changing his line of questions or the procession of witnesses as new information comes in.

Similarly, the scientific investigator needs to think in terms of sequences of experiments. The first experimental studies of the effects of participative styles of supervision on productivity gave dramatic, positive results. But the next step was to try to reproduce the same results in other companies, at other levels within the company, and even in other cultures. When the experimenters subsequently began to get a confusing mixture of results, they extended the studies to include other variables (such as workers' personalities) that might sharpen or weaken the effects of supervisory style on productivity. The final picture will be complicated but much less misleading for an executive who wants results he can apply to his organization.

Some General Principles

For success with any of the strategies for self-education, several general rules apply:

❧ The effort, whether it involves reading or reflecting on experience, should be selective and focused, guided by an agenda or goals for learning. The effort should be organized so that it can be sustained for a long enough period to show results.

❧ A learner must be willing to admit that education consists not just in acquiring new knowledge, skills, and attitudes, but also in giving up convictions and approaches to problems that may be inaccurate and outmoded.

❧ Although some learning may indeed be implicit, unplanned, and unconscious, the process of education can be facilitated by seeking opportunities to talk or write about what is being learned, to use it, and to test whether or not it works.

❧ New knowledge, skills, and attitudes are secure only when they have been integrated with those acquired earlier. Men need to translate what they read or hear into familiar terms and to seek illustrations from their own experience for the ideas and concepts involved.

For someone trying to make a real start at self-education after a period of comparative disinterest in learning, it may be easier and more encouraging for him to begin by working on something he already is strong in, rather than tackling an area in which he is weak. The accountant will usually have an easier time learning about the information-processing aspects of a computer than he will have plunging directly into the study of computer-based operations research models.

The process of learning may also be speeded by making it a group activity. Adult Bible classes and Great Books groups are effective because they involve collective commitment and an opportunity through discussion to state and test what a man thinks he is learning. Doctoral students in a graduate school often spend the final weeks before their qualifying examinations working together and testing their mastery of the material on one another. Such collective endeavors are appropriate in management, but managers' desires for status and competitive attitudes often prevent their getting started.

Organizational Climate

An individual executive who wants to learn must be aware of the importance of objectives and carefully chosen strategies. But another factor which may override both of these is the climate which his organization provides. Does his employer think enough of self-education to provide resources and incentives for learning?

The answer, as the manager who is trying to learn sees it, is often *no*. Whereas interviewees from consulting firms told of making specific time allocations for self-development and reporting to their superiors about their progress, men in business itself talked more about the environmental circumstances and company policies that hindered their efforts. They complained of lack of time, company indifference and antagonism to new ideas, and inadequate resources for learning.

Helps & Hampers

There is no easy answer to the common problem that immediate demands to keep a company going leave little time for organization-wide activities — such as long-range planning — or for individual initiative to develop new knowledge and skills. The same emphasis on current performance, though, also plagues consulting firms and universities. The difference is that consulting firms and universities have recognized that continuing self-education must be a basic organizational policy, not just an occasional subject for executive speeches.

Studies of how executives spend their time show that even senior men find it difficult to reserve time for self-education. If a manager views his career as a game which he plays against the men who grant promotions, the payoff lies in doing the things which have an immediate rather than a long-run return. The reward structure seldom emphasizes learning.

Even apparent company encouragement may have discouraging effects. One company mentioned a program of Saturday meetings to explore new topics of importance to management. This may have been effective; and since executives work overtime anyway, it may not have been too inconvenient. But overtime sessions are one more indication that self-education is something that a manager does not attempt on "company time." A comparable example of the widespread difference can be seen in company attitudes concerning support for attending evening courses (usually given) and day courses (usually denied) at nearby universities.

Another discouraging factor is managerial indifference. Even an executive who knows that massive campaigns are necessary to remind employees to control costs or prevent accidents often assumes that efforts to learn difficult new skills will be self-motivated and self-sustaining. Encouragement, when it is offered, is sometimes given to things which top executives had to learn while *their* careers were developing rather than to things which their successors, in a changed world, must know. Many interviewees felt that they had more encouragement to learn the assumptions and theory that underlay their company's existing policies and procedures than they had to study ways to reshape the policies to meet the potential which computers, foreign market opportunities, or other new factors offer.

Managements often seem conservative, too, in the kinds of self-education they will support. They are for self-education if it helps the man do his job better or represent the company better in the community. They are, at best, lukewarm about self-education if it does not contribute obviously to the organization. At the extreme, some companies have found it worthwhile to help their managers become more knowledgeable about political processes if the learners are Republicans, but not if they are Democrats. The man who wants time and assistance to study accounting is encouraged, whereas the man who wants to study the effects of computerized information systems on society may not be. By limiting the range of efforts to learn that it will endorse, a company risks getting no learning at all.

Business also errs sometimes in insisting on commitment from young men before it provides support. As an example, one of the country's major corporations is worried about its poor record in hiring good college graduates — even men whom it wooed through a carefully planned summer program. A major event of its program was a lecture by a top executive of the company about what a career with the company offered and required. Nothing was really said about the individual trainee (or his own goals

and development), although a great deal was said about what he owed the company — obligations which for the executive who spoke had clear priority over family and everything else in his life.

Dedication and commitment are important, but can they be demanded from new recruits without offering something in return? An essential element in the disappointment of many young men about business careers is their feeling that they are asked to serve on the company's terms, but are not given the kind of incentive to grow that they can find in public service or university work. One of the most important desires of college graduates is to be able to use and develop their knowledge and skills. Given an environment in which employees can develop and act, our interviews show that commitment and loyalty will usually follow.

Information & Advice

Besides incentives for self-education, companies provide many of the resources from which men learn. However, if performance appraisals are perfunctory, then some men will not recognize skills which they ought to develop. And if computer facilities are centralized at one location and the men who know computers spend little time in branch offices and factories, some of the economies of centralization may be offset by inadequate diffusion of information about what computers mean to the future of the organization. When a company library is established so that research help can be provided to managers, word of this service should be circulated in ways that will ensure that it gets beyond the attention of a small group at company headquarters.

For the sake of learning, as much as for the sake of keeping the company going, it is important that ideas and information get around the organization quickly. In-company surveys of where men turn for information and advice will often reveal hidden barriers to communications. Studies of the strategies of executives who have a reputation for keeping themselves and their departments up to date may reveal methods that other managers can use.

Some companies are betting that a major aid to managerial reeducation will be computer-based systems for "information retrieval." There is little doubt that such systems can facilitate learning, but they can be only part of the answer. A manager who wants to learn new developments in his field often lacks good guides for identifying people and publications that are likely to help him. Much more than a chemist or physician, a manager lacks a vocabulary and definition of professional needs that would enable him to specify what a retrieval system might contain. Since a great deal of managerial and professional "know-how" is diffused verbally, a major effort is needed to learn how better to structure conversational opportunities within organizations and between men in organizations and relevant outside groups. The ideal "retrieval" system for managers may be as much a file of personal contacts as a file of reports.

In addition to the problem of giving an executive access to things that have happened outside his own sphere of activity, there is the problem of giving him better access to his own local environment and personal experience. Knowledge of local conditions is a critical element in good performance. The stress, again, is to make him a keener observer and interpreter of the things he lives through — and a more aggressive explorer of new data, new insights, new experience.

If experiential and exploratory learning are to be encouraged, experience is needed that will educate and broaden rather than simply acculturate. Experience should help men learn to ask questions, rather than simply adapt to the world as it is. It should provide the chance for practice — at first simple and then more complex — in skills which are not needed now, but which will be essential in a later job. The idea of "job rotation" must give way to more systematic thinking about "job sequencing," with the emphasis not so much on variety as on cumulative evolution of knowledge and skills.

More Training?

The steps required to improve managers' capacity for self-education are difficult. We have mentioned the need for more basic research about how men learn — not in a classroom or laboratory, but from life, where most of the rewards are given for performance in the present rather than for preparation to face the future. We have described the difficulties which managers have both in defining and in

carrying through agendas for learning. We have looked at some of the inflexibilities which keep companies from providing adequate incentives and resources for learning. Perhaps the answer lies not in more emphasis on self-education, but in more frequent exposure of managers to formal training opportunities.

New Formal Programs . . .

Better opportunities for classroom education at mid-career need to be provided. Executive training is no longer something which a few affluent companies dabble with to absorb excess resources and flatter the egos of the managers who are chosen to attend. It is something toward which companies and universities must work together in order to expand and improve.[7] But, for a variety of reasons, the growth of executive training can only proceed if work is done on ways of motivating and facilitating self-education.

The first reason is that formal classroom programs are nothing more than another kind of opportunity for self-education. We talk about "management development" as if it were something that trainers or college professors do to managers. It might be more accurate to talk of "managers developing," sometimes in response to what the instructors do, but often despite their actions. We can manipulate the design of formal programs in a great many ways to shape the kinds of opportunities for learning that they provide, and theories about how to do this can now be based not only on the "know-how" of educators but also on pertinent research about how one man influences another.[8] But, in the final analysis, more seems to depend on how "student" managers see the program, what they want to gain from it, and how they respond to the opportunities that it offers.

One research study divided an executive program into two groups: those participants who had volunteered to attend and those who had been nominated by their superiors.[9] The volunteers found the program a more conflict-laden experience, but seemed much more involved in the program and in efforts at self-development. The men who had been nominated by others tended to treat the nomination as a reward for

[7] See Richard M. Cyert and William R. Dill, "The Future of Business Education," *Journal of Business,* July 1964, p. 221.

[8] See, for example, *Handbook of Research on Teaching,* edited by N. L. Gage (Chicago, Rand McNally & Company, 1965), particularly chapters 10–14; and Bernard

Berelson and Gary A. Steiner, *Human Behavior: An Inventory of Scientific Findings* (New York, Harcourt, Brace & World, Inc., 1964), particularly chapters 5, 8, and 9.

[9] Kamla Chowdhry, "Management Development Programs: Executive Needs," *Industrial Management Review,* Spring 1963, p. 31.

good performance. They were more relaxed, less involved, and less conscious of specific learning goals. Preparation for and attitudes toward self-education determined what each man derived from the program.

The second reason for linking the improvement of formal programs together with the enlargement of emphasis on self-education lies in the words already quoted from John Gardner — namely, that the goal of any teaching program is "to shift to the individual the burden of pursuing his own education." [10] Formal training programs can never provide more than a partial answer to a manager's need for learning, but they ought to do more to help him continue learning.

In the short run, executives who are now faced with the threat of personal obsolescence cannot afford to wait until appropriate classroom programs are established. Schools and companies are slow to adapt to new demands, and large-scale reorientation and expansion of mid-career programs will not develop overnight. Those who set educational policies for companies must discard the myth that really good men are irreplaceable and that good men cannot afford to leave their jobs for prolonged periods of study and research.

Mid-career programs that will be developed are more likely to be long than short, and more of them may be designed to last for periods up to a year in length. For longer programs, both in companies and in universities, something may have to be worked out concerning the awarding of degrees. Is a degree a necessary or desirable incentive for enrollment and good performance? If one is offered, what should it be? Will participants and their company sponsors accept university control of student selection and grading standards, which are normally associated with degree programs?

If new part-time and university evening programs are one line of development, special care must be taken to dissociate them from the low quality that has characterized many such programs in the past. Basic attitudes in business and in the university must be changed.

. . . Plus Informal Efforts

Even when they are extended into the longer run, formal programs are limited in their effectiveness. A great many of them are destined to remain mediocre because, in a time of increasing demand for qualified personnel at all levels

of education, the human resources needed to plan and staff programs are scarce. Even the best-staffed programs are a gamble when they try to anticipate the educational needs of a rapidly changing world. They can be *avant-garde* and still miss the mark. For the less well staffed programs, the challenge is to keep them current with the best of management practice — not put them ahead.

Classroom training can be too conservative in outlook. Good courses take time to design and implement. As group efforts which sometimes build too much on collective wisdom, formal programs sometimes founder by overlooking differences in background, ability, and interests among participants, and by downgrading the manager's desires for autonomy in laying out his own plan for growth. More often, perhaps, their range is too narrow. The hope that some employees will choose to acquire knowledge and skills that the organization does not even recognize are relevant is a powerful reason for encouraging self-education. For a company and its managers, formal training and self-education complement each other; they are not alternatives.

Conclusion

Efforts at self-education have a triple payoff:

• They produce results in the form of added knowledge and skills, including some that cannot be easily taught.

• They provide useful practice and experience in the process of learning.

• They are a source of self-confidence in facing a changing world.

All three results help a manager to deal better with the demands and opportunities of his day-to-day job, and with opportunities for formal training that he may receive. By doing more to encourage and facilitate a man's efforts to define and achieve learning objectives, business could move a long way toward establishing the image of "opportunity" for young men that it feels it lacks for college graduates today.

However, "opportunity" for the man who really wants to manage and play a part in the shaping of tomorrow's world means more than the opportunity to "be developed." It means the opportunity to continue to grow and mature in a setting where personal goals and individual differences will be recognized and respected.

[10] John W. Gardner, op. cit., p. 12.

16

DEVELOPING MANAGERS
IN DEVELOPING COUNTRIES

James A. Lee

Foreword

Any attempt to identify, select, and train future business leaders in the developing nations of Africa, Asia, and South America must take into account the fundamental differences in management development conditions between the United States and the emerging world. Here, the author pinpoints five key environmental problem areas and suggests a straightforward program of techniques for coping with them.

Since World War II, U.S. direct investment abroad has increased to about $67 billion, of which almost a third is in Africa, Asia, and South America.[1] This has produced an unparalleled need for employing foreign supervisors and managers in American-owned companies in developing countries. Since there have also been increases in local pressures to nationalize the ranks of their managements overseas, these companies will be required in the foreseeable future to identify and develop an unprecedented num-

1. Extrapolated from data given in Harlan Cleveland, et al, *The Overseas American* (New York, McGraw-Hill Book Company, Inc., 1960), and the U.S. Department of Commerce's Office of Business Economics News Release, April 21, 1967.

176

ber of potential managers of different races, from different cultures, and with different language and educational backgrounds.

The numerous emerging nations, each trying to develop the business leadership necessary for the management of its new economic units, are discovering that a competent manager cadre is not an automatic by-product of independence. They are also faced with the gigantic task of filling the leadership ranks of their own industries, government departments, and other institutions, which help deplete the small reservoir of potential managers by attracting a large percentage of the few college graduates produced in their new universities. Yet little has been written about the specific problems associated with developing local foreign nationals for management positions in American-owned companies abroad.

Environmental problems

This article identifies the five fundamental differences between management selection and development conditions in developing countries and in the United States, and suggests development techniques that take these differences into account. The key problem areas, which I shall cover in the course of this discussion, are:

1. Limited sources of managerial leadership potential.

2. Educational and technological deprivation.

3. Economic attitudes hostile to private enterprise objectives.

4. Divergent concepts of what an "ideal" manager should be.

5. Resistance to traditional American development approaches, such as face-to-face criticism.

An analysis of each of these will indicate, I believe, some techniques that are superior to "canned" American programs in producing effective results when selecting and developing managers in the emerging countries of Africa and Asia.

However, before examining these basic differences, let me say that while my own research studies have been conducted primarily in Pakistan and Ethiopia, there are similar problems in

Latin America to which my findings apply. I know this generally from the literature [2] and from visits and personal contacts in many of those countries.

1. Limited sources

Primarily because of low educational and economic levels, the sources of potential managerial talent remain extremely limited in developing countries. Consider Ethiopia, for example, with its estimated 7% adult literacy rate. There, only about half a million people have reached the minimum educational level of an average elementary school student in the United States. Moreover, that entire country of 22 million turns out less than 500 university graduates per year, all of whom have achieved an educational level roughly equivalent to that of a junior in an average American university. This is due, of course, to the cumulative effects of deprived home life, poor quality of primitive village-like schools, and substandard teaching at all levels. The secondary language (English, in Ethiopia) is used as a medium of instruction only from about seventh grade on.

This limited educational opportunity and cultural exposure produces few possible candidates for management development. Let us look briefly at the only pools of potential managers available in most underdeveloped countries.

Educated elites: This tiny pool yields a very few candidates for purely professional (nonownership) management. Members of this group are generally well-educated, quite intelligent, and free-enterprise oriented. They often have real estate holdings and a family history of high-ranking government posts. Many members of this pool are partially educated in the United States or Europe, and their home environment has been modern and characterized by much hired personal service.

Ex-military officers: This group, almost as small as the "educated elite," contains potential managers who hold many cultural values consonant with American management values. They are generally politically conservative, hardworking, reasonably logical thinkers, loyal, and quite reliable. They tend to be the most qualified source of technical management due (a) to the military selection and training system, and (b) to experience in supervision, logistics, equipment operation, and maintenance.

2. See, for example, "Management Problems and Opportunities for Management Training in Central America," a report by a survey team of Harvard Business School, Division of International Activities, December 1963; and *Elites in Latin America*, edited by Seymour M. Lipset and Aldo Solari (New York, Oxford University Press, Inc., 1967), particularly Chapter I.

University graduates: This pool, although generally too small and inadequately trained, is larger by far than the first two. Members of this group, however, are often hostile to profit and capital, and low in reasoning powers (more on this later) so necessary for business problem solving and planning. They are not motivated for decision making or economic growth planning. They tend to view their degree as an end in itself rather than to think of their higher education as a tooling up for solving challenging problems in their careers. This group contains a wide range of intellectual capabilities—from very low to very high—and most of the graduates possess what an American might term extraordinary talents for memorizing. Approximately half the members of this group aspire to work for their government on graduation.

University students in Ethiopia, for example, were asked to rank 11 occupations according to their status in society. Manager was ranked seventh and shop owner, ninth; while government official was ranked third and farmer, fourth.[3] The majority of these students see the government as the only agent to produce economic growth for their country.

High school graduates: This group, although still small by U.S. standards, is by far the most numerous. Only a few, however, have the intellectual development potential for business management. Most of them have a reading ability in English about equal to that of an American sixth grader. Moreover, they have been exposed to few of the principles of the physical world. They, like the university students, habitually learn by memorizing and drill. Thus the transition to learning for problem solving can often be slow and tedious. There is one difference between this group and the university graduates: the high school graduates seem more highly motivated. Perhaps because they do not have the ultimate laurel—a university degree—they feel that they cannot rest so comfortably on lesser accomplishment.

2. Cultural deprivation

The educationally and technologically deprived "raw materials" for management development in developing countries produce an intellectual profile very deficient in certain aptitudes vital

3. Asnake Sahlu, "Opinion Survey of University Students with Regard to Business Professions in Ethiopia," *Ethiopian Business Journal,* June 1967, p. 59.

to management performance. Most of their university graduates are seriously lacking (by American standards) in reading speed and comprehension, quantitative reasoning, and basic general science understanding. Their symbolic reasoning, numerical reasoning, and mechanical aptitude scores are usually comparable to those of Americans in the age 12 to 16 range. The use of ratios and indexes is strange to them, and consequently their decision-making habits do not usually include the use of many such tools.

Exhibit I shows the results of a five-hour bat-

Exhibit I. Intellectual profile of Ethiopian students and businessmen

Subtest	U.S. school grade equivalent of university freshmen	U.S. school grade equivalent of business managers
Verbal reasoning	9	11
Numerical ability (add, subtract, and so on)	14	14
Abstract reasoning	8	8
Clerical speed and accuracy (attention to detail)	8	8
Mechanical reasoning	6	8
Space relations	7	7
Spelling	13	14
Grammar	11	13
Reading speed/ comprehension	8	10

Note: Grade equivalents over 12 and under 8 are estimates by extrapolation.

tery of tests which I recently administered to 875 freshmen at the Haile Sellassie I University Testing Center in Addis Ababa, and to a group of 38 Ethiopians holding managerial job titles. The Ethiopian freshmen's results are comparable to those of a similar battery of tests I gave to graduate students in business administration in Pakistan in 1964. It is also interesting to note that the average English reading ability of 34 Pakistani senior managers I measured in 1967 came out at the same U.S. tenth-grade level as shown for the 38 Ethiopian managers.

The often-heard argument that such American tests are not culture-*free* seems to me irrelevant in this case. The fact remains that they are reasonably culture-*fair*. And if foreign nationals are to perform a "Western" job—e.g., supervise the maintenance of a Boeing 707, oversee the production of pharmaceuticals, or manage the distribution of 4 million gallons of gasoline per month—a Western test is a better prediction instrument than any other tool available. There is no known way to Nigerianize or Indianize a Boeing 707 or the manufacture of antibiotics.

A case example: In 1967, I devised a selection procedure for an African airline to select African pilot trainees. The employment manager, himself an African, complained that it was unfair to hold the prospective trainees to the time limits of the various American aptitude tests. I argued that because all the ground instruction, pilot training, text materials, and aircraft were American, it was more appropriate to keep the time limits than to lose the value of the comparative standards. He persisted in his argument for "fairness" until I promised to double the time limit for the tests under one condition: that he go around the world and double the length of all the runways!

The 16 African pilot trainees finally selected by the employment manager from the 700 applicants *averaged* 94 IQ on an American test. Under the direction of three flight instructors, who were experienced American instructors, the trainees required 40 hours of dual instruction to solo (compared to 8 hours for a U.S. student pilot), suffered 6 accidents including the demolishing of an aircraft, and produced 6 pilots.

In my opinion, this difficult training situation was due purely to the educational and technological deprivation that severely reduced the number of applicants with flying potential.

Translation of such tests for managerial candidates into the native language is an unsatisfactory solution at the present time for two reasons: (1) each developing country usually has several languages, and (2) few if any of these languages are rich enough to make translation practical. Even terms such as "manager," "foreign exchange," "probability," "torque," and "capital" have no equivalents in most of the languages of the developing countries. Furthermore, the written versions of the languages of most developing countries are primarily sound-making systems rather than sense-making systems. Their system of absorbing new words is usually very inefficient. For example, Urdu, Hindi, and Amharic have absorbed the words "atom" and "atomic bomb" but the root "atom" changes its written appearance when the suffix "ic" is added.

In other words, while English (or some European language) is usually a second language for most managers or potential managers in developing countries, it also is often the official government and business language. Thus it is a more effective language for most nationals to use in learning what is necessary to become a manager.

The educational system in developing countries has also conditioned the foreign national to a rote-learning approach characterized by memorizing and drill. High school and university graduates are generally superior to comparable-age Americans in straight memorizing and in computational skills like addition, subtraction, multiplication, and division. But their lack of problem-solving practice has left them generally unable to decide *whether* and *when* to add, subtract, multiply, or divide.

The average reading comprehension and speed of an English-speaking foreign national management candidate in Africa or Asia—usually a university graduate—is approximately equivalent to that of a U.S. eighth grader. (About 70% of all candidates fall between the U.S. fifth and eleventh grades in reading ability.) He is not habitually a reader, and when he reads to learn, he often simply memorizes topic sentences and paragraph headings.

3. Hostile attitudes

In most developing countries, the prevailing ideas of appropriate objectives of a business enterprise—whether governmental or privately owned—are that it be a provider of jobs and welfare. For nonowner managers and supervisors, the principle of efficiency as an economic unit is often considered a "foreign" idea, and one contrary to many of the values of the cultures of the developing countries.

There is also a general lack of economic understanding of where economic growth or new jobs come from. The role of profits, surplus, or savings is not usually understood by a large percentage of managerial employees or by the countries' opinion makers.

The results of an economic attitude survey I conducted suggest that such opinions represent the cultural values of most peoples of developing agricultural economies. *Exhibit II* shows the responses to pertinent questions in the survey of Pakistani middle managers (PM) in a petroleum company, Pakistani graduate students (PS) at the University of Karachi, Ethiopian managers (EM) from Ethiopian Air Lines, African electrical equipment salesmen (AS) from seven African

Exhibit II. Survey of economic attitudes among five groups in developing countries

					Percent of group giving this answer
Answer	PM (N=62)	PS (N=150)	EM (N=51)	AS (N=30)	ES (N=54)

What percentage of (Ethiopia's) (Pakistan's) business and industry should be in the public sector (owned by the government)?

0%	13%	5%	8%	0%	6%
25%	13	15	39	26	37
50%	24	26	20	33	30
75%	18	42	14	37	26
100%	32	13	20	3	2

Which of the following would you consider a capitalist in the most accurate sense of the word?

A factory owner	45%	67%	33%	40%	57%
A taxi driver who owns his own taxi	10	6	0	7	0
A farmer who owns 2 acres of land, 5 oxen, a wagon, and a plow	10	5	12	27	0
The holder of a paid-up life insurance policy	0	4	12	7	2
All of the above	35	18	43	20	41

Which of the following is considered by experts to be one of the most important reasons why (Ethiopia) (Pakistan) has difficulty in world exports?

Labor is too expensive	0%	2%	18%	26%	6%
(Ethiopia's) (Pakistan's) location	6	2	8	7	9
Shipping costs	6	14	12	3	17
Overpricing for too much profit	37	50	39	40	20
Trade barriers	50	32	24	23	48

What do you estimate is the annual percentage return on investment (after taxes are paid) in the textile industry?

5%	0%	5%	0%	0%	0%
10%	8	17	18	27	7
15%	50	25	29	23	37
25%	24	35	21	43	43
50%	11	18	31	7	13

What do you think is the average capital investment per employee in the ten leading manufacturing companies in (Ethiopia) (Pakistan)?

$100*	32%	25%	14%	23%	26%
$300	32	26	20	13	20
$500	8	25	51	33	30
$1,000	8	13	8	20	13
$2,000 or more	19	11	8	10	11

*Local currency equivalents were used in the original questionnaire.

Exhibit III. Ranking characteristics for survey of what the "ideal" manager should be

As it appeared in questionnaire	Abbreviation
The concern for future planning and for future problem prevention.	Future planning
The recognition of one's superior both as the source of authority and as responsible for what his subordinates do.	Respect for authority
The patient and creative searching for quantifiable variables as both a basis for and measure of decision making.	Quantifiable variables
The capacity to respond to human needs and problems, and to be sensitive to the feelings of others.	Sensitivity to others' feelings
The recognition of the importance of personal friendships in achieving overall managerial effectiveness.	Personal friendships
The ability to make accurate and timely decisions based on unlike variables, incomplete information, and incompletely understood consequences.	Decision making
The willingness to apply religious and ethical values in the conduct of business activities.	Religious-ethical values
The steady desire to develop new methods and to take new actions which improve results.	Develop new methods
The recognition of the need for active cooperation with and support of government and its programs.	Support of government
The willingness to work hard and long hours to ensure the attainment of company objectives.	Hard work
The recognition of the importance of family obligations to one's overall management career success.	Family obligations
The respect for the need to maintain appropriate status differences between manager and subordinate levels of employees.	Maintain status differences
The willingness to take economic or career risks through bold decisions.	Risk taking
The capacity to be personally loyal to a company, organization, or work group.	Capacity to be loyal
A firm belief in subordinates' capabilities to initiate action and to maintain self-control in the performance of their jobs.	Belief in subordinates

countries, and Ethiopian senior students (ES) in business administration at Haile Sellassie I University.

The socialistic attitudes reflected in this economic attitude survey—anti-private enterprise, overestimation of profits, belittlement of the role of capital, and so on—affect the "raw materials" attracted to management trainee posts. A foreign national department manager of an American overseas operation who believes that the wrong people own the company which he works for and that they are really profiteers is not likely to work very hard for its success. These attitudes, also held by many government officials, affect the freedom of the company to

discharge "mistakes." Overall, these attitudes seriously affect the motivation of the foreign national manager to help the company achieve its primary objectives—return (to America) on investment and growth.

4. Managerial concepts

Differences between concepts of the "ideal" manager held by American managers and those held by managers and students in emerging countries point up some further problems involved in developing managers abroad. In 1966-1967, I asked managers from America, Pakistan, and Ethiopia to rank 15 qualities or characteristics—selected from American business literature —of the so-called ideal manager.

(In addition, business students from Pakistan and Ethiopia were asked to rank these same characteristics to determine something of the nature of their concepts of the ideal manager. Although their comparative rankings are not included in the accompanying discussion, I would like to point out that future managers—that is, new graduates—will be no closer to the American ideals. In fact, in my research the two most different groups are the American managers and Ethiopian business students. In other words, spe-

cialized rework of many of their values will be necessary before they can be given managerial responsibilities.)

Exhibit III shows the list chosen for the questionnaire and the abbreviated forms used in the accompanying exhibits and discussion. *Exhibit IV* and *Exhibit V* compare rankings of the foreign national manager groups surveyed with American managers' rankings on each of the 15 ideal manager characteristics. Using median ranks, these characteristics are shown in order of ranking importance and connected to point up differences between American managers'

Exhibit IV. Comparative ranking of Ethiopian and American managers

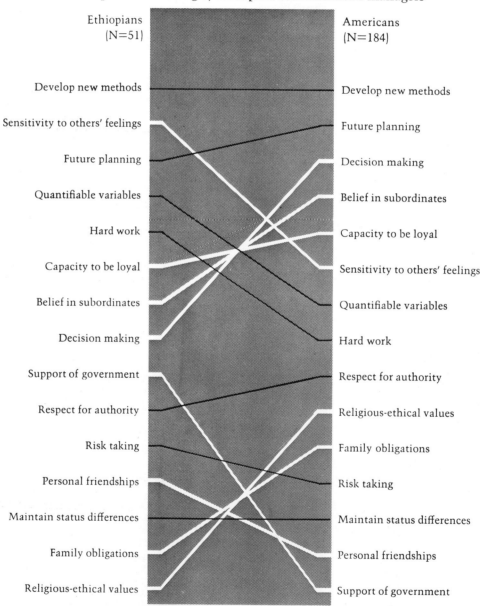

Note: White line denotes pair of ranking distributions found to be significantly different.

Exhibit V. Comparative ranking of Pakistani and American managers

Pakistanis (N=40)	Americans (N=184)
Future planning	Develop new methods
Decision making	Future planning
Develop new methods	Decision making
Sensitivity to others' feelings	Belief in subordinates
Capacity to be loyal	Capacity to be loyal
Hard work	Sensitivity to others' feelings
Quantifiable variables	Quantifiable variables
Risk taking	Hard work
Belief in subordinates	Respect for authority
Respect for authority	Religious-ethical values
Personal friendships	Family obligations
Support of government	Risk taking
Religious-ethical values	Maintain status differences
Maintain status differences	Personal friendships
Family obligations	Support of government

Note: White line denotes pair of ranking distributions found to be significantly different.

rankings and those of business managers from Pakistan and Ethiopia.

It is clear from these comparative rankings that the foreign managers surveyed do not see the "name of the game" the same as do American managers. Those from developing countries indicate they expect a manager to be very sensitive to all kinds of requests from their own subordinates. This, in turn, can lead to dire economic consequences because the supersensitivities of the foreign national managers make it difficult to say *no*. For example, because his subordinates requested rest breaks, one foreign national manager gave away two daily 15-minute coffee breaks which cost the company the equivalent of U.S. $300,000 a year. He never even considered the cost.

The foreign managers do not expect from their managerial ideal the same incorporation of ethics in management behavior as does an American manager from his ideal. Also, they see an ideal manager as having less respect for his subordinates than an American sees him. This will no doubt affect their ability to develop their own subordinates.

(A rather astounding finding, in my opinion,

was the overall agreement between divergent groups of American managers, who failed to see eye-to-eye on only 1 of the 15 characteristics. In other words, the American manager community is a subculture which is in close internal agreement on what a manager should be.)

5. *Resistance to criticism*

The most common approach to developing managers for American-owned operations in developing countries is a mixture of coaching and performance appraisal. Both of these usually involve face-to-face criticism which is often sufficiently depersonalized for an American subordinate to tolerate, but rarely impersonal enough for a foreign national. Because most of the developing world is characterized by highly personalized sensitivities, face-to-face criticism of *any* kind seldom accomplishes more than firing up various psychological defense mechanisms. Often the criticized foreign national reacts by narrowing his job responsibilities in order to prevent future error and thus to avoid more humiliation and ridicule.

Because it is not *his* (or his countryman's) company—and because he often resents this from the outset—his motivation to improve will not be the same. (In another research study, I found that only one out of eight Ethiopian and Pakistani business students are interested in future employment in a "foreign" company.)

Considering the foreign national's intellectual profile and his preference for concern with the present, his ability to anticipate or appreciate the consequences of performance errors cannot be expected to be the same as that of an American. Several Asian and African junior managers, in confidential conversations with me, have indicated that they interpreted criticism from their American bosses as an American peculiarity to live with rather than as a source of valuable information to aid them in improving their performance.

Developmental approaches

Given the five basic environmental problems we have been examining up to this point, the tailored approaches for selecting and developing managers in developing countries are almost self-indicating. Let us now turn our attention to some of the more important courses of action

open in each of these situations to American-owned companies overseas.

Problem one

The sources of managerial leadership potential are relatively few in the developing countries, as we have seen, primarily because of the limited educational opportunities and cultural exposure deficiencies. In tackling this problem, there are five courses of action:

1. Add a general aptitude test battery to the management trainee selection program.

2. Actively recruit from high schools and universities so as to increase applicant sample sizes.

3. Increase recruitment of military officers in the age 40 to 50 bracket if mature candidates are needed.

4. Give favorable consideration to applicants who have had only a high school education plus some relevant successful experience over applicants who are the garden variety university graduate—provided the former appear to be highly motivated *and* score well on aptitude tests.

5. Search for experienced local managers more in the style of U.S. executive search consultants —through extensive personal contacts rather than by formal open advertising.

Problem two

To counteract the effects of educational and technological deprivation, there are three techniques that will help to produce more effective results in the selection and development of foreign national managers:

1. American companies should consider offering a 100% refund for tuition, books, and supplies for evening extension or correspondence courses in physical science, mathematics, mechanics, logic, and engineering—whether or not these studies are directly job related.

2. In addition, American firms abroad could provide management potential with low-cost, high-interest informative reading materials at seventh- to tenth-grade reading levels, such as subscriptions to *Reader's Digest*, *Newsweek*, *Life*, *Look*, and *Time* magazines. Also, consider the distribution of special-level books on science and engineering that are printed in English.

3. Americans abroad should give maximum attention to explanations of simple mechanical and electrical functions when any explanation is necessary.

The cost per person for examples 1 and 2 just discussed would be approximately $200 to $300 per year if an employee is enrolled in one course at all times and receives three subscriptions. This would result in about 500 hours of classroom, reading, and study time for a cost per hour of learning of about 50 cents.

Problem three

In this situation where the prevailing economic attitudes are hostile toward enterprise objectives, and where there is also a general lack of understanding, there are five possible approaches:

1. Screen applicants by means of questions on attitude toward or understanding of economics. (One inventory of such questions is provided by the economic attitude questionnaire I used in my research, which can be administered to seventh-grade-level readers and up. I will send a single copy free to anyone who writes me requesting it.)

2. American companies could well distribute booklets and pamphlets to managers and pre-managerial employees which explain the roles of profit and capital in economic growth in simple English with illustrations. (Two sources of such publications in the United States are the Economics Press, West Orange, New Jersey, and Good Reading Rack Service, 505 Eighth Avenue, New York City.)

3. Support more company memberships for foreign managers in local businessmen's organizations such as Rotary and Lions clubs. Personal contact with other managers will help soften Marxian views of the management class.

4. Issue news releases to communicate changes in the company's operations, appointments, and so forth, and to explain the role of business as a valuable instrument of local and national economic development.

5. Conduct economic-understanding training programs similar to those used in the steel and copper industries in the early 1950's in the United States.

Problem four

Research studies have disclosed, then, that foreign managers do not see the "name of the game" in the same way their American counterparts do. In order to cope with the foreign national's different concepts of what a manager is and does, there are five courses of action open:

1. To help balance the supersensitivities of foreign nationals to requests from their own subordinates with organizational realities, American-owned companies can have their foreign managers practice "costing out"—that is, force them to look at the economic consequences of—various administrative decisions and policies. All fringe benefits should be costed by the foreign national managers. Extra effort should be taken to make sure that they know the approximate value of all capital equipment.

2. Incorporate, as a primary factor in any managerial performance appraisal system, the training and development of subordinates. Require periodic reports from the foreign national managers on their progress in these areas. Move in the direction of a modified management-by-objectives development program. The essential modification is that in the early stages the program objectives should be carefully "negotiated" with each foreign national manager, *beginning with a set of objectives prepared by him.*

3. Incorporate a "reliability" factor—that is, some incentive—in any performance inventory system used, and explain that the manager's reward will be based on his meeting performance deadlines and on his providing promised information or deliveries. Establish a climate of trust regarding money and valuables, but deal swiftly with clear cases of dishonesty and theft.

4. Spell out in some detail the ethics of managerial behavior as company policy. (For example, new employees will be selected from the many applicants on the basis of merit, rather than from the tribal group, ranks of relatives, or friends. The respective merits of such applicants will be determined not by rank favoritism, which is rampant today, but by as objective means as possible.)

5. American managers abroad must recognize the extensive role of local governments in economic development, and however clumsy these governments might appear to be, Americans should refrain from in-house "harping" on local government interference. In such environments, to live and let live is not enough. Where possible, actively support government programs.

Problem five

Resistance to traditional American development approaches can be effectively overcome in three basic ways:

1. Avoid *all* criticism in front of others. Private criticism should be depersonalized by fo-

cusing on methods, technical consequences, and company objectives.

2. Formal training sessions should either be concerned with the actual company problems or involve the small-team study of related business cases.

3. If not inconsistent with corporate policy, establish a management-by-objectives program in addition to the present company performance appraisal system.

In summary

Five fundamental differences between the United States and the developing world in management development circumstances have been identified as key problem areas. Any attempt to develop managers in these environments should take into account the limited sources of management potential, intellectual deprivation, economic attitudes, concepts of what a manager is and does, and resistance to face-to-face criticism. The action program recommended is a straightforward approach to these problems. It consists essentially of more extensive candidate recruiting efforts, supporting further formal education, and assessing and dealing with hostile economic attitudes by disseminating information. Such a program will help to counteract divergent views of what a manager should be.

If certain of these approaches do not seem to fit a particular management development problem in Asia, Africa, or South America, the principle of assessing the local problem carefully and tailoring a solution to fit it should remain. Another principle which should serve well in this undertaking is that more than anything else development efforts will depend primarily on identifying the management potential accurately. The guiding principle here is simply that while bright, informed, eager people do not always make good managers, people who are stupid, ignorant, and hostile never do.

LIST OF CONTRIBUTORS

KENNETH R. ANDREWS, Donald K. David Professor of Business Administration at the Harvard Business School, is an acknowledged authority on executive development. His books include *The Effectiveness of University Management Development Programs*.

MELVIN ANSHEN is Professor of Business at the Graduate School of Business, Columbia University. He has served as director of, and consultant to, many companies.

JOSEPH C. BAILEY is Professor of Human Relations, Emeritus, at the Harvard Business School and Professor of Human Relations at the Graduate School of Business, Northeastern University.

PAUL J. BROUWER has been developing industrial executives since 1945 as a member of Rohrer, Hibler & Replogle, psychological consultants. He is now General Partner in charge of the six-office Great Lakes region.

WILLIAM R. DILL and EDWIN J. ELTON are Dean and Associate Professor, respectively, at the Graduate School of Business Administration, New York University. WALLACE B.S. CROWSTON is Associate Professor of Management at the Sloan School of Management, Massachusetts Institute of Technology.

LAWRENCE L. FERGUSON was Manager of Behavioral Research Service for the General Electric Company at the time his contribution to this book was written. He is now a management consultant.

ROBERT L. KATZ is President of U.S. Natural Resources, Inc. He was formerly on the faculties of the graduate business schools at Dartmouth, Harvard, and Stanford.

JAMES A. LEE has spent much of his time in developing countries in the last decade as an industrial relations director with two U.S. companies and as a college administrator. He is now Chairman of the department of management and organizational behavior, College of Business Administration, Ohio University.

HARRY LEVINSON is Thomas Henry Carroll Ford Foundation Distinguished Visiting Professor of Business Administration, Harvard Business School, and President of the Levinson Institute. His books include *The Exceptional Executive* and *Executive Stress*.

J. STERLING LIVINGSTON has studied the early business careers of many men, as Professor of Business Administration at the Harvard Business School, as President of the Sterling Institute, and as chief executive of several other organizations.

M. SCOTT MYERS was Manager of Management Research at Texas Instruments, Inc., when he wrote the article included in this book. He is now a management consultant to Texas Instruments and other companies.

O.A. OHMANN was engaged in management development work as Assistant to the President, Standard Oil Company (Ohio), when he wrote " 'Skyhooks.' " Now retired, he continues to consult with organizations in that field.

ROBERT F. VANDELL is Professor of Business Administration at the Graduate School of Business Administration, University of Virginia. His specialty is finance, on which he has consulted and written extensively.

ABRAHAM ZALEZNIK is Cahners-Rabb Professor of Social Psychology of Management, Harvard Business School. He is also a psychoanalyst and affiliate member of the Boston Psychoanalytic Society and Institute.

INDEX